Literature, Ethics, and Aesthetics

Also by Sabrina Achilles

Waste: A Novel (1996)

Literature, Ethics, and Aesthetics
Applied Deleuze and Guattari

Sabrina Achilles

LITERATURE, ETHICS, AND AESTHETICS
Copyright © Sabrina Achilles, 2012.

First published in 2012 by
PALGRAVE MACMILLAN®
in the United States—a division of St. Martin's Press LLC,
175 Fifth Avenue, New York, NY 10010.

Where this book is distributed in the UK, Europe and the rest of the world,
this is by Palgrave Macmillan, a division of Macmillan Publishers Limited,
registered in England, company number 785998, of Houndmills,
Basingstoke, Hampshire RG21 6XS.

Palgrave Macmillan is the global academic imprint of the above companies
and has companies and representatives throughout the world.

Palgrave® and Macmillan® are registered trademarks in the United States,
the United Kingdom, Europe and other countries.

ISBN: 978–0–230–34089–3

Library of Congress Cataloging-in-Publication Data

Achilles, Sabrina.
    Literature, ethics, and aesthetics : applied Deleuze and Guattari /
Sabrina Achilles.
        p. cm.
    Includes bibliographical references.
    ISBN 978–0–230–34089–3 (hardback)
    1. Literature—Philosophy. 2. Constructivism (Philosophy) 3. Literature
and ethics. I. Title.

PN49.A24 2012
801—dc23   2011036204

A catalogue record of the book is available from the British Library.

Design by Newgen Imaging Systems (P) Ltd., Chennai, India.

First edition: March 2012

10 9 8 7 6 5 4 3 2 1

Printed in the United States of America.

For Steven Maras

Contents

Illustrations

Foreword

*L*iterature, Ethics, and Aesthetics is an original contribution to the library of work surrounding the oeuvre of Gilles Deleuze and Félix Guattari. Deleuze and Guattari individually and through their collaboration are major contributors to the revolution in philosophy during the twentieth century, associated with French post-structuralism in particular. It is no small task to make an "original" contribution to this discussion, given the extent of coverage and quality of participants engaged in unpacking, applying, and extending the innovations and insights found in the works of Deleuze and Guattari. The "revolution" refers to the work accomplished by continental philosophy in this period, which amounts to an updating of metaphysics in the broadest sense (not its "closure"), to take into account the revolutions transforming every other domain of culture dating roughly from the beginnings of the Industrial Revolution (new science, new arts, new psychology, new economics, and so forth).

The success of *Literature, Ethics, and Aesthetics* is due in part to its strategy, which selects one important theme in the oeuvre (literary function), whose explication opens out onto the entire project of Deleuze and Guattari's collaboration. A primary difficulty and frustration of Deleuze and Guattari's philosophy is the specialized vocabulary introduced and tested experimentally through a quantity of books. The vocabulary and terminology are a hybrid, reflecting a synthesis of two disciplines— philosophy (Deleuze) and psychiatry (Guattari)—formulated in an original methodology, schizoanalysis. The practice resulting from the collaboration is more than the sum of its parts, emergent rather than additive in its explanatory power, and designed not for analysis but for innovation. You could say that there is no disciplinary "expertise" on Deleuze and Guattari since anyone working on or with them is "out of field."

The originality of *Literature, Ethics, and Aesthetics* is due in part to an insight into Deleuze and Guattari's project that justifies their specialized lexicon, and in part to the contextualizing of the project in a way that translates the terms across a number of related initiatives and applications. The result is a book that is at once a service orienting newcomers to Deleuze and Guattari and a direction for further work to motivate original research and experimentation. The service role begins with an introduction to the topic that will focus the entire argument: the status of the "literary function" in the project of Deleuze and Guattari. The issue is one of general interest to the humanities disciplines, and crucial in some respects to the future of the humanities in the university and in the culture as a whole. The issue concerns the purpose, nature, and operation (function) of the "aesthetic" dimension broadly conceived (in language, experience, arts, and society). A certain line of thought with substantial credentials (Marxism and post-Marxism, taken up in the academy by cultural studies) denigrated "aesthetics" as idealist, bourgeois, escapist, defeatist, nihilistic, and ultimately fascist. The author assumes some awareness of this Marxist brief, instead using as foils the pragmatism of Richard Rorty and academic cultural studies more generally. This focus makes sense as contrasts setting up the positive role of the aesthetic in Deleuze and Guattari, because of the importance of "performance" or the "performative" (speech act) to these positions, as well as their promotion of pragmatics, referring to the reception or effect of a communication. The value of this organization is that the argument does not rely on absolute definitions of terms, extrapolated exclusively from the many texts by Deleuze and Guattari, but contextualizes terms and usage relative to similar vocabulary found in contrasting positions. A negative definition is as useful as a positive one, and together they give a satisfying feeling of "knowing one's way about" within a complex exploratory debate.

Deleuze and Guattari left the debate to the rest of us, condemning it as a waste of time or at least not the real work of philosophy. The real work of philosophy from its inception in classical Greece and continuing today is the invention of concepts. *Literature, Ethics, and Aesthetics* adopts as its focus this dimension of Deleuze and Guattari's project. In *What Is Philosophy?* Deleuze and Guattari outline a theory of concepts, or a concept of concepts, calling for and showing how to create a new kind of concept necessary for our postindustrial commodified civilization. *What Is Philosophy?*—Deleuze and Guattari's final collaboration—is their most important work, because it "saves" the concept, by adapting it to the new demands and responsibilities of contemporary conditions. The importance of *Literature, Ethics, and Aesthetics* is that it is one of the few commentaries on Deleuze and Guattari that takes this focus (Eric Alliez's *The Signature of the World* is another). This focus on the concept of concept, and the argument justifying this invention, constitute at once a service and an original contribution, opening the way for further work (the invention of more concepts of this sort). The pivot of the argument, and of the history of aesthetics, is what happened in the nineteenth century, with the avant-garde movements originating in Paris and extending to the rest of the world, the nature of which could be summarized as "pure art" or "art for art's sake." *Literature, Ethics, and Aesthetics* registers this history with a shorthand or emblematic reference to Walter Pater and the ambition of literature to achieve the status of music. To represent the fundamental misunderstanding of this pivot found in cultural studies, the author cites the Marxist Terry Eagleton's *Ideology of the Aesthetic*, in which he condemns this turn in the arts as an abandonment of responsibility by the arts for ethics and politics in the public sphere. *Literature, Ethics, and Aesthetics* refutes this reading of history and describes the embrace of aesthetics within the literary function as promoted by Deleuze and Guattari. *Literature, Ethics, and Aesthetics* shows that cultural studies, despite much surface progressivism, remains caught in the old metaphysics of subject-object epistemology, mind-body dualisms of all kinds, and representational (correspondence) models of truth. The justification for the new concept and its vocabulary (machinic assemblages and the like) is that it creates an entire lexicon to replace the representational conventions that served philosophy throughout its history up to modernity. *Literature, Ethics, and Aesthetics* demonstrates much of this shift of terms (from structures to the machinic in general), not through dry inventories but through usage demonstrated in specific contexts. Deleuze and Guattari have the opposite understanding of the importance of "pure art" (to use a shorthand phrase) than the one held by cultural studies, which is that the immanent condition of contemporary metaphysics (no transcendence of any kind, no objectivity, no representational or critical distance, but only immersion in complex dynamic becoming) is accessible to thought and communication only by means of a literary function, that is, by the devices of art, grounded in performance. They specifically embraced constructivism as their relay, but their stance may be generalized, and this is the key insight of *Literature, Ethics, and Aesthetics*—that the project of philosophy today is to do for conceptual discourse what the vanguard did for the arts: to break with mimetic realism and invent an alternative practice to support a different metaphysics capable of guiding thought in a postindustrial civilization.

The character of Deleuze and Guattari's new concept, operating through the literary function, is precisely performative, literally dramatic, introducing a fold in immanence constituting an articulation capable of thinking the event (encompassing all subject-object dualisms). *Literature, Ethics, and Aesthetics* demonstrates this positive side of the case by discussions of several theoretical instances (e.g., de Certeau's tactics and Ulmer's conduction), and by an allegorical reading of two films (*The Full Monty* and *The Sweet Hereafter*). *Literature, Ethics, and Aesthetics*, carries its argument into the relevance of media. In light of the positive case put forward, it is clear that the underlying justification for, and enabling condition of, the literary function, as the mode of discourse capable of replacing conventional propositional logic, is the hegemony of popular culture and new media in contemporary globalizing civilization. The argument calls for "performed existential refrains," or, in Lev Manovich's terms, "movies." As Manovich argued in the "Language of New Media," the general cultural interface (GCI) today is not the essay but movies, not argumentation but cinematography. Movies are not just for entertainment, but rather any sort of information may be structured cinematographically (filmic, but also as narrative or figure). *Literature, Ethics, and Aesthetics* makes this claim; the book leads up to it with the movie allegories. In reality, the misapprehension of the centrality of aesthetics to digital intelligence found in cultural studies is shared by administrators, legislators, and the general public, who treat aesthetic performance as expendable, failing to see that the future of a free democratic society depends on a public educated in the interface craft of the literary function.

GREGORY ULMER

Acknowledgments

The friends who directly or indirectly influenced this work are responsible for a considerable part of my pleasure in this project. They include Steven Maras whose rare calm and ability brought a confidence to the project before its time. Many thanks to Dimitris Vardoulakis who has a rare, enabling generosity. Hazel Smith's ongoing experimentation in writing makes her a brilliant reader. Thanks to Sara Knox for her expert editing. Gregory Ulmer's praise has been infectious. His work on electracy has been an inspiration for my own intuitive knowledge. John O'Carroll's reading assured me of the work's final veil of consistency (its completion). Peter Kirkpatrick's and Peter Hutching's most generous support toward the sabbatical in which much of this work was written was above the call of duty. Thanks to Carol Liston, head of the School of Humanities at the time of the writing of this book, for her support.

Introduction: The Literary Function

In recent neurological science, a helmet, made to stimulate neurological activity, was placed on the head of a woman with a sensory processing disorder in order to assist her own balancing capabilities. The helmet returned significant improvements; the woman could walk without wobbling and falling over. But the most astounding result was the way in which the woman continued to be able to walk without losing balance after the helmet had been removed; the brain had grown new pathways as a result of the external stimulation provided by the helmet.[1] The thesis of this book envisages the aesthetic as such a helmet. In a stand-alone text for its period, Félix Guattari writes, "Poetry today might have more to teach us than economic science, the human sciences and psychoanalysis combined" (1996:21). This book takes this baton from Guattari and considers the aesthetic not as something that expresses the world but as something that enables social, cultural, and ethical intervention. No less than the activating function of the helmet upon the body, the aesthetic regime of signs affects the bodies it comes into contact with, making the aesthetic a politically, and thereby pertinent, line of inquiry.

I use the term "literary" in place of "aesthetic" in order to focus discussion on the developments and context of the study of literature since (and including) its tarnishing by cultural studies in the 1980s and 1990s. Today, the study of literature is frequent with multiple foci as humanities departments become increasingly broad and include creative writing, philosophy, and comparative literature (apart from the usual, literary studies), all of which engage literature. Literature is also involved with interdisciplinary study, in cultural, historical, and psychoanalytical contexts. The study of literature and trauma is such an example. This book brings to this sumptuous feasting upon literature a concept referred to as the *literary function*; it takes the literary aside for a moment to consider it in its own terms and not as representation, nor as therapy, nor, indeed, as Gilles Deleuze and Guattari have dealt with "the work of art,"[2] as percepts and affects. Affect in their book *What Is Philosophy?* (1994) is thought in terms of intensity prior to ourselves. Rather, the concept developed in this work explores the literary aesthetic as performing acts, as producing affects, and by "affect" is meant an expression of a body that is the result of an action and that does not precede the action.[3] Contrary to the notion of the work of art existing "in itself,"[4] the literary function is explored for the way in which it performs an ethics of self—that includes *a concern for the self*, to borrow Foucault's expression. This self is made in the act of the literary function. Here, self, language, and the world are continuous and inseparable.

In developing this conceptual tool for the aesthetic, this book also brings a pedagogy to both literary study and creative writing practice.[5] Since its inclusion within the academy, around fifty years ago,[6] creative writing has struggled to find its own pedagogical bearing. Narratological approaches, which atomize the piece of creative writing into various parts such as genre, plot, character, tone, setting, theme, voice, and so on, add little understanding of the craft that is not predetermined.[7] At times, creative writing classes proceed in an anecdotal style as writers "talk" about their own and other writers' processes and experience of writing and reading. At best this discussion is circular and at worst, off the point. Recently, a cultural studies framing has been popular for both literary studies and creative writing as the aesthetic has continued to be viewed negatively.[8]

This book furthers the interdisciplinary relationship between creative writing and other areas within the humanities by developing a greater conceptualization for creative writing, both as a practice and as a discipline, than already exists in the humanities. In turn, the concepts developed in this book will effect the terms of the disciplines it comes into contact with. Creative writing, thus, is able to be a more active partner within its interdisciplinary "home." This conceptualization of creative writing takes place through a reconceptualization of the key terms, "aesthetic" and "literary." The frameworks used to analyze these terms are those of pragmatics and performativity, but in particular, that of a Deleuzeoguattarian approach to pragmatics and performativity.

In *A Thousand Plateaus, Capitalism and Schizophrenia* (1987:4), Deleuze and Guattari point out that the book does not exist in isolation but in conjunction with other bodies (without organs),[9] which form what they refer to as "assemblages" (4). Deleuze and Guattari, therefore, do not seek to know what a book means, "as signified or signifier" (4), but ask instead "what it functions with" (4). For Deleuze and Guattari, a book is a "little machine" (4), and they seek to know "the *relation*... of this literary machine" (4) to other machines. They give the example of a war machine, a love machine, and so on. They also note that there is an abstract machine that carries this relationship along. This work explores the literary machine and its relation to the various other machines it functions with. The relations explored are those between the literary machine and society, the literary machine and the reader, the literary machine and community, and the literary machine and subjectification. The need to consider the literary machine as an assemblage is underscored by Deleuze and Guattari's notion that "[t]here is no difference between what a book talks about and how it is made" (4). In other words, the aesthetic is as important a consideration as the social context of which it forms a part since it affects the ways in which society is "talked about." Deleuze and Guattari write:

> We will ask what (the book) functions with, in connection with what other things it does or does not transmit intensities, in which other multiplicities its own are inserted and metamorphosed, and with what bodies without organs it makes its own converge. (4)

The focus given to the literary machine in relation to society, the reader, community, and subjectification is in part due to the importance of these bodies to other, dominant approaches to text within the academy. These are also, on the whole, the bodies important to Guattari's exploration of the aesthetic. Significantly, Deleuze and Guattari's combined approach to the aesthetic[10] (which involves an interdisciplinary, or what for them is an assemblage-type approach) frees the aesthetic from the type of "autonomous realm," for which it has been criticized, while enabling its immanent study.

The Politics of Pragmatics and the Literary Machine

As Claire Parnet in *Dialogues* (1987) notes, if we consider a piece of writing on its own, "it can only turn circles around itself, falling into a black hole where the only sound forever after is the echo of the question 'What is writing? What is writing?' without anything ever coming out" (117). Deleuzeoguattarian pragmatics has no use of a study of signs in isolation since there is no universal sign system, including one belonging to language (and therefore writing). Instead, there are only regimes of signs (115), in their infinite number. Regimes of signs are neither "language [n]or a language-system" (115). They are a combination of things (which Deleuze and Guattari call fluxes and particles). For example, in the case of the anorexic regime of signs, the fluxes include food, clothing, and language. Regimes of signs also have intensities, which, in the example of the anorexic, include void and fullness (111). For Deleuze and Guattari, a regime of signs has an abstract machine that "shapes very varied combinations, emissions and continuations of fluxes" (115).[11] Rather than the language system determining the regime of signs—"There is no abstract machine internal to language" (116)—it is the "abstract machines which provide a language with a particular collective assemblage of enunciation" (116). Put otherwise, Parnet writes, it is "the regimes of signs (pragmatics) that fix the collective assemblages of enunciation in a language as flux of expression" (115).[12]

There are no "functions of language" (115), then, but rather "machinic functionings with collective assemblages" (115). In choosing to investigate the "literary function," this book investigates the literary *regime of signs* and their machinic functionings. Parnet states that Deleuze and Guattari's pragmatics proceeds by first "showing how an actual assemblage brings into play several regimes of pure signs or several abstract machines, putting them into play in one another's mechanisms" (114). Second, pragmatics entails "showing how one pure regime of signs can be translated into another, with what transformations, what unassimilable [sic] residues, what variations and innovations" (114). With respect to the first step of pragmatics, this book considers the abstract machines of the performative and of the pragmatic itself. "Performativity" and "pragmatics" are key flashpoints here since it is toward the performative utterance and act we look to theorize subjectification, singularity, the collective enunciation, and ethos, while pragmatics concerns language and writing as the ground of existence.[13] In the pages that follow, this book argues for an immanent appraisal of these terms in relation to the literary machine, asking, what is it that the literary machine does to these other machines and why it is that these terms need to be thought outside other assemblages, including pragmatics that involve the postmodern cultural-critical turn[14] and Austinian theories of performativity. While establishing the performativity and pragmatics of the literary machine, these terms are used to critique the use of these same machines by other critical and analytical regimes of signs. The critique is, on the whole, in relation to the impact of these other regimes upon the literary machine. In light of the second objective of pragmatics, the abstract machines belonging to the literary machine are analyzed in regard to the transformations, variations, and innovations they bring into effect in relation, particularly, to the abstract machines of subjectivity and community.

In adopting a Deleuzeoguattarian-style pragmatics with respect to the literary function, a political dimension is brought to the study of literary aesthetics. Such pragmatics are always political, since, as mentioned, where pragmatics are concerned there is no universal system (111). Rather, regimes of signs must be analyzed immanently. Writes Parnet, "[i]t is not the regime which presupposes signs, it is the sign which presupposes a certain regime" (105). Thus, for Parnet, "[s]emiology can only be a study of regimes, of their differences and their transformations" (105). For Deleuze, regimes of signs create the lines that go to make up our lives, and the lives of groups (125). When we engage in pragmatics we engage in making lines, and this for Deleuze is what makes pragmatics political. Writes Deleuze, "[p]olitics is active experimentation, since we do not know in advance which way a line is going to turn. Draw the line, says the account: but one can in fact draw it *anywhere*" (137). In seeking a pragmatics for the literary machine, the aim is not to turn the literary back toward the book, but to enable the book to be turned to the outside,[15] that is, such that it might be transformed into a line upon which we might find ourselves—one that is *made* available to us. In this way, the destination of the literary text is toward an ethics, in the broad sense of a way of being.

The Term "Literary Function"

The term "literary function" describes acts that Mikhail Bakhtin refers to as "verbal art" (1981:259); these include the dramatic (including cinematic), poetic, and prose forms. The "literary function" is not intended to function as a medium-specificity argument. This is contrary to Guattari, for instance, who is concerned primarily with poetry. For Guattari, the issue is one of "mental ecology," and poetry is a disappearing species that is as necessary to our survival as vitamin C (1996:114). However, this text shares with Guattari an interest in the potential of creative writing in "opening up new social, analytical and aesthetic practices" (114). The term "literary" as it is used here is also analogous to what Roland Barthes (1984) terms "trans-writing." For Barthes, trans-writing is the "antidote of myth" (168), which he describes as "thick" language that forms sociolects and idiolects. For Barthes, myth turns culture to "nature." Barthes writes:

> [T]rans-writing...(that we still refer to as "literary")...would be the extreme pole or rather the region—airy, light, spaced, open, uncentred, noble and free—where writing spreads itself against the idiolect, at its limit and fighting it. (1984:168)

Importantly, Barthes, in using the term "literary," is not restricting such writing to a genre. In "The Literary Machine," John Marks notes that

Deleuze does not approach the object of literature by genre either. Marks points out, Deleuze does not even make a "hard and fast distinction between literature and 'l'écriture'" (1998:123). Rather, Deleuze's interest in literature is in a writing that adopts a "sceptical [sic] stance with regard to language itself" (123). But of most importance to the interests of this book is Deleuze's notion of literary writers as symptomatologists, which in turn makes them theorists of ethics. Writes Marks, for Deleuze, writers are "adept at reading and creating signs. 'Signs imply ways of living, possibilities of existence, they're the symptoms of life gushing forth or draining away'" (Marks quoting Deleuze,[16] 123).

Barthes's definition of trans-writing is also of interest for the way in which writing is thought to create a "region." This resonates with Deleuzeoguattarian notions of the geological; the writing of literature is to trace lines, lines that amount to a whole cartography—that in turn becomes a geology. For Deleuze, we are able to flee via these new cartographies; we are able to find what Deleuze and Guattari refer to as a line of flight. This concept, which Deleuze and Guattari reserve for Anglo-American literature (1987:36), is a kind of fight. Quoting D. H. Lawrence, Deleuze writes: "'I tell you, old weapons go rotten: make some new ones and shoot accurately [sic]'" (36). Barthes too refers to trans-writing as writing that involves a fight (168).

So finally, on the issue of the domain of the literary function, it is necessary to consider it in the contexts to which it has migrated (as well as in its more traditional contexts), that is, beyond print media and in such cultural interfaces as movies and new media. Lev Manovich, citing Jay David Bolter, notes that all media import existing media; "All media work by 'remediating,' i.e. translating, refashioning, and reforming other media, both on the levels of content and form" (Manovich, 2001:95). The importing of literary discourse into visual media is not an exception. It is for this reason that two movies, *The Full Monty* (1997) in chapter 5 and *The Sweet Hereafter* (1997) in chapter 6 of this work, are used to allegorize the literary function. Cinema is today our new general cultural interface, GCI (2001:87). Movies might comprise optical and sound signs, but they "take on" narrative. They present a story. It is a historical fact that "cinema was constituted as such by becoming narrative... and rejecting its other possibilities" (Deleuze, 1991:25). Borrowing from Christian Metz, Deleuze ascribes to the single shot, "the smallest narrative utterance" (1991:25). However, the image/sound of film does not correspond to the system of language [langue] but rather it "condition(s) the utterance of a language [langage] (1991:25). This work will demonstrate that this is exactly the case for the literary function. Regardless of medium, the aesthetic "conditions" the utterance. Deleuze distinguishes between two types of images, one, the movement-image that seemingly adheres to, or mimics, a language system and is based in causal and logical linkages and connections. It thus performs a real, actual, and thereby legal, regime of signs. The other type of cinematic image is the time-image. The time-image stands for its own object, creates it, and erases it. This image does not correspond to a real/actual/world. Rather, it produces a virtual reality. The time-image reveals "time as everything, as 'infinite opening,' as anteriority over all normal movement defined by motivity [*motricité*]" (1991:37). However, as Deleuze says, all cinema bears the condition of the time-image. The movement-image may seem to have an independent setting to the description the camera gives it, thus making the image appear to stand for a preexisting reality, but in fact, the movement-image has "extraordinary movement. The movement-image does not reproduce a world, but constitutes an autonomous world, made up of breaks and disproportion" (1991:37). Deprived of all its centers, the movement-image addresses "itself as such to a viewer who is in himself no longer centre of his own perception" (1991:37). This movement of the infinite, as it were, thus denies the spatiotemporal coordinates that are necessary to propositional logic. The literary function conceived in this book involves the conditioning of the sign toward the infinite. Considering the passage of the literary function into cinema and new media, and the status awarded by those domains to GCI, this *literary* machine is capable of replacing conventional propositional logic. This is not what Guattari has in mind in his enormous claim for the aesthetic, but it does add weight to the need for its exploration.

In developing a conceptualization of the literary function, there is an attempt to free what Parnet refers to as "Creative functions" from machines such as marketing and journalism. Parnet notes that as writing detached from the Author function, it became "reconstituted at the periphery, regaining credit on the radio, the TV, in the newspapers, and even in the cinema (the *cinéma d'auteur*)" (1987:27). For Parnet, interest moved from the book "to newspaper articles, broadcasts, debates, colloquia" (26–27). This event took place as journalism "increasingly created the events about which it [spoke]" (29). Writes Parnet, "The journalist has discovered himself to be an author and has given reality back to a function which had fallen into discredit" (27). For Parnet, then, marketing, through "interviewers, debaters, and presenters" (27), has replaced the Author function.[17] Parnet's discussion of creative functions is in the context of a wider discussion on arborescent or origin-orientated structures (to which the Author function belongs) and non-origin-orientated structures (referred to as a rhizome). Creative functions, which Parnet also calls productive functions, are rhizomic, that is, they "proceed by intersections, crossing of lines, points of encounter in the middle" (28). Here, there is no subject "but instead collective assemblages of enunciation" (28). This book explores the literary machine as a creative function,[18] which, for instance, proceeds by intersections and results in collective assemblages of enunciation.

A Sketch of the Polemical History of the Term "Literary"

The use of the word "literary" by this text also has a polemical function, and this is why it has been chosen over other expressions such as creative writing or trans-writing. It is argued that an inquiry into the literary function has been repressed due to the treatment of the category, "literature," by recent approaches to text including contemporary pragmatics and a postmodern cultural-critical turn.[19] In other words, it is argued that due to the treatment of the term "literature" there has been a lessening of an articulation between creative writing and the other disciplines within the academy. The category "literature" came under attack in the early 1960s. Critics argued, as Andrew Milner points out (1996), that the existing study of literature failed to consider "cultural value as socially constructed" (11). It was argued that literature had been defined as a "timeless, 'aesthetic' category" (11) and was, thereby, an autonomous discourse. Housed within this autonomous discourse were ideal (human) values, beyond those of history—singular in nature.[20] For such cultural critics, both then and now, being considered a reified discourse, the literary discourse is implicit in and fundamental to a culture of discrimination, exclusion, and elitism. In other words, in being considered a high discourse it, by definition, aids in the creation of an environment of exclusivity, singularity, and intolerance—in turn adding to the production of a hierarchical structure. In fact, for Milner, it was only with the postmodern theorists that the distinction between so-called high discourse, such as literature, and low discourse, such as popular culture, is fully undermined. For Milner, postmodernism brings about a "'waning of certainty and objectivity grounded in the unquestioned hierarchy of values'" (Milner quoting Zygmunt Bauman, 10). The result is that the object of literature, as a repository of high values (the canon), has shifted ground. Texts such as Milner's *Literature, Culture & Society* (1996) map this shift from literary to cultural studies.[21]

Milner makes a distinction between cultural theorists who have embraced postmodernism and those who have not. For Milner, cultural theorists prior to (or those who take up a position different from that of the theorists who have embraced) postmodernism retained "literature" as an alternative to mass and commodity culture. They saw in high modernism a "'redemptive' function" (56). Such theorists of culture include those of the Frankfurt School, the initiators of the Anglo-American shift from literary to cultural studies (Richard Hoggart and Raymond Williams),[22] and post-structuralists, of whom he says there is doubt as to their endorsement of the idea of the postmodern. Milner points out, "French post-structuralism was generally far too preoccupied with the high modernist canon to accord any serious attention to a contemporary culture that had acquired an increasingly postmodern complexion" (55). With respect to Michel Foucault, Milner writes, "In so far as Foucault's archaeology is able to envisage a 'post-modern' episteme, it is only that inaugurated by high structuralism itself" (55).

With the shift from literary into cultural studies, the category of the "literary," as an object of study, has largely disappeared.[23] This is because the term has become synonymous with aesthetic autonomy and an elitist discourse. Terry Eagleton (1985) notes that the New Critics aided in giving the term this negative connotation since they reduced the study of literature to poetry, and "poetry is of all literary genres the one most apparently sealed from history" (1985:51). Thus, theorists and critics moved on in the nomenclature of their discipline. In his chapter "From Literary to Cultural Studies: The Sociological Turn," Milner writes, "[b]y 'cultural studies' I mean...a particular academic discipline, that discourse about 'culture,' as distinct from 'literature'" (1996:11). For Antony Easthope, "Literary studies...fell into crisis and...transformed into something else, cultural studies," fifty years after it began and with the work of Terry Eagleton, in particular (1991:5). Milner notes that it was first with Hoggart (1957)[24] that "criticism shifted emphasis from 'literature' to 'culture'" (15). Milner describes this as the "sociological turn." In the place of the "Leavisite notion of a distinctly valuable minority culture" (15), culture was now being seen as "'a whole way of life'" (Milner quoting Raymond Williams, 15). The view of cultural studies in this context is that the value of a text is made in and through history and by "the valuing community" (23). The study of any cultural object, therefore, should involve the study of the institutions (discursive, formal, social, etc.) within which the cultural object is embedded. Milner notes:

> For Bennett and for much of contemporary cultural studies, a recognition of the social constructedness of literature thus leads to a kind of cultural populism, which deliberately turns *against literature*. (1996:24)

(Milner notes that *Against Literature* was apparently the original title of Tony Bennett's own book [24].) In such an environment, a distinction between literary and nonliterary texts collapses. Writes Milner, "For Bennett, aesthetic discourse is…merely one discourse of value amongst many others, for example sports or cuisine" (23). These discourses, in their text form, may all be "analyzable according to analogous intellectual procedures and operations" (11). For both Milner and Bennett, the problem with "philosophical aesthetics" (23) is that it fetishizes the object valued rather than the valuing process. The common view found in cultural criticism, contrary to the formalist view, is that "literariness" "is not a property of a certain type of writing, but rather a function of the ways in which different kinds of writing are socially processed" (22).

Immanence and Pragmatics

Clearly, Guattari's view of poetry is of a discourse worthy of study in its own right. However, Guattari's approach to the aesthetic is along lines different from those of the philosophical aesthetics described by Bennett. Bennett calls philosophical aesthetics a "discourse of disqualification" (1990:160) in that its edicts suppose a standard one can fail to achieve. As mentioned above, such aesthetics promote a culture of universality, a culture singular in nature. This text pursues a nuanced approach to the aesthetic, which does not draw an aesthetic/cultural opposition. It explores the thinking of Deleuze and Guattari and Foucault as that which considers the aesthetic as intrinsic to modes of existence. On one occasion, Deleuze questions whether, in fact, "the intrinsic aesthetic of modes of existence" could be the "ultimate dimension of social apparatuses" (1992:163). This text explores the literary aesthetic in relation to modes of existence after the importance Guattari, Deleuze, and Foucault all give to the aesthetic. As Deleuze writes, "Foucault…makes allusion to 'aesthetic' criteria, which are understood as criteria for life and replace on each occasion the claims of transcendental judgement with an immanent evaluation" (163). The approach to the literary aesthetic by this text, then, is one of "pragmatism, functionalism, positivism (and) pluralism" (162), to borrow Deleuze's description of Foucault's own philosophical approach. The literary aesthetic is assessed according to what Deleuze calls "content of 'possibility'"(163)—which is referred to in this text as potential—and in terms of "liberty" and "creativity," among other criteria. For Deleuze, such criteria are important to the thinking of modes of existence in an immanent manner. They are, for Deleuze, immanent criteria. Immanent evaluation, for Deleuze, replaces transcendental judgment (163).

The immanent concept of the literary function developed here also takes heed of Deleuze and Guattari's *empiricist* notions of the concept.[25] According to Peter Cook in his paper "Thinking the Concept Otherwise: Deleuze and Expression" (1998), the concept in Deleuze and Guattari's empiricism is the *expressed* of an event. Cook distinguishes between an expressive utterance in Deleuze and Guattari's empiricism and the descriptive utterance of the abstract concept. In Deleuze and Guattari's empiricism, the concept is the *expressed* of the immanent (inexpressible) event and does not preexist this. As Deleuze himself says, empiricism involves "analysing states of things, in such a way that non-pre-existent concepts can be extracted from them" (Deleuze and Parnet, 1987:vii). In *What Is Philosophy?* Deleuze and Guattari write, "Every concept is a combination that did not exist before" (1994:75). This immanent nature of the concept thus makes it unsuitable to the *universal description* of an object or class of objects, as with an abstract concept. In fact, there is no place for a subject and an object within the empiricist concept. Rather, it expresses an event/action (the literary *function*) that is itself "immaterial and unpresentable" (Cook, 1998:28).

For Deleuze and Guattari, the image of thought—also referred to as the plane of immanence—is itself eventlike, being referred to by Deleuze and Guattari as movement of the infinite. (It is the image of thought and the plane of immanence of the literary function that this text expresses.) Both the event and the plane of immanence are "immaterial and unpresentable." They are, therefore, virtual. Both belong to "a different form of time" (as Cook says of the event). And as Deleuze and Guattari say of thought:

> Movement of the infinite does not refer to spatiotemporal coordinates that define the successive positions of a moving object and the fixed reference points in relation to which these positions vary. "To orientate oneself in thought" implies neither objective reference point nor moving object that experiences itself as a subject and that as such strives for or needs the infinite. Movement takes in everything, and there is no place for a subject and an object that can only be concepts. (1994:37)

Such an engagement with the concept takes the literary function beyond both literary criticism with its descriptive language, and cultural criticism, which, it is argued below, has progressively moved away from such a notion of an immanent concept and has distanced itself from the category of the aesthetic. Formalism's immanent approach to the study of the literary is of particular importance to the construction of the concept of the literary function; it is considered a crucial step in understanding the virtual nature of the literary. It is argued that while "formalism" is often the name used to signal an opposition to a pragmatic approach to literature—prevalent in the postmodern cultural-criticism turn—the thinking of structural linguist Louis Hjelmslev is crucial to understanding the question of the pragmatic in relation to the literary. Hjelmslev's thinking helps to theorize the literary as an immanent concept. However, the formalist project is not reemployed en bloc, rather, there are clues from within it that furthers exploration of the aesthetic.

The pursuit of the literary function is distinct from that of Milner, Eagleton, and Williams, who (unlike Bennett) advocate retaining the category of literature but within the broader umbrella of *cultural* studies. For Milner, "Literature matters precisely *because* its value is made in and through history" (1996:24). For Milner literature, "in the sense of writing" and reading, is worthy of academic study since it is the "particular fashion" by which "'*narrative*...the central function or *instance* of the human mind' comes to be socially institutionalised" (10).[26] Moreover, for Milner, Williams, and Eagleton, literature matters because it *is* valued "by the valuing community, rather than as an inherent property of the valued text itself" (25). In other words, this text pursues an immanent, ethico-aesthetic approach to the category of the literary. It seeks a pragmatics (regime of signs) for the literary machine. In this it is distinct from a postmodern cultural-critical approach to the category of the literary.

There is, of course, no denying the legitimacy of the turn to cultural studies. The focus of cultural studies on the so-called literary mode of production, including the ideological and historical forces surrounding literature, has eroded transcendental judgment born of the variety of autonomous approaches to text existing in the history of literary studies. Cultural studies has been party to the decentralist moves within the humanities, including feminist and postcolonial theories, which have opened analysis to a vastly broader array of texts, including those belonging to contemporary and popular culture and those of non–Anglo-American origin. This move has eroded the imperialistic canon that, in part at least, has been responsible for racial and class domination. Cultural studies has brought invaluable initiatives in the area of multiculturalism to textual studies and analysis, as it has with the issues of gender and sexual preference. And cultural studies has called into question theoretical approaches to text where they lack a pragmatic end. While these achievements have been unquestionably worthwhile, they have been at the expense of an important exploration into the ethics and affects belonging to the literary machine.

While the literary function has been clearly informed by the pragmatics of Deleuze and Guattari, it does not use their work as a model.
Parnet, in talking about Barthes's text *Sade/Fourier/Loyola*, notes that
as a pragmatics it comprises fluxes and particles, which, as such, are
capable of being modified and "coloured-in" (1987:116). This work,
Literature, Ethics, and Aesthetics, has found much in the work of Deleuze
and Guattari (and at times Foucault) to be colored-in, and from out of
which new fluxes and particles could be formed. It has used the concepts
of Deleuze, Guattari, and Foucault as so many tools in its own pragmatic
and political experimentation. Guattari evokes such a process in relation to his own work. For Guattari, his process is that of the artist creating "new forms from the palette" (1995:7). He asks that the reader not
take his own work as a model, saying: "[j]ust as an artist borrows from
his precursors and contemporaries the traits which suit him, I invite
those who read me to take or reject my concepts freely" (1995:12). The
result of Guattari's ethico-aesthetics is a production of singularities and
autonomy and not a repetitious model. Guattari declares his perspective to involve "shifting the human and social sciences from scientific
paradigms toward ethico-aesthetic paradigms." For Guattari, models of
any description (including Freudian and Lacanian models of the unconscious) are not of interest in determining scientific answers to the problems of the psyche but along with models in general they should only
be "considered in terms of the production of subjectivity—inseparable
as much from technical and institutional apparatuses which promote
it as from their impact on psychiatry, university teaching or the mass
media" (1995:11). Guattari adds that in

a more general way, one has to admit that every individual and social
group conveys its own system of modelising subjectivity; that is, a certain
cartography—composed of cognitive references—with which it positions
itself in relation to its affects and anguishes, and attempts to manage its
inhibitions and drives. (1995:11)

The Chapters

In chapter 1, "Being Constructivist," it is in respect to constructivism
that the endeavor to create a concept for the literary function is justified
and where the grounds for a new pedagogical approach to literary texts
is founded. In this chapter, key aspects of the way forward are identified,
namely, in the link between pragmatics, the literary, and performativity.
It is here that the philosophical rationale behind Deleuze and Guattari's

approach to pragmatics, and how this differs from other pragmatic approaches, is also explained.

Where chapter 1 explores the necessity to construct a concept for the literary function in order to explore this regime of signs and its affects, chapter 2, "Rethinking the Performative in Pragmatics," discusses the way in which a rejection of the construction of theoretical concepts by some areas of pragmatics today has limited such exploration. Contemporary pragmatics is explored as a diverse field, theorists discussed include Richard Rorty, and thereby the American tradition and Deleuze and Guattari. Linguistic pragmatists include J. L. Austin, Charles Morris, and Jacques Lacan.

Chapter 3, "The Literary Function and the Cartographic Turn: Performative Philosophy," extends the previous chapter's exploration into the performative but in this instance it is in relation to analytic cartography—or what is referred to by one writer as the cartographic turn. The cartographic turn is seen to have arisen out of a need to address ecological concerns that old paradigms are unable to do—for example, those involving subject and object as the basic framework of thought. The literary regime of signs is seen as a powerful force in such an endeavor—a force that is, however, denied by cartographies that maintain constraining links between reality and representation. The chapter considers the work of Michel Foucault, Bruno Bosteels, Gregory Ulmer, Deleuze and Guattari, and Michel de Certeau in discussing the literary function in relation to performative cartographic practice.

Chapter 4, "The Literary Function and Society I: Affirmation of Immanent Aesthetics" begins an exploration into the literary function in relation to other domains—society, the subject, community—which continues across the next three chapters. This chapter explores the problem of the relationship between text and society as it is expressed across certain instances of postmodern cultural criticism. The postmodern cultural critics discussed in this chapter represent a thinking trend in literary and cultural criticism and theory between the mid-1970s and the mid-1990s, which, it is argued, has influenced approaches to the category of the literary today. These critics include Fred Pfeil, Pierre Bourdieu, and Lance Olsen. In chapter 3, the literary function is considered as a transformative process in which signs become a-signifying and an "ontological affirmation." The literary functions to turn signifying regimes to matter, or to what Deleuze and Guattari also call *phylum* (1987:437). Chapter 4 explores the way in which certain postmodern cultural criticism captures this process by tending toward what Deleuze and Guattari refer to as "models of realization" (1987:434). Models of realization function to capture phylum—or what Deleuze and Guattari also refer to as "decoded

flows" (434). However, it is argued in chapter 5, "The Literary Function
and Society II: Community and Subjectification," that the literary function performs its own capture when it takes the signs of culture within its
folds and returns them to phylum.

Chapter 5 explores the literary function in terms of the production
of subjectification and community, which are considered to counter the
forces of models of realization and operate at the boundaries of social
apparatuses, producing lines of fracture responsible for the transformation of one social apparatus into another. Bakhtin's theory of the act is
crucial here, as is Guattari's concept of processual subjectivity and de
Certeau's notion of speech and the collective. This chapter includes a
reading of Peter Cattaneo's film *The Full Monty* (1997).

Chapter 6, "The Reader and the Event of Fiction," brings together the
literary function, subjectification, and a concern for the Self as an ethics,
and the relationship of all this to the formation of community. The literary function is seen to provide an ethics that overcomes the individuation and subjugation of the subject. This chapter looks at narratological
approaches to fiction, in particular in the work of Marie MacLean, which
theorizes narrative fiction in relation to performance, and finds in such
approaches an inability to theorize literary discourse as a transformative
body, and, thereby, as a production of Self outside the Law (which is discussed in terms of language and structure). The chapter ends with an
extensive reading of Atom Egoyan's film *The Sweet Hereafter* (1997).

I

Being Constructivist

In the pragmatics of Richard Rorty there is a continuation of the thinking that texts are made distinct by the valuing community. This can be found in *Consequences of Pragmatism* (1982). Rorty aligns his activity with "culture criticism" (xI) and describes his own context as postphilosophical. The task of the "culture critic" (xI), as Rorty refers to himself, is to study the comparative "advantages and disadvantages of various ways of talking which our race has invented" (xI). In other words, for Rorty, the value of the text depends upon the valuing community; our culture, purpose, and institutions "cannot be supported except conversationally" (167). Rorty is entirely skeptical of what he refers to as "vocabularies," by which he means philosophical theories of the type that attempt "to ground some element of our practices on something external to these practices" (167). He cites Platonic and Kantian philosophies as examples of such theories. Rorty refutes the tag of relativism when directed at cultural criticism (167). But he does embrace the "meta-philosophical relativists" (167) William James and John Dewey for the way "they think there is no way to choose, and no point in choosing, between incompatible philosophical theories" (167). Perhaps it is due to Rorty's relativistic-type objection to philosophy that a tendency to curtail the activity of philosophical thinking and the construction of concepts has prevailed. But constructivism enables the production of immanent thought, or put otherwise, a concept, and this is what we need for an approach to literature if literature is not to be taken as an *obvious* object by the different valuing communities. What is risked in such circumstances is no less than a return to positivist thinking.

What differentiates Deleuze and Guattari's thought from the postmodern cultural-critical turn is their notion of constructivism. For Deleuze and Guattari, philosophy is a type of constructivism (1994:35). Thought, for Deleuze and Guattari, is material, it may be experimented with, and it is capable of bringing about social and political transformation—of being a veritable war machine. This notion compares with the constructivism of the avant-garde, commencing with Vladimir Tatlin around 1913. Here, constructivism emphasized a relationship between art and life, experimenting with materials for utilitarian ends and in ways that promoted social and political change.

Behind Deleuze and Guattari's notion of constructivism is their notion of, and insistence on, the plane of immanence. The plane of immanence is a "prephilosophy" or a "nonphilosophy" (1994:41); it is an absolute horizon upon which the concepts of philosophy take hold, "populate." And since the plane of immanence of philosophy is a "prephilosophy," the activity of philosophy (the creation of concepts) involves "a sort of groping experimentation" (41). That is, there is an experimentation with the "materials" of philosophy as there is with the materials used by avant-garde constructivism. For Deleuze and Guattari, the plane is immanent since thought and substance are immanent (as substance and thought are immanent in the constructivism of the avant-garde). The plane of immanence is, for Deleuze and Guattari, "the image of thought" (37). Other spatial descriptions are given to the plane of immanence; it is *"a point of absolute survey"* (21). Concepts are "'absolute surfaces or volumes,' forms whose only object is the inseparability of distinct variations" (21). For Deleuze and Guattari, then, the plane of immanence is a plane of "selection" and "specification," "due to thought by right" (50).

Added to this seemingly already immanent nature of the plane (i.e., added to its geological "dimension") is the aspect of movement. "Thought demands 'only' movement that can be carried to infinity" or, "the movement of the infinite" (37). This movement of thought becomes substance or being since in "turning towards" a horizon (truth) thought must thereby turn back on itself, creating a fold. (Deleuze and Guattari give the image of immanence being woven like a gigantic shuttle.) Say Deleuze and Guattari, "[i]nfinite movement is double, and there is only a fold from one to the other. It is in this sense that thinking and being are said to be one and the same" (38). For Deleuze and Guattari, "[m]ovement is not the image of thought without being also the substance of thought" (38). "The plane of immanence has two facets," then, which are described as Thought and Nature, or, *Nous* and *Physis* (38). In other words, the plane of immanence describes a continuum between thought, the world of things, and events. From this continuity the category of thought cannot be left out. However, this has often been the case since Literature's fall.

In considering the literary regime of signs from the point of view of a plane of immanence, then, it must be viewed as an event and as *substance*—not as a linguistic category. Deleuze and Guattari add to their thinking about the plane of immanence similar thinking found in a letter to Herodotus from Epicurus: "'[t]he atom will traverse space with the speed of thought'" (38). Immanence is then, immanent to itself—the literary event cannot be thought outside *its own* thought—and this fact is most perfectly exhibited, for Deleuze and Guattari, in the thinking of Spinoza:

> In his last book of the *Ethics* (Spinoza) produced the movement of the infinite and gave infinite speeds to thought.... There he attains incredible speeds, with such lightning compression that one can only speak of music, of tornadoes, of wind and strings. (1994:48)

For Deleuze and Guattari, this book of Spinoza's, in fact, satisfied philosophy's prephilosophical presupposition.

For Deleuze and Guattari, because it is immanent, that which "pertains to thought as such must be distinguished from contingent features of the brain or historical opinions" (37). They add:

> Movement of the infinite does not refer to spatiotemporal coordinates that define the successive positions of a moving object and the fixed reference points in relation to which these positions vary. "To orientate oneself in thought" implies neither objective reference point nor moving object that experiences itself as a subject and that as such strives for or needs the infinite. Movement takes in everything, and there is no place for a subject and an object that can only be concepts. (1994:37)

Rorty is the most recent commentator in the American tradition of pragmatics, and he is against transcendental philosophy precisely for its material play. He is against what he calls the "vocabularies" of philosophy, rejecting the "mapping," the "picturing" of our world by philosophy and the creating of a "vocabulary." Rorty finds that "picturing" is the desire of, or belief in, the representation of an a priori truth, an ahistorical aesthetic. For Rorty, the "anti-pragmatist" strives for the atemporal, for an "escape from time and history" (1982:174). In the place of mapping, he advocates "conversation." For Rorty, conversation keeps a discourse out of the unsavory domain of aesthetics—and by definition ahistoricism—since the "conversation constraints" (also referred to by Rorty as objections) (1982:164) determine the direction of "meaning." In other words, conversational constraints keep a discourse lodged within its time and out of the ahistorical category.

But Deleuze and Guattari avoid transcendence in their thinking by distinguishing the plane of immanence from simply immanence, considered not as a *plane* but as immanent *to* something else. They argue that the notion of immanence to something introduces the transcendent (1994:45). They give the example of consciousness; in the Greek world, consciousness belonged to no one and was considered as a plane of immanence (by Descartes, Kant, and Husserl). However, increasingly it became the domain of a Christian consciousness (46).

The Geological Nature of Thought

In their notion of constructivism, Deleuze and Guattari offer an alternative to this capture of picturing by American philosophical pragmatics. For Deleuze and Guarttari, philosophy involves an image of thought that has its own time outside history. The image of thought is geological in formation.[1] "[C]onstructivism has two qualitatively different complementary aspects: the creation of concepts and the laying out of a plane (of immanence)" (1994:36). (This must be compared to Rorty's notion of conversation, which is the opposite of a plane, since, for Rorty, due to the floating nature of language, conversation is all that is possible.) The plane has "diagrammatic features," and these involve the "infinite movements of thought" (40). It has "*directions* that are fractal in nature" (40). And it has intuitions that are "the envelopment of infinite movements of thought that constantly pass through the plane of immanence" (40). Thus, it is that the plane of immanence is described as "the *image* of thought" (37, my italics). Concepts are intensive ordinates of the movements of the plane. They are "differential positions: finite movements in which the infinite is now only speed and each of which constitutes a surface or a volume, an irregular contour marking the halt in the degree of proliferation" (40). They are "absolute dimensions" (40).

For Deleuze and Guattari, philosophy proceeds by the superimposition of the images of thought—a philosophy-becoming—resulting in a "*stratigraphic* time." It does *not* proceed by "the succession of systems" (59) as with the history of philosophy. The stratigraphic time, also referred to as "philosophical time" (59), is a "grandiose time of coexistence that does not exclude the before and after but superimposes them in a stratigraphic order" (59). It is "an infinite becoming of philosophy that crosscuts its history without being confused with it" (59).[2] Thus, with the stratigraphic, is thought considered as an image immanent to its own time; as a *substance* that defines its own time. The formation of thought is a formed substance that sits on the landscape of thinking uniquely, principally because it does not belong to History:

> Certain paths (movements [of thought]) take on a sense of direction only as the shortcuts or detours of faded paths; a variable curvature can appear only as the transformation of one or more others.... Mental landscapes do not change haphazardly through the ages: a mountain had to rise here or a river to flow by there again recently for the ground, now dry and flat, to have a particular appearance and texture... very old strata can rise to the surface again, can cut a path through the formations that covered them. (1994:58)

In other words, it is the geographic that makes for a philosophy-becoming, and, equally, it is a philosophy-becoming that makes the plane of immanence geographic, or the *image* of thought. The philosophy-becoming, coexistence, involving as it does, the best and worst of philosophy, is ultimately a movement toward the nonthought of thought—toward thought's immanence (59). For Deleuze and Guattari, the plane of immanence is "that which cannot be thought and yet must be thought" (60). It is the outside *of thought,* thought's utmost intimacy.

To further make this point of immanence of the concept and the plane, Deleuze and Guattari point out that the "nonphilosophical" (the plane of immanence) "is perhaps closer to the heart of philosophy than philosophy itself" (1994:41). That is, it has its own thought/being. "This means that philosophy cannot be content to be understood only philosophically or conceptually, but is addressed essentially to non-philosophers as well" (41).[3] This addressing of philosophers to nonphilosophers can be responsible for interdisciplinarity—or the becoming of thought—not considered in Rorty's objection to "vocabularies."

Deleuze and Guattari's image of thought, then, is neither an act of representation or transcendentalism. This is because it forms an immanent plane. On the other hand, Rorty's pragmatism, we could say, in fact makes immanence, immanent *to* something—that being, the *"social norm"* (1982:165). Rorty advocates "conformity to social norms" and "social context." Rorty criticizes the philosopher for wanting to be "constrained not merely by the disciplines of the day, but by the ahistorical and nonhuman nature of reality itself" (165). For Rorty, the issue "is between those who think our culture, or purpose, or intuitions cannot be supported except conversationally, and people who still hope for other sorts of support" (167).

But in fact, Deleuze rejects conversation. In "A Conversation: What Is It? What Is It For?" [*sic*] (Deleuze and Parnet, 1987), he says, "[i]t is very hard to 'explain oneself'—an interview, a dialogue, a conversation. Most of the time, when someone asks me a question, even one which relates to me, I see that, strictly, I don't have anything to say" (1). For Deleuze, if you aren't allowed to invent your questions, a question is hard to answer because, as Deleuze says, it is "constructed" or "invented" with "elements from all over the place, from never mind where" (1). (They are themselves already vocabularies, pictures.)

Deleuze's awkwardness in the face of conversation counters Rorty's dependence upon conversation. For Rorty, a conversation is possible when one accepts "the ordinary, retail, detailed, concrete reasons which have brought one to one's present view" (1982:165). The "retail" figure used here by Rorty refers to "criteria" agreed upon by interlocutors over time and with use. The criteria, for Rorty, does away with the Platonic-Kantian habit of attempting to determine criteria—of truth, knowledge, and morality—outside of discursive formations. Rorty also uses the economic metaphor of "paid off" to speak about these well-entrenched criteria. In a sense criteria are the glue of conversationality and where talking has left the *discipline*—of aesthetics or philosophy—and is communing about something besides itself, a social norm. This is why Rorty is able to say, "There are no constraints on inquiry save conversational ones" (1982:165).[4] This quite clearly is opposed to Deleuze and Guattari's notion of the plane of immanence in which, as they say, "[m]ental landscapes do not change haphazardly" (1994:59). Conversational constraints are also referred to by Rorty, as mentioned above, as "objections" (1982:165). But for Deleuze, objections are "even worse" (1987:1) than conversations. For Deleuze, objections have never contributed anything. Says Deleuze: "Every time someone puts an objection to me, I want to say: 'OK, OK, let's go on to something else" (1987:1). In other words, conversation and objections are not philosophy (the construction of concepts). For Deleuze and Guattari, "Those who do not renew the image of thought are not philosophers but functionaries who, enjoying a ready-made thought, are not even conscious of the problem and are unaware even of the efforts of those they claim to take as their models" (1994:51).

The Turn to Culture and Genealogy

In Rorty, conversational constraints come about (and replace vocabularies) because of the "ungrounded," "floating" nature of the conversations for both "members" (174). Conversation is ungrounded because language goes all the way down. Conversational constraint results in metaphilosophy, and or genealogy. For example, for Rorty, the issue is what to make of the history of philosophy, of what to make of "the place within the intellectual history of the West of the particular series of texts which raise the "deep" Philosophical problems which realists want to preserve" (xxix). A finding of genealogy might be to note that the "familiarity of terminology is a criterion of theory-choice in physical science," or that "coherence with the institutions of the surviving parliamentary democracies is a criterion in social philosophy" (166), and so on.

But, says Deleuze, too much attention is given to history. He writes, "[w]e think too much in terms of history, whether personal or universal" (Deleuze and Parnet, 1987:2). Contrary to this, for Deleuze and Guattari, "[p]hilosophers carry out a vast diversion of wisdom (their stratigraphy); they place it at the service of pure immanence" (1994:44). In doing so, "[t]hey replaced genealogy with a geology" (44). The philosophers may have, at times, donned a (transcendent) mask over the plane of immanence, but as Deleuze and Guattari say, "How could philosophy not disguise itself in its early stages?" (44). How could philosophy not profit from instituting a prephilosophical plane? (44). However, the point is that in pursuing immanence, they did institute a plane that sieve-like "stretched over chaos" (43), and in the process it made a ground[5] upon which friendship could be founded—friendship being the beginning of thinking minus idols and Kings. Say Deleuze and Guattari: "Only friends can set out a plane of immanence from which idols have been cleared" (43).

For Rorty, philosophy is a succession of systems, of "incompatible philosophical theories" (1982:167) that attempt to "ground our practices on something external to these practices" (167). His particular pragmatism does not attempt to choose between "incompatible philosophical theories" (167). On the other hand, for Deleuze and Guattari, this notion of incompatible philosophical theories is one belonging to the history of philosophy, to the notion of philosophy as a succession of systems, and it misses the stratigraphic, philosophy-becoming. Says Deleuze, philosophy-becoming "has nothing to do with the history of philosophy and…happens through those who the history of philosophy does not manage to classify" (Deleuze and Parnet, 1987:2).[6] Contrary to Rorty's horror (as a genealogist) in the ground of philosophy, the stratigraphic, the philosophy-becoming depends precisely upon the ground of the plane of immanence it constitutes. The plane of immanence is the earth or deterritorialization on which philosophy creates its concepts (1994:93–95). In Deleuze and Guattari, philosophy cannot be reduced to history because its practice is to wrest itself from history as it creates new concepts. In contrast, "[h]istory today still designates only the set of conditions, however recent they may be, from which one turns away in order to become, that is to say, in order to create something new (96).

A New Approach to the Literary Text

Daniel Smith, in discussing the place of ethics in Deleuze's philosophy states that what Deleuze "calls 'ethics' is…a set of 'facilitative' (*facultative*) rules that evaluates what we do, say, and think according to the immanent mode of existence that it implies" (1998:252). What is needed is an immanent exploration of the literary aesthetic facilitating a certain mode of existence or ethics. The concept of the literary function that this book constructs is hewn from prior concepts of performativity and pragmatics. As has already been shown with respect to pragmatics, the field of performativity too is anything but unified. "Pragmatics," when used by some cultural commentators, has been used to describe the postmodern turn in general, as with the Lance Olsen's reference to the American tradition of James and Dewy.[7] Olsen's reading of the American tradition, for instance, creates the instance of a unity of postmodernism and pragmatics (Deleuze and Guattari's is nonpostmodern pragmatics) and at the same time a unified field of pragmatics. The different pragmatics have a vastly different bearing on a literary function and discourse; for example, postmodern pragmatics, in the form as described by Olsen, results in the transmigration of "the literary" into "the cultural."

However, the uneven terrain of contemporary pragmatics—which involves linguistic pragmatics, philosophical pragmatism, postmodern pragmatics, and Deleuze and Guattari's schizopragmatics—provides a rich terrain for the mining of a literary function. And the literary function, as it emerges out of this "field" of pragmatics, in fact, becomes a point of critique of some aspects of the domain. For example, the linguistic category of the performative belongs to linguistic pragmatics; however, by pursuing the performative beyond its linguistic context, definitional problems of this pragmatics can be demonstrated. In turn, the literary function serves to open up performativity beyond its disciplinary and linguistic base.[8] In fact, in the proceeding chapters it is the linguistic nature of a variety of pragmatics to which definitional problems are attributed.

In what follows, the concepts of performativity and pragmatics open up the ethical and political questions housed within the aesthetic, which, it is argued, the shift of some pragmatics (linguistic, philosophical pragmatism) into the field of contemporary cultural theory and criticism, have at times foreclosed. This emphasis upon the aesthetic brings criticism to bear on pragmatics that fail to be truly immanent. In the process an inherent relationship between pragmatics and immanence is missed. Such a relationship emphasizes the continuum between life and the (literary) aesthetic and the importance of furthering exploration into the literary function as a result. The literary function, then, as it is developed in this book, also becomes a critique of nonimmanent modes of cultural criticism.

Finally, it is important to note that this book does not seek an exhaustive account of—nor a definitive, universal vocabulary for—the literary function. Instead, its practice is that of empiricism. Empiricism, says Deleuze, is the analysis of "the states of things in such a way that non-pre-existent concepts can be extracted from them" (Deleuze and Parnet, 1987:vii). According to Deleuze, empiricism does not refer terms or elements back to an abstract concept such as the One, the Subject, or the Whole (vii), and I would add to this "the literary." Rather, it takes abstract terms—such as the "literary," the "performative," and the "pragmatic"—and examines them. It examines not "unities," "totalities," but the *relation between* elements. Thus, its "object" is multiple rather than a Subject/abstraction. The result is the creation of a plane—also referred to by Deleuze and Guattari as a "concept" and an "event." Say Deleuze and Guattari, "[t]he event . . . is related to the immanent survey of a field without a subject" (1994:48).

2

Rethinking the Performative in Pragmatics

Hence the necessity of a return to pragmatics, in which language never has universality in itself, self-sufficient formalization, a general semiology, or a meta-language.

(Deleuze and Guattari, A Thousand Plateaus:
Capitalism and Schizophrenia)

Certain pragmatic approaches block an investigation of aesthetics, and as an ethics, while other approaches enable such an investigation. This chapter considers the category of the performative in relation to pragmatics and rethinks the performative in order to theorize the literary function in ways pragmatic approaches belonging to the postmodern-cultural-critical turn are unable to do. It is only by rethinking the performative that we can arrive at a pragmatics for the literary function that enable an exploration into the ethics of aesthetics. By considering the performative in relation to pragmatics we can eventually look at the storytelling situation, the production of singularity and subjectification, and the production of community. In other words, the performative helps us understand the literary function in terms of affect and not in terms of representation.

Contemporary pragmatics has a common root in pragmatism, which involves an attack both on positivistic and transcendental philosophical thought. However, pragmatism is also plural. There are French and German pragmatists including Jacques Derrida, François Lyotard,[1] Hans-Georg Gadamer, Foucault, and Deleuze and Guattari, who have a common point of departure in Nietzsche and Heidegger, while there exists an American tradition of pragmatism with its point of departure in William James and John Dewey. Richard Rorty, Charles Sanders Peirce, and Wilfrid Sellars belong with the contemporary American pragmatists. As mentioned, certain types of pragmatics block the way to the possibility of "new analytical, aesthetic and social practices," as Guattari says of postmodernism itself (1996:112). This chapter will raise the issue of the definitional problems of pragmatics that give rise to a turning away from the aesthetic. Such pragmatics explored include philosophical pragmatism, linguistic pragmatics, and certain aspects of postmodern pragmatics. The definitional problems that are the focus of this chapter, and that lead to a foreclosure upon the aesthetic, are ultimately traced to the different approaches to performativity within these instances of pragmatics. The chapter, therefore, considers, and reconsiders, the significance of the performative in the context of pragmatics and in relation to the literary function.

Rorty is of particular importance to this chapter because of his discussion of the articulation between (his) philosophical pragmatism and literary and cultural criticism. For Rorty, pragmatism is a kind of literary criticism because it is happy to grasp its own time in thought, to merely "interpret interpretations," to be a "historicism," and not, as positivist philosophy requires, to attempt to lay down any "true propositions... for the human race unto all generations" (1982:xli). In fact, for Rorty, our century is marked by the breakdown of the distinction between criticism and philosophy by "people who write as if there were nothing but texts" (1982:139). These "textualists" include the "Yale school" of literary criticism, Harold Bloom, Geoffrey Hartmann, J. Hills Miller, and Paul De Man and French thinkers such as Jacques Derrida and Michel Foucault. It should also be noted, however, that thinking such as Rorty's has taken literary criticism in the direction of philosophical pragmatism, nee cultural criticism, and away from its former autonomous and universalist activities. It is because of the role Rorty plays in exploring the boundaries between philosophical pragmatism and criticism that his is the first pragmatics to come under scrutiny in this chapter.

Rorty's Pragmatism and/as Literary Studies

In *Consequences of Pragmatism* (1982), Rorty puts forward a treatise for the contemporary pragmatist. For Rorty, pragmatism is philosophy without the presupposition of the transcendental philosophy of Plato, Kant, and Hegel and the empirical philosophy of Hobbes and Marx. Rorty indicates the difference between the former and latter kinds of philosophy with a small "p" and a big "P," respectively. (I retain such a distinction when referring to Rorty's argument.) For Rorty, Philosophy argues that certain sentences correspond to a truth, an essence, a transcendent universal, either within a spatiotemporal reality or without. Such Philosophy is an epistemology of the picture. For Rorty, language is paired off "with bits of what one takes the world to be.... [Thus,] we can rap out routine undeliberated reports like 'This is water,' 'That's red,' 'That ugly'" (162), and so on, and these "short categorical sentences can easily be thought of as pictures, or as symbols which fit together to make a map" (162). Rorty refers to this as a "correspondence theory of truth."

For "technical realists" and "intuitive realists" (as Rorty dubs the two camps of contemporary proponents of the "correspondence theory of truth"), the true sentence corresponds to a piece of Truth itself. The central presupposition of the Realists, as Rorty calls the nonpragmatists, is: "that true sentences divide into an upper and a lower division—the sentences which correspond to something and those which are 'true' only by courtesy of convention" (1982:xviii). For Rorty, it is in the elimination of these classes of language that correspondence theory is brought down. For Rorty's pragmatism, truth is entirely a property of certain sentences. "(T)rue sentences are not true because they correspond to reality, and so there is no need to worry what sort of reality, if any, a given sentence corresponds to—no need to worry about what 'makes' it true" (1982:xvi).

Rorty's pragmatism is squarely, then, in the tradition of the "linguistic turn," in which analytic philosophers of language, such as "Wittgenstein-Sellars-Quine-Davidson," in a postpositivistic mode see truth as conventional and contingent *due* to language's ubiquity and thereby noncorrespondence. For Rorty, language is not "a *tertium quid* between Subject and Object, nor...a medium in which we try to form pictures of reality" (1982:xviii).

Far from corresponding to Reality, language, for Rorty's pragmatism, is a coping device for its users. The behavioral aspect of its users becomes proof of language's pragmatic ends. Or, put differently, language is "part of the behaviour of human beings" (1982:xviii).[2] Where the technical realist claims that the statement "X is ø" is only possible by discovering what "X" refers to and then seeing if that is similar in kind to ø, a pragmatist would say that "X is ø," as a statement, is dependent on how useful a belief it is to have. For the pragmatist, all truths are intratheoretical, meaning they are dependent on their belief systems. Therefore, in the place of truth, Dewey's "warranted assertibility" is preferred as a notion. William James defined the true as "the name of whatever proves itself to be good," either by way of belief or by way of "definite, assignable reasons" (Rorty paraphrasing James, xxv). Rorty says of James's view: "'True' resembles 'good' or 'rational' in being a normative notion, a compliment paid to sentences that seem to be paying their way and that fit in with other sentences which are doing so" (1982:xxv).

In the end, pragmatists are not interested in the validity of their debate when compared to the debate of realist philosophers. Rather, they are concerned about what is *at stake* in either argument. As Rorty says, what is important is that the sentence is paying its way. For Rorty, it is this pragmatic criterion that is missing from Western realist Philosophy and that, therefore, makes its success questionable. Western realist Philosophy is ultimately driven by Moral Law—to bring to the fore a universal community based upon shared intuitions. The aim is for an "intellectual justice" that is reached by finding theses that "do justice to *everybody's* intuitions" (xxx). Intuitions are our potential, and it is the philanthropic duty of the realist philosopher to bring them to universality with dialectical thought and synthesis. Rorty's pragmatist rejects this project on the grounds that, first, it presupposes that "language does *not* go all the way down" (1982:xxx), that, "some intuitions at least, are *not* a function of the way one has been brought up to talk, of the texts and people one has encountered" (xxx). And second, pragmatism is a critique of universalism. Realist Philosophy finds common elements from different vocabularies that house different intuitions, such as Homeric warriors, Buddhist sages, contemporary French literary critics, and so on. The realists formulate theses that, says Rorty, "would be rational for all these people to accept" (xxx). However, for Rorty, these theses reduce and skew the vocabularies. The thesis is skewed because it is blind to its own frame, its presuppositions. For instance, Cartesian thought is able to arrive at the notion of the *human being* with the aid of the theoretical tool of synthesis and thus ignore its own frame and presupposition of the Modern West. For Rorty's pragmatist, understanding intuitions in situ, a kind of "historicism" or "quasi-anthropology,"...is a necessary and honest acknowledgment of the nontranscendental nature of thought.

For Rorty, the pragmatist envisages a universal community only if it is based upon a "hybridization" of thought—by hybridization he means different vocabularies. This opposes the notion put forward by intuitive realism that a universal community is possible due to shared intuitions and a resulting synthesis of thought evolved by Philosophy to express these shared intuitions. As already mentioned, the pragmatist doesn't claim a viability for arguments with an opposing philosophical theory since " '[a]ll awareness is a linguistic affair' " (Rorty quoting Sellers, xxxvi), and " '[t]he meaning of a proposition is its method of verification' " (Rorty quoting Sellers, xxxvi). The pragmatist cannot disclaim intuition, "[t]here are no fast little arguments to show that there are no such things as intuitions—arguments which are themselves not based on something stronger than intuitions" (1982:xxxvii). The pragmatist opposes realist philosophy, based on "the Kantian vocabulary of morals" (xxxvii) and "the Cartesian vocabulary in philosophy of the mind" (xxxvii), because she finds these intuitions and vocabularies an "incubus" (xxxvii). Simply, pragmatically, they have not paid off.

In pragmatism, no one discourse has the ability to connect with an ineffable Truth or reality. In particular, Rorty disparages Thomas Nagel's claim for an intuitive self. This self is something "we cannot learn about by believing true propositions but only by *being* like that" (xxxvi). For Rorty, there is no isolable thing, such as an essence of being, "against which to test vocabularies and cultures" (xxxvi). Rather, vocabularies and cultures are (seemingly) self-improving as a result of coming up against other vocabularies and cultures. Rather than attempting to express the ineffable, then, the job of the philosopher, for Rorty, is to "see how things hang together" (xl). What the pragmatist will pass on to the next generation is not truthful propositions, as has been the Philosopher's goal, but descriptions of ways of seeing, that is, descriptions of descriptions. She uses names to denote sets of descriptions, symbol-systems, and ways of seeing. Her specialty is seeing similarities and differences between great big pictures, between attempts to see how things hang together (xl).

This genealogical-type approach involves the "bookish intellectual" in what Rorty refers to as the "literary-historical-anthropological-political merry-go-round" of thought (xxxviii). The pragmatist does not go beyond this interdisciplinary mode. There are no "transdisciplinary, transcultural, ahistorical criteria" (1982:xxxviii). Thus, the realist Philosophers with their "scientific" discourse are replaced by a "culture critic" whose discourse is eclectic. The critic may "comment on anything at all" (xl). For Rorty:

> Such a culture would, doubtless, contain specialists in seeing how things hang together. But these specialists would be people who had no special "problems" to solve, nor any special "method" to apply, abide by no particular disciplinary standards, had no collective self-image as a "profession." (xxxix)

The critic's "highest hope is to grasp their time in thought" (xli), and, as already mentioned, not to offer any perennial propositions. Being bounded by the ubiquity of language, the new "culture criticism" may only be "a study of the comparative advantages and disadvantages of the various ways of talking which our race has invented" (xl).

For Rorty, pragmatism is about getting things done. He is against end-less interpretation because it gets in the way of getting things done (xli). He states that comparison and contrast of "vocabularies," in a search for the final, universal vocabulary should be abandoned for the general acceptance of a criterion—something that all sides agree "would count as resolving disputes" (xli). Rorty's point is that there can be no univer-sal criterion as we create criterion in the course of creating a practice. The problem with literary intellectuals of the scientific kind, for Rorty, "is their inability to...agree on what would count as resolving disputes, on the criterion to which all sides must appeal" (xli). For Rorty, once a criterion is agreed upon, "vigorous argumentation" can follow—and things can be done (see also, 1982:xlii).

Thus, for Rorty, all discourses have an equal status—none are privy to the Truth; rather, each has a role in "trying to cope with various bits of the universe" (xliii). Literature and the arts, for Rorty, help ethics do its job in attending to the universe. Literature and the arts, therefore, act as inquiries and are "on the same footing as scientific inquires," for instance (xliii). Some inquiries produce propositions, and "[t]he ques-tions about what propositions to assert" are "questions about what will help us get what we want (or...what we *should* want)" (xliii). Literature and the arts help ethics do its job by guiding us in what narratives to listen to and comment on and retell.

Language All the Way Down

The problem with Rorty's contemporary philosophical pragmatism is that it closes the door upon conceptual exploration, including the exploration of the literary aesthetic and function. This is because Rorty's pragmatics is governed by the universality of language. His notion of the *ubiquity of language* is a development written up by Rorty as the linguistic turn. Writes Rorty, "Language goes all the way down," making philosophy "a kind of writing" (1982:90). However, Rorty's discussion of language is not nuanced enough; when language is posited as ubiquitous, from which there is no outside, it becomes universal and thereby the new transcenden-tal signifier to replace intuition. Thus, Rorty's pragmatics does not escape the pitfalls of Philosophy. For Rorty, linguistic awareness is an "affair" unto itself, but Rorty does not speak of other affairs: there are incorpo-real, bodily, nonlinguistic, a-signifying affairs,[3] of which I will elaborate on later in the chapter. To not make this distinction is to give language a universality to which Rorty is supposedly opposed. But as Deleuze and

Guattari say, "Language never has universality in itself" (1987:111). For Deleuze and Guattari, what is needed is a kind of geological pragmatics, not a linguistic pragmatics, since "there is always a form of content that is simultaneously inseparable from the form of expression" (1987:111). Say Deleuze and Guattari:

> If we call the signifying semiotic system semiology, then semiology is only one regime of signs among others, and not the most important one. Hence the necessity of a return to pragmatics, in which language never has universality in itself, self-sufficient formalization, a general semiology, or a metalanguage. (111)

When Rorty says that language is ubiquitous and that "[a]ll aware-ness is a linguistic affair" (1982:xxxvi), he concludes that "theory" and "contemplation" (162) are not useful but mere ruminations (on an intuition).[4] Rorty's position divides language into language that is theo-retical (and useless) and language that is practical, and, more particu-larly, useful. Writes Rorty: "It is the vocabulary of practice rather than theory, or action rather than contemplation, in which we can say some-thing useful about truth" (1982:162). For Rorty, language pared back to the sentence (he suggests individual sentences should replace vocabular-ies and theories) is more capable of "utility, convenience, and likelihood of getting what we want" (1982:163). For Rorty, because it is ubiquitous, language is a tyrannical force that must be tamed; the user must stay away from concepts and theories and use "sentences" only, and in par-ticular, sentences that have proven themselves worthy because they are useful. To quote Rorty paraphrasing James: "'True' resembles 'good' or 'rational' in being a normative notion, a compliment paid to sentences that seem to be paying their way and that fit in with other sentences which are doing so" (1982:xxv).[5]

Rorty's position on language, then, means abandoning the limitations of language, that is, its ubiquity, by favoring actions over vocabularies. In Rorty, the act, or the practice, solves the problem of the vicissitudinous nature of language, and vocabularies become redundant. The problem with this idea, however, is that it prefigures the act and practice outside language. Rorty wishes to appeal to history when he says we must use only sentences that have paid their way; however, this reading of history is imagined outside lan-guage. Rorty's notion of "the good action" seems, paradoxically, to be both humanist and pre-structuralist as well as post-structuralist. Rorty actually says that the accomplished contemporary pragmatists, in doing what they do, are "simply people who [are] good at being human" (xxxix). Elsewhere, he accuses nonpragmatists of being interested in the nonhuman nature of reality (165). Rorty's pragmatics, then, is a humanist approach to philosophy that, ironically, results from a notion of the ubiquity of language.

Rorty's approach to language is dialectical, which ineluctably steers Rorty's philosophy in the direction of Philosophy. When the contemporary pragmatist refers to sets of descriptions in order to know how they hang together and "in the hope of making it hang together with everything else" (1982:xxxix), he is engaging in a dialectical approach to language. Rorty notes that Philosophy has sought to make language adequate to the Truth, but his own dialectical approach to descriptions (his description of descriptions) now makes Truth adequate to language. According to Timothy Gould, J. L. Austin refers to Philosophy's obsession with the Descriptive Fallacy:

> It was for too long the assumption of philosophers that the business of a "statement" can only be to "describe" some state of affairs, or to "state some fact," which it must do either truly or falsely.... The idea that the business of language shows up in a form of utterance that is, in a sense, designed to be true or false has its counterpart in a philosopher's picture of the world—a world in which the (interesting) conditions are to be thought of as "facts," to which our (interesting) utterances must correspond (or fail to). (Gould, 1995:22–23)[6]

Rorty himself is against the correspondence between statement and world, but he does not avoid this paradigm when comparing sets of descriptions in order to arrive at a signified world outside them. Ironically, it is due to the vicissitudinous nature of language, its ubiquity, that this quasi-dialecticism happens (albeit by default rather than by design).

Theory, Practice, and the Performative

Rorty's pragmatics is suspicious of conceptualization because it does not operate with a developed sense of performativity. Instead, Rorty's linguistic-based pragmatics is representative—where pragmatics that bring forth conceptualizations function performatively, that is, as actions and geological formations. To illustrate the difference between representative pragmatics and conceptual pragmatics, it is helpful to compare Rorty's notion of "tool" to Deleuze and Guattari's notion of "tool." "We must be careful *not* to...suggest that one can separate the tool, Language, from its users and inquire as to its 'adequacy' to achieve our purposes" (Rorty, 1982:xix). Here, language must meet goals seemingly originated from outside it, as though there was a subject it represented. The pragmatists Deleuze and Guattari also use the word "tool." Their usage differs from Rorty's, however. In Deleuze and Guattari, the word "tool" refers to their theory, and not to language and the sentence, as it does in Rorty. For them, the role of theory is not to be representative but *to act as a relay point that forms networks that produce conditions.*[7] In other words, theory or conceptualization is performative, and by that I mean it produces conditions and is not representative. Deleuze's work was once criticized by a Maoist for not representing the *purposes* of Maoism, where other theorists, such as Sartre and Foucault, seemingly did (Foucault, 1977:205). But for Deleuze the role of theory is not to be representative: "A theorising intellectual . . . is no longer a subject, a representing or representative consciousness" (Deleuze in Foucault, 1977:206).[8] For the intellectual to take up the position of the representative is to install a division of power and a distribution of power (Deleuze in Foucault, 209).[9]

For Deleuze, theory does not operate by way of representation because "theory is always local and related to a limited field. . . . Moreover, from the moment a theory moves into its proper domain, it begins to encounter obstacles, walls, and blockages which require its relay by another type of discourse" (Deleuze in Foucault, 205). For Deleuze "[t]he relationship which holds in the application of a theory is never one of resemblance" (Deleuze in Foucault, 205) because both theory and practice are partial and fragmented. Therefore, the relationship between theory and practice is not one in which practice is the application of theory or theory the application of practice. Rather than being representative, theory, like practice, serves as a relay point that forms networks that produce conditions. This conceptualization differs from Rorty's in not thinking of language as being outside of theory—there is no "purpose" that the language must prove adequate to. Rather, theory and practice are both actions, "theoretical actions and practical actions" (Deleuze in Foucault, 207). Deleuze gives the example of Foucault's "theoretical analysis of the context of confinement," which then functioned as a relay to "the information group for prisoners (GIP)," which in turn "creat(ed) conditions that permit(ted) the prisoners themselves to speak" (Deleuze in Foucault, 206).

Deleuze's notion of the relationship between theory and practice differs from Rorty's. When Rorty states that the role of literature is to aid ethics in doing its job by acting as an inquiry, which produces propositions (1982:xliii), he envisages a relationship between theory and practice as one in which theory is considered an application of practice. For Deleuze, this is an old approach to the relationship of practice and theory and is a totalizing process (Foucault, 1977:205). Such a notion requires a "judge" or "decoder" or "enunciative subject," to borrow Barthes's terms, and is a notion of the text as transparent and not as immanent. "Immanent," here, pertains not only to the limited field of the theory or practice but also to its performative quality. Michael Clark points out that in Barthes's notion of Text the word is not situated in the world, as it is for historicists, nor is the world situated in the word, as it is for formalists, but rather the word is treated as world (2000:7). The difference between Deleuze and Rorty is, then, between Deleuze's notion of textual practice creating conditions, and Rorty's notion of it producing propositions.[10]

For Deleuze, theory is a regional system in the struggle against systems of power. It does not totalize (as power does) but is rather an "instrument for multiplication and it also multiplies itself" (Deleuze in Foucault, 1977:208). It is theory that the intellectual uses in the "struggle against the forms of power that transform him into its object and instrument in the sphere of 'knowledge,' 'truth,' 'consciousness,' and 'discourse'" (Deleuze, in Foucault, 208). Theory is "necessarily an instrument of combat.... If no one uses it, beginning with the theoretician himself... then the theory is worthless or the moment is inappropriate" (Deleuze in Foucault, 208). In Deleuze, then, it is not language that is a tool, neither is it sentences that are tools, but theory is a tool. "A theory is exactly like a box of tools," writes Deleuze (Deleuze in Foucault, 208). This distinction between language and theory is highly significant, it marks the difference between a theory of language (which is Deleuze and Guattari's) and a humanistic approach to language (which is Rorty's). Language (in Rorty) is totalizing because language serves to represent the subject/purpose while in Deleuze, theory aids in the struggle against such forms of power due to its multiplying function. In his forward to Deleuze and Guattari's *A Thousand Plateaus, Capitalism and Schizophrenia*, Brian Massumi says, "[Deleuze] calls his kind of philosophy 'pragmatics' because its goal is the invention of concepts that do not add up to a system of belief or an architecture of propositions that you either enter or you don't" (Deleuze and Guattari, 1987:xv). In this way, Deleuze and Guattari and Rorty are alike. However, Massumi goes on to say that the concept (in Deleuze) packs "a potential in the way a crowbar in a willing hand envelops an energy of prying" (1987:xv). It is this transformative and performative quality attached to theory that is missing from the representative mode of Rorty's language and sentences.

It is in respect to its representative function, its descriptive function, then, that Rorty's pragmatism can also be described as a kind of "scientific" positivism, despite Rorty's own idea that pragmatism is a step away from positivism. Rorty's pragmatism continues the Philosophical paradigm (despite its linguistic turn) when it opposes history to the definitive vocabulary of Philosophy. The historical—which is where things get done—is of primary importance for Rorty, and it is where he sees

Philosophy has failed. Rorty says that for philosophical pragmatics the historical is a shifting ground due to its linguistic nature and the role practice has in formulating criteria. However, it is no less historical for that. *The historical becomes the-criterion-to-which-all-sides-must-appeal*, since vocabularies cannot be relied upon in this case. The historical, in Rorty, is that which stabilizes the vicissitudinous nature of language. It is where its *value* can and should be judged. In Rorty, language is the mere tool of history, and history is placed in (*binary*) opposition to Philosophy's definitive vocabulary.

Despite Rorty's call for conversation, his tone puts forward a commitment to history in the (Marxist) Philosophical sense—as that which has a (unified) purpose. It is the criterion (upon which the pragmatists must agree from the outset) that makes the purpose unified. Rorty further adds to this quite modernist sense of history when he sees contemporary pragmatics as progressive and itself belonging to an evolution:

> [T]he Enlightenment thought, rightly, that what would succeed religion would be *better*. The pragmatist is betting that what succeeds the "scientific," positivist culture which the Enlightenment produced will be *better*. (1982:xxxviii)

To conclude this section on Rorty's pragmatics, the definitional problem with Rorty's normative style of pragmatics results when he attempts to distinguish between lower and upper 'p' philosophy via philosophical linguistics. On the one hand Rorty states that language goes all the way down, and this is why there can be no definitive utterances, but on the other hand Rorty's philosophy imagines language as able to be a mere bit player, seconded to an economy and realm outside it, namely history. Consequently, Rorty's philosophy forecloses upon the performative in relation to pragmatics—as this is constituted in the philosophy of Foucault and Deleuze and Guattari, for example. Rorty's philosophy attempts to keep the vicissitudinous nature of language at bay through a dialecticism of language itself. Sentences can only be trusted when they link with other sentences that do the same. Deleuze and Guattari describe certain philosophers as paranoid, and Rorty fits this description: their regime of signs is a paranoid regime of signs.[11] Such philosophers fear the "deterritorialized sign assailing [them] from every direction in the gliding atmosphere" of the chain of signifiers (1987:112). Ironically, however, this makes these philosophers masters of the "superpower of the signifier" (112). Deleuze and Guattari note that it is the "royal feeling of wrath" these philosophers assume that makes them "master(s) of the network spreading through the atmosphere" (112).[12] Deleuze and Guattari have dramatized the paranoid despotic regime thus: "They are attacking me and making me suffer, but I can guess what they're up to, I'm one step ahead of them. I've always known, I have power even in my impotence. 'I'll get them'" (112). The definitional problem with Rorty's contemporary philosophical pragmatism, the reason for its all too close association with transcendent philosophy, is its focus upon the ubiquity of language and thus the chain of signifiers. Ironically, this has resulted in a humanistic discourse. Rorty's criteria, to which all sides agree, as well the representative function of his pragmatics, make it capable of being a totalizing discourse. But above all, Rorty's pragmatist is unable to explore regimes of signs in their immanence, but only as they correspond to pregiven criteria. He is unable to explore regimes of signs as they multiply and transform, as they carry out, for example, the literary function.

Linguistic Pragmatics

Philosophical pragmatism is not the only tradition of pragmatics. The pragmatics belonging to linguistics is largely attributable to J. L. Austin and his theory of the performative utterance.[13] His notion of the performative is crucial to a concept of the literary function (as it is for Deleuze and Guattari's pragmatics), particularly its attribute of virtuality. This section will explore Austin's notion of the performative, but it will also point to a shortfall in this field of pragmatics.

Since Charles Morris made the distinction between "syntax, semantics, and pragmatics" (Recanati, 1987:2)[14] pragmatics has referred to the *affective* attributes of utterances. François Recanati says of Morris's thoughts on the subject: "The part of meaning involving speaker and hearer—what the sign 'expresses' or 'evokes'—is its pragmatic meaning, as against its representational content or semantic meaning" (2). Because the expressive meaning is thought by Morris to be extrinsic to the sentence itself and variable in nature, it was concluded that it is specific to the context of the utterance. For Austin as well, it is context that "defines" the pragmatic meaning of the utterance. (There are echoes here of Rorty's thinking also.)[15] Says Recanati, Peirce, in theorizing the semantic and expressive functions, made the distinction between the sign as a *type* and the sign as a *token*. The sign-type is the sign's *symbolic* function, the sign as it "is conventionally associated with the things it represents." The sign-token on the other hand is *indexical*, and it is associated with the referent by way of fact rather than convention, as with the example of the child's tears, which being caused by distress can stand as a sign for that distress, in the same way smoke is a sign of fire. Thus, the sign-token has an empirical or causal relation between sign and thing (Recanati, 1987:4). This so-called factual rather than conventional association between sign and referent is referred to as "existential." A further early definition of the pragmatic utterance is that it involves the use value—what a speaker does with words—rather than the meaning of words. (Here too, there are echoes of Rorty.) Thus, early pragmatic studies was occupied with areas external to language itself, such as psychology or sociology.

Austin, however, extended the pragmatic to "the fold of linguistics proper" (Recanati, 1987:9) with his notion of the illocutionary. The illocutionary refers to the social aspect of language—when a speaker speaks with serious intent he or she performs a social act, for example, an order, a question, advice, the expression of a wish, and so on. The performative is considered to be a subset of the illocutionary; rather than action being accomplished in *speaking*, as in the case of the illocutionary, in the performative, actions are accomplished by *saying* them. For example, I make promises when I say "I love you."[16] Austin opposes the performative utterance to the constative utterance, which, according to Austin, is descriptive; it describes an event only. The performative, on the other hand, both describes the action of the speaker while at the same time accomplishing that action. "[L]anguage, in Austin's view, is an institution used to perform acts that can exist only within and by virtue of that institution" (1987:9). (We have echoes of Rorty here too.) These acts Austin refers to as "speech acts."[17]

Deleuze and Guattari's Critique of Structural Linguistics and Its Effect upon the Definition of Performative

Deleuze and Guattari pursue the performative further, and, in particular, the existential function, to which I will shortly turn. They make a connection between the performative and immanence, and the result is a critique of structural linguistics—and the (referring) signifier. In Deleuze and Guattari's work, pragmatics shifts from an outcome-oriented pragmatics, seen in Rorty, to a much more humble cause, that of mapping regimes of signs. Say Deleuze and Guattari, all signs are pragmatic, in that they cause affects, and are performative, but it is not the role of pragmatics to state whether these are good or bad, either naturally or *necessarily* (1987:227). The object is to study the dangers of the regimes "to the extent that (pragmatics) undertakes not to represent, interpret, or symbolize, but only to make maps and draw lines, marking (the regimes) mixtures as well as their distinctions"(227). This is also known as "micropolitics." Mapping in Deleuze and Guattari does not correlate to the map of Philosophy referred to by Rorty. The map in Deleuze and Guattari is not correspondent but immanent. Deleuze and Guattari compare their mapping to tracing, which derives from "the oldest form of thought" and involves "genetic axis and profound structure" (1987:12). These act as models to which subjective instances may be traced. For Deleuze and Guattari, "[w]hat distinguishes the map from the tracing is that it is entirely oriented toward an experimentation in contact with the real. Their famous example is of the wasp and the orchid. "The orchid does not reproduce the tracing of the wasp; it forms a map with the wasp" (12). This example, found in nature, is an example of a process in which alliance, and not evolution (or filiation), is at work. Such mappings are creative, they form new "lines," meaning, they create new formations. Deleuze and Guattari also refer to this process of alliance as one of becoming. They give their example of the alliance of the cat and the baboon that results in a C virus (238). The nonfilial nature of mapping (or becoming) means, then, that it does not result in a model or structure, as the trace does. For example, from the orchid-wasp alliance no wasp-orchid eventuates (238). The map, then, "is open and connectable in all of its dimensions; it is detachable, reversible, susceptible to constant modification... (it) has multiple entryways, as opposed to the tracing, which always comes back 'to the same'" (12). And finally and importantly: "[t]he map has to do with performance, whereas the tracing always involves an alleged 'competence'" (12–13).

Unlike Austin, Deleuze and Guattari do not countenance the traditional "division of labour" between semantic meaning and pragmatic affect. For Deleuze and Guattari, "There are no universals or invariants of language...separate from 'performances.'" However, for Deleuze and Guattari, pragmatics involves the mapping of mixed semiotics (rather than linguistic semiotics—or history), and this is where they part company with both Austin and Rorty. This assemblage of semiotics forms an abstract machine that provides a language with a particular collective assemblage of enunciation—a speech act, a performative. In saying there is no invariant to language, Deleuze and Guattari are saying there is "no abstract machine internal to language" and therefore no subject of enunciation either. Deleuze and Guattari's pragmatics is, therefore, an extralinguistic pragmatics, and, correspondingly, it is empiricist and involves immanence. This is unlike Austinian-type pragmatics, which, by definition, is dependent on the subject of enunciation to make it context specific. And it differs from philosophical pragmatism and its implicit subject—being at the heart of its moral, humanistic "social norm," to which all sides must appeal.

Deleuze and Guattari's distinction between the *plane* of immanence and immanence that is immanent *to* something is crucial in considering the difference between Deleuzeoguattarian pragmatics and linguistic-based pragmatics. Immanence to something is immanence that presents "a flux of the lived that is immanent to the subject and individualized in that which belongs to the self" (1994:47). The speech act conceptualized linguistically is made immanent *to* something. In Rorty, sentences must "fit" with other sentences and thus become the criterion to which all sides must appeal for the sake of getting what *we* want. Here, the sentences are made immanent *to* something: the subject, history. Austin's "context" also becomes "a flux of the lived" that the performative is immanent *to*. For Deleuze and Guattari, however, the performative is precisely the concept of the *plane* of immanence—it is a collective assemblage of enunciation, without a subject of enunciation. For Deleuze and Guattari, when immanence is made immanent to something, it is automatically a transcendentalism—which is why Rorty's and Austin's concept of pragmatics remains humanist[18]—and language is captured by the transcendentalism to which it is made immanent.

Guattari's Existential Function Highlights the Problem with Rorty's Pragmatism, Linguistic Pragmatics, and Postmodern Pragmatics

Félix Guattari's critique of those forms of pragmatics derived from the linguistic turn is that they fail to take the lessons of the performative nature of language far enough. As a result, they become caught up in the philosophical tradition of description and categorization. With respect to approaches to the performative, Peirce, for example, sees the performative as indexical, associated with the referent by way of fact rather than convention. It has an empirical or causal relation between the sign and the thing. For Deleuze and Guattari, this is not the performative but merely what they call the noncorporeal attribute, that which is the "expressed" of statements (as, e.g., in the case of the crime, there is "the body of property, the body of the victim, the body of the convict" (1987:80), etc.).[19] For Deleuze and Guattari, philosophy too has been in the habit of producing propositions and concepts that are really the expressed of events—that remain for Deleuze and Guattari unpresentable and immaterial (see Cook, 1998:28). For Guattari, postmodern pragmatics fails due to its tie to linguistics and linguistics-descriptive modeling of language. Writes Guattari:

> The linguists specializing in declaration and speech acts have pointed out the fact that certain linguistic elements acquire another function parallel to the traditionally recognized one of signification and denotation, which is a particular pragmatic, by causing the respective positions of the speaking subject to crystallize, or by introducing, de facto, certain situational frameworks. (A classical example: The president who declares "the meeting is called to order" and who, by doing so, really calls the meeting to order.) However, even these have decided that they must limit the influence of their discovery to the category of their speciality. Whereas in reality, this third "existentialist" function, on which they place the accent, should logically imply a final crack in the structuralist straight-jacket within which they continue to bind their language. (1986:41)

In other words, for Guattari, all speech acts belong to the "'existentialist' function"—the performative, in Austinian terms—and thereby are immanent and unpresentable and cannot be categorized. John Searle further galvanized Austin's protostructuralist approach to the performative when he set forth to determine the different categories of performatives (such as the performative of promising). This structuralist/descriptive approach to language is further shown to be a folly by Cook. Calling on Derrida's critique of Searle, Cook points out that Searle's approach to the performative fails since on all repetitions of the speech act it repeats differently. This is the case since, like all linguistic acts, it is determined by *différance*—deferring and differing from other such acts. This makes categorization impossible (Cook, 1998).

Deleuze and Guattari's notion that the philosophical concept, proposition, or statement, is the expressed of events, which are unpresentable, can be traced to Deleuze's work in *The Logic of Sense*. Here, Deleuze revisits the thinking of the Stoics who make a "'distinction between bodies and events: between the knife that cuts and the cutting as an event'" (Cook quoting Deleuze, 1998:28).[20] For the Stoics, "Bodies and their qualities are material which can exist in the present, events are immaterial and unpresentable... [and] for this reason (the Stoics) assign events a different form of time and a different ontological status" (28). Furthermore, events have a "different relation to language than do bodies"(28). Bodies are "describable, denotable," but events are "'sayables'" (28). To quote Cook in full:

> To say an event is, firstly, not to describe it. For an event cannot be described as a body can be. The event of greening, for instance, can be located by

describing the changing of colours of a leaf, or by distinguishing its varying degrees of chlorophyll content. This, however, is not strictly a description of the event itself, but rather just of the body transformed by it. And it
is noteworthy that any such description of the circumstances in which an
event occurs does not suffice to comprehend the event itself. (28)

For Guattari and Deleuze, then, what is needed to escape the descriptive
bind of philosophy and to think the performative, among other concepts,
is no less than a new concept of the concept. For Deleuze and Guattari,
as well as for Derrida (see Patton, 1996), the new concept of the concept
entails thinking of concepts not as bearing a necessary relation to an
object, or as the creation of a speaker (a subject of enunciation), but as
being created by language itself. In both Deleuze and Guattari and
Derrida, "there is no proper relation to the object" (Patton, 123) to be
found in language. (Rorty's criteria to which all sides agree presuppose
the attitudes toward language that Deleuze and Guattari reject.) Rather,
new concepts are made when concepts are used differently, according "to the particular problem field in which they operate" (123). For
Deleuze and Guattari, terms that mark concepts are not metaphors but
deterritorializations that occur when a term is transferred to a "foreign
domain" (124). Derrida uses the term, and quasi-concept, "catachresis" to
describe the process in which a concept discovers and names "content not
previously known" (125). Writes Patton, quoting Fontanier:

> "Catachresis" consists in "the imposition of a sign upon a meaning
> which did not yet have its own proper sign in language." This is not, as in
> Aristotle's definition of metaphor, the transfer of a name which properly
> belongs to one thing onto something else, but rather the forced extension
> of a sign so that it stands for some content that did not previously have its
> own sign. (125)

As the above section begins to make clear, in order to think the concept
(including the concept of the performative) outside of description, the
performative needs to be thought extralinguistically, that is, as creating a
new territory, and not as (mere) metaphor. It needs to be thought in terms
of its ability to affect, its ability to cause "positions of the speaking subject
to crystallize" (Guattari, 1986:41), for example. To this point, the existential function and/or performative has been associated with that which
is external to language. For Morris, the existential function was that
which was extrinsic to the sentence and thereby specific to the context; it
was something beyond the "representational content or semantic meaning" and something that evoked or expressed something for individual
speakers and hearers. And, as has already been mentioned, for Peirce, the

existential function is associated with the referent by way of fact rather than convention; it has an empirical or causal relation between the sign and the thing. However, neither these nonlinguistic nor linguistic explanations of the performative explain the performative's affective powers. For Austin, language is an "institution used to perform acts that can exist only within and by virtue of that institution" (1987:9). However, to say language is an institution, to give a linguistic/structural explanation, does not explain the category's affective powers; it does not answer *why* it becomes an institution. To understand this, we need to address the performative, not linguistically or nonlinguistically, but *extralinguistically*.

In order to address the performative extralinguistically, I turn to Guattari's notion of autopoiesis. For Guattari the existential function— the way in which language may cause the "position of the speaking subject to crystallize"—is the result of the autonomized, irreversibility of the aesthetic object, which Guattari refers to as "autopoiesis."[21] Autopoiesis is found in music and poetry, but for Guattari the notion of autopoiesis is "necessary to the analysis of Unconscious formations, pedagogy, psychiatry and more generally to a social field devastated by capitalist subjectivity" (1995:15). The autopoietic is detached from universal time and resides instead in "the category of 'existential refrains'"(15). Existential refrains are a crystallization of "the most deterritorialized existential Territories" (16).[22] The refrains are "hyper-complex" (16) and both musical (keepers of time) and diagrammatic—"highly relative existential synchronies"(16) that mark out a "well defined functional space" (15).

In the existential refrain, "time ceases to be exterior in order to become an intensive nucleus [*foyer*] of temporalization"(Guattari, 16). For Guattari, these existential refrains are accountable for subjectivations,[23] and the territory they mark out is governed by its own speeds and slownesses. The refrains are immanent and virtual, not actual and universal. They constitute a nonsymbolic semiotization because they are movement based—even when the refrain is linguistic. Their idiosyncratic temporalization produces a rhythm that in turn is the refrain and the existential territory. For example, the signature, its authoring/style performs such a "space" (territory). In my signature are the letters L and S. The 'Ls' and 'Ss' are lines and circling movements, crossing one another, like masts and sails. My signature is a "sailing ship" on an ocean. This "ship" is my "home." In the chapter "The Geology of Morals," *A Thousand Plateaus: Capitalism and Schizophrenia* (1987), Deleuze and Guattari make the point that when disparate things and signs meet, like these letters and ships, "there is no 'like,'" no saying the letters are like ships' masts. Rather, there is a consistency between these things, forming what Deleuze and Guattari refer to as "the plane of consistency" (1987:69). "[T]he plane of consistency is the abolition of all metaphor" (Deleuze and Guattari, 69). This is significant in that it places the existential refrain beyond description and in a virtual realm since the relationship between things is not representational and there is therefore no point of origin—only movement. For Deleuze and Guattari, what makes for a consistency between things is that they have been "uprooted from their strata, destratified, decoded, deterritorialized, and this is what makes their proximity and interpenetration in the plane of consistency possible" (1987:69).[24] Deleuze and Guattari refer to this virtual realm of the plane of consistency (and by implication, the existential refrain) as Real: "All that consists is Real" (Deleuze and Guattari, 69). This "Real"

> knows nothing of differences in level, orders of magnitude, or distances. It knows nothing of the difference between the artificial and the natural. It knows nothing of the distinction between contents and expressions, or that between forms and formed substances. (Deleuze and Guattari, 1987:69-70)

The plane of consistency and existential refrain, then, is bound up with territory. It is a "milieu in which change occurs" (69). From this account of the plane of consistency and existential refrain, we are left with a theory of the performative that explains its affective powers and its virtual, immanent, and Real nature. It is not possible to apply a descriptive or categorizing theory to the performative within Guattari's regime of signs belonging to the existential refrain. To return to the example of the signature, as with Foucault's "discursive author," the signature does not indicate a person or a subject (i.e., the signature is not a metaphor for the author, it is not an index for the author). It is "the constituting mark of a domain, an abode" (Deleuze and Guattari, 1987:316). The artist/author performs a territory with his or her oeuvre—which is not the smallest meaning unit, but the smallest moving unit, an act(ion).[25]

The existential function, then, deterritorializes the linguistic sign. The refrain's idiosyncratic rhythm/timing (its polychronic nature) creates a crystallized deterritorialized territory[26] and is highly functional (e.g., the territory bird songs map). The form of expression—the refrain of the bird song—becomes the form of content, the territory. And the territory or form of content thus becomes the form of expression. To quote Guattari:

> Content participates in subjectivity by giving consistency to the ontological quality of Expression (as exhibited with the example of my signature). It is in this reversibility of Content and Expression where what I call the existentialising function resides. (1995:22)

In other words, this existential function (resulting from the reversibility of content and expression) is the function of the performative. The performative function.[27]

Postmodern Pragmatism and Equivalence

Rorty's theory does not allow an inquiry into anything other than the signifying regime of the sign. Deleuze and Guattari bemoan the attention given to the signifier and taken away from existential territories and the sign. In Guattari's eyes, this obsession with the "limitlessness of significance" is responsible for postmodern noncommitment. For Guattari, the signifier reterritorializes content into a mere exchange economy, or what is also referred to as an economy of equivalence. This economy of equivalence (an economy of the Same) is what is responsible for postmodernism's "ethics of non-commitment" (Guattari, 1986:40).[28]

Jacques Lacan has been instrumental in figuring this emphasis on the signifier. As Guattari points out, Lacan says, "'A signifier represents a subject for another signifier'" (Guattari quoting Lacan, 1986:41). This image is that of a hall of mirrors in phase (a mirror phase), notwithstanding an infinite regression that supports the charge of the subject's deferment. Here, in phase, "I" am a reflection only—the reflective process itself, a phantasm. In the chapter "The Line And Light," *The Four Fundamental Concepts of Psycho-Analysis* (1991), Lacan relays an anecdote of a fishing trip in which his fisherman companion points to a sardine can floating on the water and says: "*You see that can? Do you see it? Well, it doesn't see you!*" (1991:95). Lacan goes on to explain what is for him a certain irony in this playful statement by concluding that although the notion that the can can see him at all is absurd, it, in fact, does see him, in the sense that its reflection (of light that carried the image) was looking in the place of "him," looking for him. Lacan makes the point that "I am not simply that punctiform being located at the geometral [*sic*] point from which the perspective is grasped. No doubt, in the depths of my eye, the picture is painted. The picture, certainly, is in my eye. But I am not in the picture" (1991:96).

The fisherman's point (which becomes metonymic of Lacan's point about the subject in general) is that Lacan was out of the picture, out of the fisherman's scene altogether—a fish out of water. The can (signifier) takes the place of Lacan (the subject) for another signifier (LACAN). That is, "I" (the subject) am the "scene" (signifier) that *reflects* (signifier) me.

The "scene" does not constitute a signified, a picture, or a landscape, productive of a position where "I" might be rendered at the geometrical point of its third dimension. Rather, it is something a lot less definite; it is reflection itself. Lacan compares the point of the gaze to the screen, to a light source. It operates to "grasp," to "solicit," the subject precisely because it isn't traversable, as the geometrical space is. It operates because it is opaque. Says Lacan, "It is always that gleam of light… which prevents me, at each point, from being a screen, from making the light appear as an iridescence that overflows it. In short, the point of gaze always participates in the ambiguity of the jewel" (1991:96). The gleam of light prevents me from being a signified, instead "I," "my" gaze participates in the transcendental signifier—the jewel—for which there is no signified.

Thus the signifier (the can) that comes to represent the subject (Lacan) for another signifier (LACAN), operates (within) an economy of equivalence. The subject is cast along a chain of signifiers; A = B, B = C, C = D, D = E, E =, and so on. The form of expression (the signifier, the can, that comes to take the place of the subject) is devoid, emptied of content because the signifier reterritorializes content into an exchange economy. As mentioned above, for Guattari, this economy of equivalence is what is responsible for postmodernism's ethics of noncommitment. In an ethics of noncommitment, all are equal because all are dependent on a (central) signifier, a truth that is necessarily opaque, the nontruth of truth.[29] Deleuze and Guattari thus bemoan this "so-called" signifying chain because it replaces an emphasis on the sign. In their words, because of the "limitlessness of significance… not much attention is paid to… the territorial states of things constituting the designatable" (1987:112).

The Performative as Critique of Equivalence and Exchange

The performative critiques the theme of equivalence and exchange that has dominated much of contemporary critical thought, including that of Rorty, Lacan, and the postmodernism of, for instance, Baudrillard. Rorty praises a system that judges a sign according to other signs—or rather, signifiers. Sentences can only be trusted when they link with other sentences that have paid their way. To requote Rorty:

> "True" resembles "good" or "rational" in being a normative notion, a compliment paid to sentences that seem to be paying their way and that fit in with other sentences which are doing so. (1982:xxv)

In the chapter "Is There Any Poetic Writing?" (1968), Roland Barthes criticizes classical poetry for exactly that which James and Rorty praise

in philosophical pragmatism. In classical poetry, says Barthes, all signifiers are made to *equate* to a transcendental signified by being similar.
Each signifier is made valid by its "natural" tie to the next one, to the network of signifiers. These signifiers, in fact, must not stand out alone, their
interconnection and concurrence being evidence of a signified—that is,
together they add up to a signified. This thinking that Barthes ascribes to
classical poetry has an uncanny resonance with the thinking generated
by the linguistic turn, such as Rorty's. Deleuze and Guattari say of this
thinking that it is not a question of what a sign signifies but "to which
other signs it refers" (1987:112). They add:

> One can forgo the notion of the sign, for what is retained is not principally
> the sign's relation to a state of things it designates, or to an entity it signifies,
> but only the formal relation of sign to sign insofar as it defines a so-called
> signifying chain. (1987:112)

Deleuze and Guattari refer to this regime of signs as "the signifying regime
of signs or "the signifying sign" (1987:112). In other words, with this
gesture of the linguistic—signifying regime of the sign—the immanent
nature of the sign is disguised. Within the signifying sign:

> [n]ot much attention is paid to *indexes*, in other words, the territorial states
> of things constituting the designatable. Not much attention is paid to *icons*,
> that is, operations of reterritorialization constituting the signifiable. Thus
> the sign has already attained a high degree of relative deterritorialization;
> it is thought of as a *symbol* in a constant movement of referral from sign to
> sign. (Deleuze and Guattari, 1987:112)

The sentences Rorty speaks of (Deleuze and Guattari refer to the network
of signs) form, for Deleuze and Guattari, "an amorphous continuum that
for the moment plays the role of the 'signified'" (112); the "signified" in
Rorty being the criterion-to-which-all-sides-must-appeal, and the "normative notion" of which Rorty, after William James, speaks. Deleuze and
Guattari talk about this "amorphous continuum" as a wall or medium,
in which, they say, "the specific forms of all contents dissolve" (112). It is
a "mundanization of contents" (112). But, say Deleuze and Guattari, the
signified "continually glides beneath the signifier"—the signifier in Rorty
being evidenced by the sentences as they are made equivalent to, that is,
made to "fit in with other sentences." (Hence my criticism that in Rorty
the signifier becomes a transcendental figure.)

Rorty's fear of vocabularies means that the literary must be considered
as a sign in relation to other signs—this forms the central criterion to
which all sides agree. Literary criticism that does not agree on a criterion

(1982:xli), and considers the literary as a separate regime of signs, gives in to the vicissitudinous nature of language. For Rorty, the accomplishment of the user's aims is put forward as an indication of language's truth, its validity. In this regard *literature must act as an inquiry*. This provides a *context* for the literary and positions it outside the slippery sign (including that of Philosophy). However, Rorty's approach to literature means that its sign, including its form of expression and form of content (i.e., its difference), is "dissolved" into an "atmospheric continuum" (which, in Rorty, is the criterion-to-which-all-sides-must-appeal, and, "the user's aims"). This, it should be noted, amounts to a literary mimesis.[30] Literature's signs are turned to signifiers as it is made to be equivalent to the general criterion or signified. This utilitarian function of the literary makes the literary, in fact, redundant. Its form of content (as is all content) is dissolved and abstracted by the signifying regime of signs (Deleuze and Guattari, 1987:112). Along with all other regimes of signs, then, the literary vocabulary is made "the same"—equivalent, within the binary, Philosophy/philosophical, paradigm. Here, all vocabularies are no more than signifiers—"*just* fiction"—the same, an infinitely malleable "atmospheric continuum," a goo we can wind around our finger to get what we want.

Rorty's pragmatism, due to its dependence on the equivalence and exchangeability of the signifier, results in the abstract and indefinite values or intuitions that have underscored Philosophy. When language is not viewed within individual vocabularies or within regimes of signs but sentence by sentence (as they are exchangeable and equivalent), the purpose must be—if not to supersede language—then to belong to an invisible sign (as with Barthes's notion of classicism). Rorty as much as says that his own contemporary pragmatism and Philosophy have very little between them. Both, he says, are based on intuition—there is nothing to say what side is right or wrong. The difference, states Rorty, is that for philosophy the indefinable values are not the object of study, but more provisional questions are. However, context—the difference between eternal and provisional questions—is still within the realm of a transcendental signified, that is, the invisible sign.

In his article "The Post Modern Dead End" (1986), Guattari criticizes postmodernism's ethics of noncommitment, attributing it to a structuralist interpretation of pragmatics taken up by postmodern philosophers. Guattari asks for a commitment to a regime of signs, to immanence, in the place of the current designation of equivalence. He suggests that postmodern thinking, being based upon the "Royal Place" of the signifier, cannot "articulate subjective facts with unconscious formations, esthetic problematics and micropolitics" (1986:41). Deleuze and Guattari note that in the signifying regime of signs, "[n]ot only do signs form an infinite network, but the network of signs is infinitely circular. The statement survives its object, the name survives its owner" (1987:112). Though at first it may not appear so, this describes Rorty's project. When Rorty states that the tool, Language, must not be separated from its users when we inquire into its adequacy to achieve our purpose, the purpose *works in this case as a statement*. It *qualifies* the sign making the sign equivalent and exchangeable. It may then fit with other signs/sentences that have "paid their way." This sign is seen to *work* because it fulfills the requirements of the user. That is, because the purpose governs what the sign means the statement/situation survives its object. Its objects/sentences are what Deleuze and Guattari call "overcoding."

The Performative and the Real

From their notion of the performative or the existential function, Deleuze and Guattari, then, consider the sign in the light of an a-signifying state. They share this approach with other thinkers such as Derrida and Foucault. Here, an a-signifying state constitutes territoriality, the real, and is distinguished from the signifier. As, mentioned, the performative has traditionally involved a connection between language and various versions of the real, however, there are crucial differences between the real according to Deleuze and Guattari, Derrida, and Foucault, and this tradition. For example, in Austin's theory of the performative, "context"—which the performative act brings about—enables full meaning. Here, the real is equated with the complete "free consciousness present to the totality of the operation, and of absolutely meaningful speech" (Derrida, 1988:15).[31] For Austin, things happen in the performative speech act: language, time, and space are coterminous. But as Derrida has argued,[32] this theory disregards the connection between the subject and the sign and imagines a subject outside the sign. Thus, it depends upon a metaphysical notion of time/space and full presence.[33] Deleuze and Guattari's polychronic existential refrain belongs to the event that is unpresentable and immaterial, as discussed earlier. In order to theorize the sign's relationship with the real—another description for the performative—it is helpful to consider, in more depth, what Deleuze and Guattari replace the signifier with.

The signifier is replaced with *the regime of signs*. A regime of signs is made up of form of content and form of expression.[34] These do not equate with the signified and the signifier: "[T]he form of expression is reducible not to words but to a set of statements arising in the social field considered as a stratum" (1987:66). Equally, "[t]he form of content is reducible not to a thing but to a complex state of things as a formation of power" (66). Deleuze and Guattari give the example of the prison—as Foucault analyzed it—as an example of the form of content. Deleuze and Guattari's point is that, unlike the simple designatory and indicative function of the signifier and the signified, *the form of content and the form of expression have an affective function within themselves and in relationship to one another.* The form of content is a complex *state* of things and the form of expression a set of statements arising in the social field considered as a *stratum.* The regime of signs, then, has attributes, affects, in the way the performative category is said to have. Here is where the regime of signs leaves the abstract and descriptive linguistic realm of the signifier. Taking the example of the prison, Deleuze and Guattari make the point that the thing or form of the prison does not refer back to the word "prison" (as the signified is made to conform and be subordinate to the signifier). Rather, the form of the prison refers "to entirely different words and concepts, such as 'delinquent' and 'delinquency'" (66). "Delinquency," a form of expression (because it is discursive), "is in no way a signifier...the signified of which would be the prison" (66). Their relationship is affective rather than indicative; they affect one another. The regime of signs, then, has a performative function, in that it accomplishes something, rather than a *constative* function, which involves assertions, considered as true or false descriptions of facts.[35] Alone, the form of content, the prison, is not reducible to a single thing either, but is a "complex state of things" that are "*form*ations of power"—that is, they are also affective. Deleuze and Guattari give the example of architecture and regimentation as formations of power.

Unlike a signifier then, which refers back to a thing, the form of content is considered not as a thing, but as a "state of things," which have an affectivity—their "formation of power." And the form of expression is considered, not linguistically but as something real, a stratum. Belonging to the social it is also thereby an affective body. The regimes of signs, then, are not informational or communicational but affective, in the same way the performative is traditionally thought to be language that accomplishes an action (1987:77–78).[36]

Deleuze and Guattari do not restrict "formations of power" to forms of content—or, rather, we must keep in mind that forms of expression become forms of content in the existential refrains. The "discursive multiplicities" of the forms of expression, and the "nondiscursive multiplicities" of the forms of content, are attributes of bodies of a society, as mentioned. However, in addition, these bodies are *incorporeal* because of their characteristic of an action that transforms.[37] Thus they are known by Deleuze and Guattari as *incorporeal transformations*. Deleuze and Guattari distinguish between *non*corporeal attributes and *in*corporeal attributes or transformations. Noncorporeal attributes are the "expressed" of the statement, for example, in the case of the crime, there is "the body of property, the body of the victim, the body of the convict, the body of the prison" (1987:80), however, it is in the transformative mode (in which the "accused" becomes a "convict," say) that the incorporeal attribute lies. The noncorporeal attributes, which are the expressed of the statement, are a redundancy of the statement, but a necessary redundancy. That is, beyond the statement there is no or little information, truth or fact—as there is for science that tries to rid redundancy from the statement (theorem). Moreover, the noncorporeal attributes are necessary for the incorporeal attributes.

Incorporeal attributes, then, are virtual and real. For Deleuze and Guattari, it is in their action, in their demands,[38] that words or statements function. Words cease to be linguistic, but become real, incorporeal bodies, continuous with life. Incorporeal attributes are the implicit function of speech, a nondiscursive presupposition—beyond the signifier, and, "opposed to the potentially explicit assumptions by which a statement refers to other statements or an external action" (1987:77).

* * *

Deleuze and Guattari, therefore, bring together linguistic pragmatics and a philosophy of pure immanence (or, as they put it, a radical empiricism, resulting in a particular pragmatics).[39] Here, only events are presented as concepts. This pragmatics affects a critique of both philosophical pragmatism and pragmatics belonging to linguistics: the former's dependence on the metaphysical sign of a general "criteria" (and conversation) and the latter's dependence on the metaphysical sign of "context." The result is not merely to have pointed to definitional problems with pragmatics but to have produced an ethico-aesthetics—that is, a critical practice involving aesthetics, not shunning it.[40] To go forward without the aesthetic is to once again imagine a subject outside the sign. In Deleuze and Guattari, the aesthetic—or autopoiesis—is entirely bound to their immanent, virtual, nonlinguistic form of critique that forecloses not the literary but the "explicit assumption (found in Rorty) by which a statement refers to other statements or an external action" (1987:77). In ethico-aesthetics, there can be no singular, linear, discursive act enabling this referring statement (or sentence, as it is with Rorty). Rather, each statement is in fact a set of statements forming a stratum and a complex state of things. Deleuze and Guattari refer to a "complex assemblage" to describe this "phenomena" because the incorporeal body is, in fact, ultimately nondiscursive. The performative and the illocutionary explain the nondiscursive nature of the "complex assemblage." The performative, with its attributes of movement and force, results in indirect discourse—voices and tongues that are incorporeal transformations: acts (77). The illocutionary further illustrates the nondiscursive since each speech act is discursively multiple and nonsubjective. Even though the illocutionary statement is self-referential (because, according to Emile Benveniste (1971), it carries the speaker in the form of shifters), it is fundamentally a nonsubjective statement because the "I" in my statement cannot be separated from the rest of the complex assemblage (whose formations of power enable my act). Thus, say Deleuze and Guattari, "the role and range of the subjective morphemes"(1987:78) are delimited—there is no singular, linear discursive act. "There is not even a subject of enunciation" (1987:79).

What must be distinguished between is a pragmatics of the sign (what in Guattari is ethico-aesthetics and what in this context is the pragmatics of the literary function) and linguistic-based pragmatics. A Deleuzeoguattarian approach to the performative is crucial to the concept of the pragmatics of the sign. Linguistic or traditional-style pragmatics suppress the transformative attributes of the performative act, what Deleuze and Guattari refer to as the attributes of movement and force. In other words, traditional pragmatics suppress performance and the result is a favoring of context and equivalence. In Austin, "context" brings meaning to the (performative) utterance, and in Rorty's philosophical pragmatism, "context" is ushered in the back door with its dependence on a general criterion, conversation, and its historicist tendency. Postmodern pragmatics' emphasis on a deferring signifier (found in Rorty) inevitably involves a nostalgia for presence when it, like Austin's pragmatics, presumes a "consciousness present to the totality of the operation" (Derrida, 1988:15). Nonliterary or aesthetic-based pragmatics have resulted in a nonaesthetic-based study of culture, including the culture of literature. In the following chapters, this shortfall is addressed. To begin with, we turn toward performativity and the cartographic and consider performative philosophy in relation to the literary function.

3

The Literary Function and the Cartographic Turn: Performative Philosophy

The cartographic raises the problem of thinking that is configured as a line drawn between subject and object, as well as temporally as opposed to spatially. Thinking that does not engage cartographically is unable to become an empiricism; it reduces thinking to the Same, to the One, and at that point thinking becomes self-fulfilling. For example, at a recent symposium on writing and trauma, a line was popularly drawn between Silence (the subject) and Trauma (the object). The silence, however, is self-fulfilling because the thinking of the trauma is in the subject rather than everywhere around it, in the relationship of the territory to the earth. This chapter explores the literary function in relation to the cartographic. It resituates and reconfigures literary theory on an axis different from that of the subject and the object. Here, the literary and its performative function work as a metatheory as the literary function is thought through various moments in post-structural theory, criticism, and philosophy, including an engagement with work of Bruno Bosteels, Gregory Ulmer, Michel de Certeau, and Michel Foucault. In mapping the literary function across a series of contemporary theoretical and philosophical acts, the poetics and rhetoric of the literary are changed and broadened. What is at stake here is not a mere recapture of territory belonging to the book, arguably lost to the literary since the postmodern cultural-critical turn, but a foray into the literary function within the cartographic turn. This chapter also maps the way in which the inadequate attention given to the literary function by cultural criticism is responsible for what Bosteels (1998) sees as poor cartographic practice.

What Is Meant by Cartographic?

Deleuze, in *Foucault* (1988), introduces Foucault's writing as both cartographic and theatrical, drawing a parallel between these terms. For Deleuze, Foucault's analysis is theatrical—he refers to *Discipline and Punish, Birth of the Prison* (1979) and "The Divine Comedy of Punishment" (1988:23)—due to Foucault's use of illustration and the meticulous nature of his description, including "(a) whole chain of phenomena, from anti-masturbation machines for children to the mechanics of prison for adults" (23). The horrors depicted by Foucault (such as "the botched torture of Damien") to Deleuze seem "lovingly rendered" (23), bringing to Foucault's books "a joy or jubilation"—a kind of divine comedy. The loving, meticulous description evokes, in Deleuze, unexpected "fits of laughter" (23), which is a "joy of wanting to destroy whatever mutilates life" (23). Foucault's "theatrical analyses" Deleuze refers to as cartography. *In other words, the cartographic methodology is performative.* With this in mind, it may be said that Foucault has written some of the best plays, the best novels, of this half of the century. Although the subject matter of *Discipline and Punish* articulates a new conception of power, this subject matter is only touched upon in the first few pages of the book. Instead, Foucault "adopts a method that is completely different from the 'thesis.' He is content to suggest abandoning a certain number of postulates which have traditionally marked the position of the left" (Deleuze, 1988:24–25). Instead, Foucault uses cartographic methodology (also referred to as "functional analysis") that

> becomes increasingly microphysical and the illustrations increasingly physical, expressing the "effects" of analysis, not in a causal way but through the use of optics and colour: the red on red of the tortured inmates contrasts with the grey on grey of prison. Analysis and illustration go hand in hand, offering us a microphysics of power and a political investment of the body. These illustrations are coloured in on a minutely drawn map. (Deleuze, 1988:24)

Foucault's new theatrical methodology, then, used in analyzing power, allows him to bring about a whole new conception of power; it is no longer perceived as an "analogy, homology or univocality," not as "homogeneous," but as a strategy, a continuity between "the particular points through which it passes" (25).

The Lack of Performative Cartography in
Cultural Studies

In his essay, "From Text to Territory" (1998), Bruno Bosteels notes a shift in the post-1970s "theoretical vanguards" "from text to territory" (145).

For Bosteels that shift is due to a growing awareness of ever-pressing ecological concerns as well as the move in philosophical thought and modern
human sciences in which the subject (who also comes to be the privileged
object) becomes the basic framework of thought. To quote Bosteels:

> More recently, the alternative to this characteristic redoubling of subject
> and object is no longer the continuous flow of experience cherished by
> both phenomenologists and philosophers of life alike, nor is it just the
> radical free play of difference celebrated by some poststructuralist and
> deconstructive philosophers of language. (1998:145)

Bosteels mentions that these new thinkers, who include Guy Debord,
Deleuze and Guattari, Foucault, Henri Lefebvre, and de Certeau, do
not automatically deny the results of the previous criticism (145).
However, writes Bosteels—quoting from Deleuze and Guattari's, *What
Is Philosophy?*—"(s)ubject and object give a poor approximation of
thought.... Thinking is neither a line drawn between subject and object
nor a revolving of one around another. Rather thinking takes place in the
relationship of territory to earth" (1998:145). In the critical and theoretical inquiries of today, says Bosteels, there is a shift away from the "rhetoric of temporality most typical of deconstruction" toward "a general
politics of spatiality" (146). (Bosteels refers to textual-oriented criticism
as early post-structuralism.) This new thinking, which ushers in a type
of criticism described as cartography, has an emphasis on "places, spaces,
sites, fields, maps, and charts both real and metaphorical" (146). This distinction, between text and cartography and between early and late post-
structuralism, is not upheld here. This matter will be addressed by the
analysis of Foucault's early cartography, employed here to theorize the
relationship between the literary function and cartography. For Bosteels,
the textual analysis of writing, as with the ethical discussion of acting,
are both still modeled upon the ontological analysis of being. Replacing
this is "the cultural study of literary, artistic, and ideological forms of
mapping" (146). However, for Bosteels, there is, within cultural studies,
an undesirable and unspoken "critical social theory of causality" (146). To
quote Bosteels in full:

> Across the board, in fact, all kinds of places, spaces, sites, fields, maps, and
> charts both real and metaphorical are fast becoming tiresomely ubiquitous.
> Aside from what is undoubtedly just another passing fad, the fresh allure
> of such images and metaphors also hides an unfinished task, perhaps even
> an unconsciously avoided one of conceptual elaboration.... I would like
> to submit the following thought as a working hypothesis: Behind almost
> every recent use and abuse of the cartographic metaphor there lies—like a
> trauma that must be repressed—an unspoken theory of articulation, more

specifically a critical social theory of causality, parading in the guise of a generic statement about the current fashion of cultural studies. Unless this missing link with theories of causality somehow becomes conceptually explicit, what could mark the onset of a veritable cartographic turn will only have been just another lost opportunity to guide the contemporary debates along a welcome sweep of hitherto unbeaten paths. (1998:146)

The reason Bosteels gives for the conceptual missing link is the lack of attention given to the performative nature of mapping. This oversight explains why there is a critical social theory of causality in much of cultural studies. Bosteels's hypothesis is important if we are to conceptualize the performative nature of mapping and to question, at least, the cultural study of literary mapping. For Bosteels cartography is all too often "realist"; it falls into the modes of reflection, mimesis, and interpretation. He cites Christian Jacob, who suggests that we ought to apply strategies of "deconstruction" to the cartographies in order "to break the exclusive and constraining link between reality and representation which has dominated cartographic thinking and constitutes the implicit epistemology of its history" (Bosteels, 1998:147).

In response to Bosteels and Jacob's objection to mimetic mapping, it is helpful to consider, here, Foucault's notion of the map. For Foucault the map (or several maps, actually) makes up a society's diagrams, and these are informal in dimension. Foucault refers to these as abstract machines. The abstract machine belongs to the social (before the technical). In his book on Foucault, Deleuze writes:

> The *diagram* is no longer an auditory or visual archive but a map, a cartography that is coextensive with the whole social field.... It is defined by its informal functions and matter and in terms of form makes no distinction between content and expression, a discursive formation and a non-discursive formation. It is a machine that is almost blind and mute. (1988:34)

Further to this, Deleuze writes:

> The diagram or abstract machine is the map of relations between forces, a map of destiny, or intensity, which proceeds by primary non-localizable relations and at every moment passes through every point, "or rather in every relation from one point to another." (1988:36)

For Deleuze, abstract machines are the cause of concrete assemblages. Concrete assemblages execute the relations of the abstract machines so that "these relations between forces take place 'not above' but within the very tissue of the assemblage they produce" (1988:37). Deleuze refers to the abstract machine as an immanent cause since it "is a cause which is realized, integrated and distinguished in its effect. In this way there is a correlation or mutual presupposition between cause and effect, between abstract machine and concrete assemblages" (1988:37).

Bosteels, then, is correct to point out that a map "is never just a mirror of nature. It is neither an adequate imitation nor a transparent reflection of a stable territory already existing elsewhere" (1998:147). Bosteels opposes Deleuze and Guattari's schizoanalytic cartography to realist mapping. The schizoanalytic cartography is a performative map, says Bosteels (159). The map is not an "'indefinitely tracing off the same complexes or the same universal mathemes,'" rather it explores and experiments with a *mobilization* of the unconscious (Bosteels quoting Deleuze and Guattari, 1998:159). Deleuze and Guattari's theory of the unconscious is no longer a theory of the subject, the person, and objects but deals with the production of trajectories and becomings (159). "'[I]t is nothing else but the rhizome of machinic interactions'" (Bosteels quoting Guattari, 1998:154). For Bosteels, these machinic interactions articulate us "'to the system of force and the formations of power that surround us'" (Bosteels quoting Guattari, 154). "Mapping the unconscious now involves the interlocking of four abstract domains, or ontological factors: machinic phylums, energetic fluxes, incorporeal universes, and existential territories" (155).[1] Bosteels points out that causality is not within the domain of schizoanalysis because schizoanalysis is constructivist and seeks a line of flight. Constructivism is both performative and helps to define the performative as virtual. Says Guattari, "'I repeat, the analytic map...can no longer be distinguished from the existential territory that it engenders! The object of knowledge and the subject of enunciation coincide in this kind of assemblage'" (Bosteels quoting Guattari, 166). And, a "'schizoanalytic cartography is not 'second' with regard to the existential territories it brings forth; one cannot even say, properly speaking, that it represents them, since here it is the map that, somehow, engenders the territories in question'" (Bosteels quoting Guattari, 167). For instance, for Deleuze, Foucault's cartography engenders "a triple definition of writing: to write is to struggle and resist; to write is to become; to write is to draw a map: 'I am a cartographer'" (Deleuze, 1988:44).

To further emphasize the performative nature of mapping, Bosteels notes that although schizoanalysis and cartography are dependent upon the assemblage, it is in "enactment" (a term Bosteels borrows from Francisco Varela) that schizoanalysis takes place. For Varela, the "'cognitive faculties are inextricably linked to the history of what is lived, just as hitherto inexistent paths appear in the walking'" (Bosteels quoting

Varela, 1998:166). Bosteels concludes from Varela's emphasis upon the performative that, " '[t]o enact' " is in fact more appropriate than " 'to assemble' " (166). At this point analysis becomes creative, a kind of auto-production (166). To quote Bosteels quoting Guattari, "[n]ot only does the map start to refer indefinitely to its own cartography…but it is the distinction between the map and the territory (the map and 'the thing mapped' which tends to disappear" (166). Deleuze and Guattari's own writing is an excellent example of performative mapping.

Bosteels's criticism of many contemporary cartographic practices, however, is that

> maps are still frequently evaluated in terms of their referential and scientific accuracy in relation to the represented objects, instead of being judged like works of art for their ontological and pragmatic efficacy in making and unmaking the environment, setting up existential territories, or bringing forth entire worlds from the uneven surface of the earth. (1998:147)

In other words, much of the so-called cartographic writing has been judged as nonperformative. The shift from "text to territory" within literary studies[2] has also often not escaped realist tendencies. Anthony Easthope (1991) identifies the move from literary to cultural stud-ies with the publications of *Culture and Society* by Raymond Williams (1958) and Roland Barthes's *Mythologies* (1957)[3]. For Easthope, a focus on *context* has replaced literary studies (and this he defines as literary formalism, including New Criticism and structuralism). Certain "terms" produce "a new paradigm" for cultural studies, and these "terms" pro-vide cultural studies with a context within which the text is taken up and a reading constructed (Easthope, 1991:141). Easthope tells us that he has garnered these terms in a historical survey, and they include: Sign System, Ideology, Gender, Identification and Subject Position, The Other, Institution, The Problem of Readership, Escaping Mastery, a Pedagogic Reason. For Easthope, "a concern with signification which attempted to treat it apart from the question of ideology would rightly incur the charge of formalism" (130). Easthope's cultural studies, in acknowledg-ing that the "context" in which a reading is constructed is in fact that of the "terms," seems to be a performative gesture (or at least mindful of deconstruction). However, what is not understood by this cultural studies is the realist nature of the "terms" since they are presented as the same complexes or universal mathemes, to repeat Deleuze and Guattari above, against which the map is indefinitely traced off. For instance, under the term "Identification and Subject Position" Easthope identifies a kind of analysis "[n]ow obligatory for the study of signifying practice." This kind

of practice includes Laura Mulvey's notion that "men are offered a position of dominant specularity as active bearers of the look while women
are accorded a position of identification with images of themselves as pas-
sive objects" (Easthope, 1991:133). Hal Foster, in *Return of the Real: The
Avant-Garde at the End of the Century* (1996) notes that the gaze in Laçan
is in fact not gendered, that it is the world that looks at us, rather than our
looking at it. The illustration of this point may appear to amount to no
more than a semantic argument but it is the way in which knowledge is
taken that is at issue here, not the veracity of the statements. Approaches
to signifying practice involving universal mathemes (against which the
map is indefinitely traced off) are causal in nature and not performative.
In other words, it is not a matter of criticism and theory being friendly
or open to the performative but of being performative in itself. (Schizo)
analysis is not object but territory.[4]

One way to address the way knowledge is taken up by cultural studies
(such as that practiced by Easthope) is to compare its objective with that
of performative mapping. For Easthope the objective of cultural studies is
to "understand signifying practice" (1991:131) while taking into account
the notion that textuality is not a secondary and subsequent effect. He
points out that cultural studies is forced to reject

> an understanding of popular culture and its texts in the over-arching
> concept of hegemony or indeed any conceptualization starting from a
> would-be masterful account of the social formation of which textuality is
> to be seen as a secondary and subsequent effect. (1991:129)

However, while envisaging a textualist analytic practice, Easthope's practice becomes mimetic when he employs "terms" that become the "universal mathemes" or "the same complexes" from which the signifying
practices are traced. For Deleuze and Guattari such a mode of analysis is
structuralist in kind and they critique the structuralist mode of analysis
for considering structures and their mechanics as being causal in relation to the phenomenal landscape.[5] For Guattari, a structuralist mode of
analysis seeks to

> bracket out the problematics of the signified, the icon, the Imago and the
> imaginary, to the advantage of syntagmatic articulations. Attention [is]
> focused on interactional, structural mechanics, which supposedly ani-
> mate...the phenomenal landscape. (1995:59)

(Deleuze cites those modes of analysis opposed to performative mapping as "vertical parallelism" or "primary relations of expression," and

"a horizontal causality" or "secondary relations of reflection" [Bosteels, 1998:152].)

Contrary to this approach, the objective for performative mapping would be to produce a pathic knowledge. A pathic knowledge operates as "a refrain of ontological affirmation" (Guattari, 1995:60). Guattari posits four ontological functions: "Universe, machinic Phylum, Flux and Territory" (1995:59). For Guattari, the ontological crystallization is a monad, that is, it has a "knowledge of being-in-the-world, of a sphere of for-itself" (1995:60). What "authorises the erection of enunciative monads" (60), that is, what "gives consistency to these discursive systems" (60) is to be found on the side of content. Guattari quickly qualifies content as the existential function. "[T]aking support from certain discursive links [the existential function] diverts them from their signifying, denotational and propositional incidences, making them play the role of a refrain of ontological affirmation" (60). A pathic apprehension, then

> escapes energetico-spatio-temporal coordinates (productive of the concept of "context"). Knowledge here is first of all existential transference, non-discursive transitivism. The enunciation of this transference always occurs through the diversion of a narration whose primary function is *not to engender a rational explanation* but to promote complex refrains, supports of an intensive, memorial persistence and an event-centred consistency. (1995:61, my italics)

Pathic knowledge, though nondiscursive and escaping energetico-spatio-temporal coordinates, is achieved "*through* energetico-spatio-temporal coordinates, in the world of language and through multiple mediations" (1995:25, my italics). What produces pathic knowledge is the apprehension of a "pseudo-discursivity, a detournement of discursivity" (1995:26).

Pathic Knowledge and Literariness

This notion of pathic knowledge, as a detournement of discursivity, provides for a redefinition of the specificity of the literary discourse, once referred to by the formalists as literariness. This in turn provides further conceptualization for the literary function. In order to think pathic knowledge in regard to literariness, it is necessary to return, in more depth, to the concept of the diagram. In Deleuze and Guattari, the diagram consists of matter and function and it, therefore, comes before substance and that which comprises substance: forms of expression and forms of content. The diagrammatic as matter is referred to as abstract (machines) and functional; "it operates by *matter*, not by substance; by function, not by form" (Deleuze and Guattari, 1987:141). The diagram is a conjugation of deterritorialized content and expression, which are referred to as traits of content and traits of expression. These diagrams are therefore not signifying signs but presignifying, and they do not, therefore, belong to strata, where forms of expression and forms of content reside. To quote Deleuze and Guattari:

> Strictly speaking…there are no regimes of signs on the diagrammatic level…because form of expression is no longer really distinct from form of content. The diagram knows only traits and cutting edges that are still elements of content insofar as they are material and of expression insofar as they are functional, but which draw one another along, form relays, and meld in a shared deterritorialization: particles-signs. (1987:142)

For Deleuze and Guattari, strata are formed by the double articulation between forms of expression and forms of content. Substances, or forms of content and forms of expression, are the formalization of *traits* of expression and *traits* of content.

The conjugations that produce these diagrams—for example, the meeting of voice and instrument in Wagner—result in a double deterritorialization (of voice and instrument). The diagram, then, "does not function to *represent*, even something real" (142, my italics). Artists and authors' names designate matters and functions. Write Deleuze and Guattari, "[t]he name of a musician or scientist is used in the same way as a painter's name designates a color, nuance, tone, or intensity: it is always a question of a conjunction of Matter and Function" (142). Rather than representation or double articulation, then, the diagrams construct "a real that is yet to come, a new type of reality" (142). For Deleuze and Guattari, the diagrammatic, which is absolute deterritorialization, is "identical to the earth itself" (143). When Guattari says that pathic knowledge does not function to engender rational explanation, this is because it is diagrammatic.

"Literariness" has been described by formalists as "a function of the differential relations between one sort of discourse and another" (Eagleton, 1983:6). In this way it is diagrammatic. In functioning to show the differential relations between discourses, literariness exposes the material, the matter of discourse. It draws content and expression from their home in the stratographic into (material) play, where, as matter, they can intermix in "a shared deterritorialization: particle-signs" (Deleuze and Guattari, 1987:142). Here, the literary functions not as representative but as pathic knowledge—that is, diagrammatically. The detournement of discursivity "constitutes points of creation or potentiality" (1987:142), which does not "stand outside history but is instead always 'prior to' history" (142). This is where the concept of literariness comes to inform the concept of the literary function, that is, as a form of pathic knowledge. And it is where the concept of the literary function has an application beyond fiction and the book and toward an ethics.

Pseudodiscursivity and a detournement of discursivity, then, divert signifying, denotational, and propositional incidences. Guattari refers to such a function as existential and autopoietic; it produces an irreversible sign because it is diagrammatic, and it is, thereby, also a-signifying and thereby a territory in relation to the earth. Bosteels notes that Guattari opposes "a-signifying, diagrammatic semiotics" to

> signifying semiologies [which] subordinate the content to the expression, while overcoding the latter in the name of the sole expression-substance of the linguistic signifier (for example, the instance of the letter, the signifying chain in structuralism, textuality in early poststructuralism). (Bosteels, 1998:162)

The literary function, when viewed in the light of the existential function, begins to take on an entirely different meaning from that given to it by cultural criticism, and, ironically, by Eagleton himself, who fails to grasp the performative—that is, the existential, ontological, and event-centered dimensions of the literary. For those, like Eagleton, who mark cultural studies as a progression from literary studies, formalism simply got it wrong. Eagleton notes that the essence of formalism was the notion of "making strange" (1983:6), but, he argues, that formalism was misguided since in other nonliterary contexts texts can appear strange. For Eagleton, it is (once again) to the social and cultural *context* that we must turn, this time, in order to resolve the estranging qualities of the text. Estrangement is contextual, not textual and certainly not existential. Eagleton gives the example of a drunk reading a sign in the London underground system. The sign reads: "Dogs must be carried on the escalator." The drunk reads the sign to mean something of general, even cosmic significance, to which the drunk's retort is, "how true!" "Dogs must..." is an example of ambiguous writing. Context determines the reading convention appropriate to it, and thus the meaning of the sign. Eagleton further illustrates his point by focusing on a literary text that—read in another context—could be taken in a nonliterary way. Eagleton imagines someone at a nearby pub uttering the expression, "This is awfully squiggly handwriting!" Although this line is from Knut Hamsun's novel *Hunger*, the speaker would not think it literary or indeed out of place in this context. For Eagleton it is the *institution* of the novel that tells him to read it as fictional. That the text might be on university literature syllabuses also makes *Hunger* literary. Eagleton writes: "[t]he *context* tells me that it is literary; but the language itself has no inherent properties or qualities which might distinguish it from other kinds of discourse" (1983:6).

In Eagleton, then, as with other practitioners of cultural criticism (see Schirato and Yell, 2000), "context" functions as "a horizontal causality" (Bosteels, 1998:152) and or "syntagmatic articulation" (Guattari, 1995:59), to use Guattari's interchangeable expressions. Horizontal causality and syntagmatic articulations are methodologies that maintain a "constraining link between reality and representation" (Bosteels, 147). "Content" functions to focus attention on the "interactional, structural mechanics" (Guattari, 1995:52). To requote Guattari, such mechanics "supposedly animate the phenomenal landscape" (1995:52). These mimetic and representational forms of criticism capture the molecular insurgencies of the literary (their lines of flight).[6]

Deleuze and Guattari address such capture with their notion of articulation. In the chapter "The Geology of Morals" (1987), Deleuze and Guattari say articulation happens in two steps, the first, to which we can compare pathic knowledge, the second, the knowledge of cultural criticism. To quote Deleuze and Guattari in full:

> The first articulation chooses or deducts, from unstable particle-flows, metastable molecular or quasi-molecular units (*substances*) upon which it imposes a statistical order of connections and successions (*forms*). The second articulation [known as double articulation] establishes functional, compact, stable structures (*forms*), and constructs the molar compounds in which these structures are simultaneously actualized (*substances*). (1987:40–41)

For Deleuze and Guattari, "The first articulation is not lacking in systematic interactions" (1987:41). Secondary articulations are phenomena that constitute an overcoding and are "phenomena of centering, unification, totalization, integration, hierarchization, and finalization" (1987:41). (The "terms" within Easthope's cultural studies can be said to establish "functional, compact, stable structures.")

For Deleuze and Guattari, double articulation (which involves the secondary articulation referred to above) is responsible for the three great strata that bind us. These they list as "the organism, signifiance, and subjectification" (1987:159). What is most important is the interconnection between the phenomena since it is this that produces double articulation. We can see this triad in operation in Easthope's notion of ideology. In this, meaning is socially constituted, "It is the social not individual being which determines consciousness" (1991:130). Ideology is also responsible, however, for "the transformation of a sense of social being into a version of personal consciousness" (1991:130–132). Ideology determines the organism. Through a process of subjectification that organism is given signifiance. Ideology as a term, then, is the overcoding of ontological crystallizations, otherwise referred to as subjectivations. Ideology functions to capture these existential refrains. Deleuze and Guattari warn of such double articulation:

> You will be organized, you will be an organism, you will articulate your body—otherwise you're just depraved. You will be signifier and signified, interpreter and interpreted—otherwise you're just a deviant. You will be subject, nailed down as one, a subject of enunciation recoiled into a subject of the statement—otherwise you're just a tramp. (1987:159)

Easthope's notion of ideology is an example of the use of energetico-spatio-temporal coordinates: subjectivation "caught" within the spatiotemporal coordinate of the organism. Easthope's terms, "Identification" and "Subject Position" are another example of double articulation and the formation of the *organism*. Easthope gives the example of the act of reading to demonstrate the formation of Identification and Subject Position. "(S)ince a text positions its reader on the basis of the signifier/signified relation... [it thereby] functions at its deeper level to institute individual rather than social consciousness, to promote a position for the supposedly transcendent and self-sufficient individual" (Easthope, 1991:133). Eagleton's approach to the literary also achieves a double articulation that binds subjectivation (and text). "We" are displaced into the "functional, compact, stable structures (forms)" of discourse, genre, narrative, institution, context, etc.[7]

Double articulation is opposed to the literary function, to pathic knowledge. It is a process of emptying, or disenabling first-step articulation with its connections and successions. In other words, cultural studies (as discussed above), has succeeded in emptying the literary from literary studies. This new direction halted the possibilities of the revolutionary mode of the literary so energetically begun by the Formalists.

The Logic of Electronic Learning: Ulmer's Literary Cartography

Ulmer has been interested in the cartographic turn for some time. *Applied Grammatology* (Ulmer, 1985), analyzes the significance of spatiality in

Derrida's grammatological work. Ulmer notes that before Derrida, anything in grammatology that resisted linearity was suppressed (1985:8). For Ulmer, Derrida's work rescues the humanities from redundancy, which was imminent because the humanities gave primacy to the word and to the verbal (9), enclosing "reality within language" (9). Threatening the significance of the word was the mathematical script. However, as Ulmer writes, Derrida looked to the "nonphonetic features of mathematical operations for exploring the resources of spacing in writing" (9). For Ulmer, "[t]he resurgence of the graphic element, escaping from the domination of the spoken word, is a symptom of the end of the metaphysical era" (9).

For Derrida, then, writing was spatial. It functioned by way of the trace (of the inscription). This element Derrida also calls "the *gramme*, or the *grapheme*" (Ulmer, 1985:10). Furthermore, Derrida's theory of writing considers *writing as performative*:

> "Now we tend to say 'writing'[8] ... to designate not only the physical gestures of literal pictographic or ideographic inscription, but also the totality of what makes it possible; and also, beyond the signifying face, the signified face itself. And thus we say 'writing' for all that gives rise to an inscription in general, whether it is literal or not and even if what it distributes in space is alien to the order of the voice: cinematography, choreography, of course, but also pictorial, musical, sculptural 'writing.' One might also speak of athletic writing, and with every greater certainty of military or political writing in view of the techniques that govern those domains today. All this to describe not only the system of notation secondarily connected with these activities but the *essence and the content of these activities themselves*." (Ulmer quoting Derrida, 9, my italics)

Grammatology marks a departure from the thinking that an "'escape from logocentrism is impossible because the language we use to criticize or to formulate alternatives works according to the principles being contested'" (Ulmer quoting Jonathan Culler, 5). Thus, "a review of Derrida's program at the level of grammatology will reveal a mode of writing, and ultimately of pedagogical practice, that is designed to overcome the logocentric limitations of discourse" (Ulmer, 5).

As though taking his cue from Derrida's grammatological project, J. David Bolter has said that "electronic writing will require a simpler, more *positive* literary theory" (Bolter, 1990 my italics). In his use of the word "positive" there is resonance with Derrida's spatial grammatology. Of interest is the degree to which this "more positive literary theory" involves the literary. In what way might the literary theory of electronic writing inform desirable practice in cartographic mapping? In an attempt to answer these questions I have turned to Ulmer's essay, "The Miranda Warnings: An Experiment in Hyperrhetoric" (1994). In this text, Ulmer seeks guidelines for a hyperrhetoric for electronic literacy and in so doing he explores the history of analytic practice—he eventually finds a desirable model in the literary.

Analytic modes of representation begin, for Ulmer, with the advent of literacy (and the literary, to which I shall turn later):

> Analytical thinking…emerged in the process of thinking about a specific experience—justice—within the new alphabetic apparatus. Justice was the first concept, the first practice, to pass from the oral mode of representation (dramatized as an event, performed as the actions of a hero) to a literate mode (abstract definition couched in a logical syntax). (Ulmer, 1994:347)

Ulmer writes of the birth of conceptual thinking by the Greeks: "'Hesiod weaves together the two justices of the *Illiad* and *Odyssey* (those of Achilles and Odysseus) to compose his own story of justice'" (Ulmer quoting E. A. Havelock, 347).[9] It seems that it is the technology of writing (alphabetical writing) that enables Hesiod to produce his own story of justice. Hesiod's methodology entails focusing upon two terms—*dike and hubris*—that are "buried deep in the oral matrix" (347) and without writing, these terms would be hard to recollect and to collect (347). However, writing places the "story visibly before the eye, so that the flow (of language) *is arrestable [sic] and the words become fixed shapes, and the process of selection and collection can begin*" (347, my italics). Ulmer writes:

> Hesiod builds "his own semi-connected discourse out of disconnected bits and pieces contained in oral discourse, either some pieces in which the term *dike* happened for whatever reason to occur, or others in which incidents occurred that he felt were appropriate to connect with the word." (Ulmer quoting Havelock, 1994:347)

Ulmer makes the point that Hesiod's methodology is compositional rather than ideological, and he sets out to return to and repeat Hesiod's experiment (346). Following Hesiod, analytic modes of representation become increasingly ideological and abstract. Solon—described as the "'first statesman on the European scene'" (Ulmer quoting Havelock, 348)—has a more abstract law code than Hesiod. His provides "justice as due process protection for all" (Ulmer, 348). Finally, Plato makes an ultimate departure from Hesiod when he moves away from "the specifics of legal situations" (348) (which Solon still considered). Plato sought the invention of conceptual thinking, moving away from dramatization of an event fully into the creation of an abstract topic, in which narrative turns into logic, persons into generalised entities of classes with properties and attributes, in which "to do" is replaced by "to be." (1994:348)

In devising his own hyperrhetoric for electronic literacy, Ulmer repeats Hesiod's experiment, "formally and conceptually" (348). He follows the example of Hesiod whose conceptual thinking uses three registers:

> In the same way that alphabetic literacy made conceptual thinking possible, electronic literacy requires another means for arranging diverse particulars into classes and sets (1). The new arrangement has to be invented out of the old one, involving a new form and a new style of reasoning (2). The process of invention cannot occur in general, but, as in the passage from oral to the alphabetic, must evolve in terms of a specific action and topic (3). (1994:348)[10]

Ultimately, Ulmer is seeking an electronic supplement for philosophy (348). Electronic classification could be to the "concept what Hesiod's dike is to Homer's heroes" (348). With a methodology developed from Hesiod's thinking, Ulmer is able to achieve Bolter's "more positive (literary) theory." Hesiod's "methodology" involves the production of an event; the process must evolve in terms of a specific action and topic and be a dramatization—hitherto peculiar to oral representation and narrative. In other words, the methodology is performative—producing a more positive theory than with Plato's abstract reasoning.

The new rhetoric, then, involves what Ulmer refers to as "conduction." Conduction is where series of semantic fields cross or meet—the alphabetic field with the conceptual field, for instance—leaving a gap. While "'language is a code that pairs phonetic and semantic representations of sentences,'" there is, however, "'a gap between the semantic representations of sentences and the thought actually communicated by utterances. This gap is filled not by more coding, but by inference.'" (Ulmer, quoting D. Sperber and D. Wilson, 346). So inference does not "communicate messages, *it orients me in a certain direction* by means of evocation" (Ulmer, 346, my italics). Conduction, then, brings together writing and intuition: "[t]o the deduction and induction of the natural sciences, and the abduction of the cultural sciences, hyperrhetoric adds conduction, bringing together writing and intuition (including the 'unconscious')" (346). Ulmer's hyperrhetoric, then, is the research of something—in this case justice—which remains to be discovered (348). It is "a feeling, an intuition, difficult to name" (347).

For Ulmer, the mode of "connectionism" offered by the database produces a conductive mode of research. Connectionism operates without a set of rules, instead there is a "distributed memory, a memory triggered by a cue that spreads through the encyclopedia, [*sic*] the library, the data base" (346). Thus, in connectionism there is no "central processor," one is directed by evocation. It is a more positive approach to conceptual problems. Writes Ulmer, "I am learning to write with this remembering, outside of my head, working a prosthesis…. There is something I want to research using this invention, working the library like a data base" (346). This, for Ulmer, is hyperrhetoric.

Ulmer points out that he can name his intuition if he uses "the circulation of signs through the four educational discourse institutions of our culture—discipline, school, family, entertainment" (347). He points out that the "discipline name of [his] feeling is "justice," or perhaps "injustice" (347). However, using such "institutions" defeats the mode of the new writing, and this, primarily, is invention. Writes Ulmer: "[t]he feeling I want to research has something to do with justice, in a sense that remains to be discovered" (348). (There are obvious resonances here with Deleuze and Guattari's notion of pathic knowledge and as that is a knowledge yet to be discovered, "a real that is yet to come" (1987:142)). In order to "discover" the feeling, produced by two incommensurate series (the electronic and pedagogy), Ulmer must set up a "field" or map that becomes something positive and specific. In setting up a field, Ulmer is once again copying Hesiod. Hesiod discovered that in the epics there "was a 'field' of meaning that he called a dike" (1994:347). From these fields of meaning, he tried to assemble his own field of meaning. This process Ulmer refers to as "compositional" (as opposed to "ideological").

Ulmer further illustrates what he means by compositional when he relates this methodology directly to a literary source. Richard Foreman's "How to Write a Play," provides Ulmer with a topology of the compositional:

> Make a kind of beauty that isn't an ALTERNATIVE to a certain environment (beauty, adventure, romance, dream, drama all take you out of your real world and into their own in the hope you'll return refreshed, wiser, more compassionate, etc.) but rather make GAPS in the non-beautiful, look carefully at the structure of the non-beautiful, whatever it is (and remember that structure is always a combination of the THING and the PERCEIVING of it) and see where there are small points, gaps, unarticulated or un-mapped places within it (the non-beautiful) which must be the very places where beauty CAN be planted. (Ulmer quoting Richard Foreman, 346)

Ulmer's new writing, his conductive methodology, is really the old writing of *literary* composition (as articulated by Foreman). The new writing evolves in terms of a specific action and topic and is dramatized, as oral representation and narrative were dramatized prior to Plato's abstract reasoning. Here, incommensurate series are connected—the mapped and the unmapped, the thing being perceived and the perceiving of it. The literary is thus nonlogocentric (without a central processor). *This is a topology for the performative mode of the literary.* Again, this compositional/intuitional writing is in part explained by Guattari's notion of pathic knowledge. Such knowledge is not concerned to engender "rational explanation but to promote complex refrains, supports of intensive, memorial persistence and an event-centred consistency" (Guattari, 1995:61). Such writing is an "ontological crystallization," it has a "knowledge of being-in-the-world, of a sphere of for-itself" (Guattari, 61). It is an existential refrain, "concerned" with the performed. Within post-structural theory there has been debate about which modes of narrative speech representation are the least logocentric: direct discourse, indirect discourse, or free indirect discourse (see Belsey, 1991; and Lodge, 1996). However, these narratological approaches to fiction overlook the pathic knowledge belonging to the literary, which is nondiscursive, a detournement of discursivity. The literary functions to produce an ontological crystalization, an event-centered consistency. To describe "direct discourse" or "indirect discourse" in relation to fiction is to engage in "structural mechanics" and thus to engage in representational analytic practices.

A Case in Point …

In "The Miranda Warnings," Ulmer sets up a field of meaning (he maps) "justice" in just this compositional way. In doing this, he further *builds* upon the intuitive-compositional nature of the hyperrhetoric—remembering that what he is doing in "The Miranda Warnings" is *inventing* a form of writing (cartography) based upon a serial form of composition (1994:352). Ulmer begins by taking a leaf out of Seymour Papert's book *Mindstorms: Children, Computers, and Powerful Ideas.* Papert has sought how to "debug" our intuitions, believing that intuitive knowledge is used by experts in their given fields in order to take their fields forward[11]. Papert developed this "know-how" in his students by finding practical "habits of exploration from personal lives" and transferring them " 'to the formal domain of scientific theory construction'" or formal knowledge (Ulmer quoting Papert, 351). For example, Papert notes that the processes of juggling and essay writing are similar. For Papert, "The model for the new school institution involving electronic schooling, is the Brazilian samba school" (352):

> "At the core of the famous carnival in Rio de Janeiro is a twelve-hour-long procession of song, dance, and street theater. One troop of players after another presents its piece. Usually the piece is a dramatization through music and dance of a historical event or folk tale." Each troop represents a social club that may have thousands of members of all ages and skills, who work together as a kind of community during the year preparing for carnival. (Ulmer quoting Papert, 352)

Ulmer decides that part of the model for hyperrhetoric is "like dancing the samba" (352):

> The kind of writing I want to learn, or that I am inventing—hyperrhetoric— is like dancing the samba. (352)

Ulmer then introduces a second metaphor: "In the scenario of literacy, finding out something, doing research, learning the truth, is like giving somebody the third degree" (354). Seeing an ad for electronic schooling evokes in Ulmer a "quotidian intuitive" (349) response. The ad is for the company *Digital* and depicts a film-noir style image of three detectives interrogating a man. One detective holds a clump of the man's hair. The man being interrogated is sitting in a chair and looks up at the detectives surrounding him with a worried expression. Next to the word *Digital* is the caption "*Announcing A Painless Way To Get The Information You Need.*" Below this caption is another caption: "*Digital. The Open Advantage*" (344). Ulmer decides to use this ad as a prosthesis in order to follow the sequence of his intuitive understanding and to come up with a "disciplinary intuition" for hyperrhetoric:

> The methodology, rather, is to use the semantic domain of the samba as one half of a figure, whose other half must come from the other domain of the ad, in order to produce a field within which to evoke the emerging thought of justice. (1994:352)

Ulmer points out that the "photograph in the *Digital* ad, depicting a scene of the third degree, is a metonym for this allegory of truth" (355). In the electronic scenario, on the other hand, learning the truth is like dancing the samba with someone. Ulmer points out that the scenario in which learning the truth is a torture goes back two millennia. It has a circuitous root, but in early philosophy the truth was considered to be hidden, buried—a secret that needed to be extracted. The association of truth with interrogation seems to have gone hand in hand from there. Referring to W. E. B. Du Bois, Ulmer writes: "'Logic and dialectic are police arts. Philosophy becomes a method of arrest and discipline; philosophical argument is a dividing, a splitting, a fracturing of the logical body, a process that resembles torture'" (Ulmer quoting Du Bois, 355). Ulmer notes that intuitive-writing is "thought of as knowing-how rather than knowing-that," in other words, it is "in the style of acquiring a skill rather than solving a problem" (350).

Ulmer then considers the effect of the Miranda warning upon the police interrogation process. The Miranda warning is the warning given to a suspect during a custodial interrogation. It tells him or her of their right to an attorney, their right against self-incrimination, and their right to remain silent. "If a suspect is taken into custody by police and questioned without advising him of his Miranda rights, his responses cannot be used in evidence against him to establish his guilt" (357). Ulmer points out the Miranda warning is a constitutional right against self-incrimination, it "invokes the need for protection from 'torture'" (359). Ulmer goes on to point out that fourteen years after the Miranda legislation, the court broadened its definition of interrogation. The court-declared interrogation included

> "techniques of persuasion," such as staged lineups, intended to evoke statements from a suspect. Indeed, said the Court, interrogation occurs any time police use words or actions "that they should have known were reasonably likely to elicit an incriminating response from a suspect." (Ulmer quoting E. Witt, 359)

For Ulmer, the "crucial point for hyperrhetoric, looking for an alternative to the third degree, in all its forms and styles, as the figure of research, is the definition of interrogation provided by the Court, to clarify the application of Miranda" (359). For Ulmer, "Miranda makes rhetoric unconstitutional, at least when it comes to interrogation" (360). This brings Ulmer, recursively, back to his theme of justice, and in particular, the relationship of justice to techniques of writing. Ulmer has (re)thought the process of justice, not abstractly, but performatively, compositionally, following Hesiod's methodological footsteps. This is a performative cartographic and pedagogical approach. Most notably, this new pedagogy, this performative analysis, the new writing technology, must involve a passage from previous writing technologies. Ulmer's writing method has its roots in preabstract thought, in the conceptual thinking of Hesiod. Hesiod's methodology borrowed from the previous "writing" technologies including oral, narrative, and dramatic. In other words, such methodology is a process of invention and cannot occur in general but as a passage from one series to another, and in terms of a "specific action and topic" (Ulmer, 1994:348). It involves *previous forms and concepts*. Ulmer's step back from Platonic abstract thought to Hesiodian connectionism has links with the literary and may help form pedagogical approaches to the literary. Alphabetical writing, spatial writing, places the "story visibly before the eye, so that the flow (of language) is arrestable [*sic*] and the words become fixed shapes, and the process of selection and collection can begin" (Ulmer, 1994:347). This process accords with Deleuze and Guattari's "first level articulation," which, to recap, "chooses or deducts, from unstable particle-flows, metastable molecular or quasi-molecular units (*substances*) upon which it imposes a statistical order of connections and successions (*forms*)" (1987:40). It also accords with Deleuze and Guattari's notion of the diagrammatic, which "operates by *matter*, not by substances; by function, not by form" (1987:141). The point to this order of language is not to "engender rational explanation but to promote complex refrains, supports of a intensive, memorial persistence and an event-centred consistency" (Guattari, 1995:61). The formalists might, simply, have said: this is language's literariness.

Continuing on with his samba series, Ulmer remembers Carmen Miranda, the Brazilian performer who made the samba famous outside of Brazil. For Ulmer, the meaning of samba music is precisely, freedom (362). He guesses Carmen Miranda chose her name (originally Marie do Carmo Miranda da Cunha) because it evoked the famous Brazilian freedom fighter, Francisco Miranda. For Ulmer, that lineage "qualifies her to serve as guide to this new relationship to information, replacing the search for truth" (360). "Miranda...moves between the two series, two styles of memory and freedom in the Digital ad, defensive on one side (the right to silence) and affirming on the other (overcoming enforced silence)" (362).

Ulmer organizes the series he has generated "by the gap between [these] two paradigms of inquiry" (363) into a coherent pattern, addressing a problem Plato addressed in the *Cratylus*: "the problem of the motivation of meanings; the relation of the material of language and discourse to the materiality of nature and culture" (Ulmer, 360). His answer lies in his making of a pattern, that is, in his electronic methodology, his hyperrhetoric: "The key to the electronic methodology is the recognition and formation of pattern" (Ulmer, 370). His idea is to experiment with making a pattern, which he calls a "Miranda": "the name for this specific pattern, and perhaps for the method of gathering diverse items into a set of electronic reasoning" (371). In creating his own Miranda pattern, Ulmer brings together Carmen Miranda and Ludwig Wittgenstein. He has them each take up a role in a musical comedy of his own making.

Ulmer's interest in Wittgenstein is primarily due to Wittgenstein's own fascination with a kind of electronic reasoning similar to Ulmer's "Miranda." Wittgenstein had rejected a two-valued logic in the design of electrical circuits put forward by Bertrand Russell and Alfred North Whitehead in *Principia* (367–368). Wittgenstein noted in his "picture theory" that there was a "common logical pattern to things" (369). The famous common logical pattern is shown in what could be termed Wittgenstein's "Miranda" pattern: duck-rabbit, from *Philosophical Investigations*[12] (fig. 3.1):

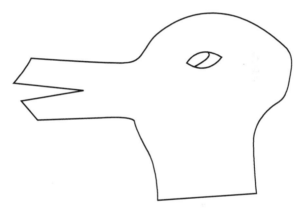

Figure 3.1   Wittgenstein's "Miranda" pattern: Duck-rabbit, from *Philosophical Investigations*.

"A gramophone record, the musical idea, the written notes, and the sound-waves, all stand to one another in the same internal relation of depicting that holds between language and the world. They are all constructed according to a common logical pattern." (Ulmer quoting Wittgenstein's *Prototractatus*, 369)[13]

For Ulmer, the great significance of Wittgenstein's work is that understanding philosophy is not a matter of the production of a concept, nor

"the discovery of facts, nor the drawing of logically valid inferences from accepted premises—nor, still less, the construction of theories—but, rather, the right point of view (from which to 'see' the joke, to hear the expression in the music or to see your way out of the philosophical fog)." (Ulmer quoting Wittgenstein, 369)

But we can only partly agree with Ulmer and Wittgenstein here. Concepts and theories are the result of a concatenation of philosophical thought (see Deleuze and Guattari, *What Is Philosophy?* (1994) and the previous chapter that bears out such thinking).[14] That is, they are surface-like, a transversalization, an arrangement of more than one series of thought. Ulmer's "Miranda" is both a methodology and a concept; it theorizes knowledge just as Guattari does with his pathic, nonpathic distinction. Knowledge, it seems, is the problem here, at least as that presupposes a fog; a buried or hidden secret that needs to be extracted; a splitting and fracturing of a (logical) body; and a process that resembles torture. But where we can concur with Ulmer and Wittgenstein is with the notion of getting the joke. For Ulmer, "[t]his 'getting a joke' as the aspect from which to revise conceptual thinking is in fact the common ground on which the Wittgenstein Miranda affair [is]...played out" (1994:369). By "the Wittgenstein Miranda affair," he is referring to his own musical comedy in which Miranda and Wittgenstein play *opposite* one another. (This doubling is, of course, also present in, and responsible for, literary irony.) Ulmer uses the structure of a musical comedy to arrange his Miranda pattern. "My experiment...is shown, if not told, as if in the style choreographed by Busby Berkeley" (370). The musical comedy offers Ulmer a plot structure "organized around a romance in which the two partners in the couple-to-be begin in a state of diametrical opposition, in a dualism that is harmonised through the course of a courtship" (366). (The use of the literary *form* must not be considered coincidental here. It is necessary and it is what gives expression to Ulmer's Miranda/pattern.) Into the diametrical opposition of the two partners, Ulmer may put his two series. As Ulmer himself puts it: "[t]he intent of my musical is not to confirm the myth of marriage but to find a point of contact between two models of information access, represented in the characters of Wittgenstein and Miranda" (366).[15] Ulmer opposes his Miranda pattern to "the methodology of truth by interrogation" belonging to the Western tradition. (He notes that Wittgenstein's book *Philosophicus* marks the closure of this methodology.) "What is at stake is not the literal dance (of Miranda teaching Wittgenstein) but the figurative one, changing our cultural style of turning information into knowledge" (Ulmer, 367).

By following his intuition, Ulmer invents an electronic methodology and discipline (hyperrhetoric, "Miranda") that changes the nature of learning—from a basis in knowledge and interrogation to learning modeled upon the samba. It takes (at least) two to tango, that is, at least more than one series, to arrive at a "Miranda." And so Ulmer has left behind the torture of "knowing" for working the prothesis of the electronic database. Ulmer began by comparing technologies of writing. He compared the oral to literacy and ended by adding the technology of the electronic. Looking at the work of Hesiod, he saw how literacy might provide a visual shape that could be harvested into concepts, such as "justice" and "Miranda." (Literacy arrests the flow of language, the words become fixed shapes, enabling the process of selection and collection to begin.) Justice went hand in hand with literacy. Buried in the knowledge, justice and truth were nevertheless always going to be a torturous affair. With the new electronic technology, Ulmer has sought to reinvent justice. Ulmer describes his Miranda as "a word-thing evoking a feeling. Mood" (371). His Miranda solves "the problem of the motivation of meanings: the relation of the material of language and discourse to the materiality of nature and culture."

For Ulmer, "[t]he feeling associated with this Miranda, that names and motivates the new elaboration of justice in the coming electronic era, is *saudade*" (371). This Brazilian word suggests "'a kind of bittersweet longing which means, in a way, 'glad to be feeling.' (We have no word in English for this concept)'" (Ulmer quoting P. Winter, 362). The word-thing *saudade* is the performed: the affect of performative mapping. But moreover, this is also the literary. Ulmer's aesthetics extends the poetics of the literary. The literary function, as in the Miranda, involves the production of affect, of word-things, which have never involved torturous justice.[16] As Ulmer says of his own literary act—his "musical comedy" staring Carmen Miranda and Ludwig Wittgenstein—"The purpose of my experiment is not to play the imitation game straight...but to devise a replacement for it" (366). Here, we have the detournement of the literary.

De Certeau's Performative Stories

While there has been a turn away from the literary due to an emphasis that cultural criticism has placed upon *context*, the cartographic turn has also involved a turning back to the literary. The literary is being used to break through old "top-down" theoretical models, as with the notion of a postmodern equivalence of signs, and post-structuralist and structuralist notions of interpellation. The new theory is of the performative. As de Certeau writes in his analysis of the spatial ordering of stories: "[o]ur investigation...moves from structures to actions" (1988:16). And to once again remind ourselves of Guattari's words: "Poetry today might have more to teach us than economic science, the human sciences and psychoanalysis combined" (1995:21). The new writing involves a micropolitics and microinsurgencies, which are literary *acts*. The microinsurgencies of Miranda Carmen are meticulously noted by Ulmer: her change of name, her wearing of a hat full of fruit (in a deterritorialization of her father's fruit business), the five-inch heels she had designed so that her dancing partners couldn't flirt with the women behind her. And so on. These become a part of Ulmer's "little story"—to allude to Lyotard here—of justice. de Certeau has considered the importance of stories to micropolitics. Says de Certeau, all stories are travel stories, *they enable us to get around.* He likens stories to a means of transportation, noting that the buses in Athens are called *metaphorai.* Says de Certeau, "[s]tories could take this noble name (metaphorai): every day, they traverse and organize places; they select and link them together; they make sentences and itineraries out of them. They are spatial trajectories" (1988:115). To quote de Certeau in full:

> Narrative structures have the status of spatial syntaxes. By means of a whole panoply of codes, ordered ways of proceeding and constraints, they regulate changes in space (or moves from one place to another) made by stories in the form of places put in linear or interlaced series: from here (Paris), one goes there (Montargis); etc. More than that, when they are represented in descriptions or acted out by actors (a foreigner, a city-dweller, a ghost), these places are linked together more or less tightly or easily by "modalities" that specify the kind of passage leading from the one to the other: the transition can be given an "epistemological" modality concerning knowledge (for example: "it's not certain that this is the Place de la Republique"), an "alethic" one concerning existence (for example, "the land of milk and honey is an improbable end-point"), or a deontic one concerning obligation (for example: "from this point, you have to go over to that one").... These are only a few notations among many others, and serve only to indicate with what subtle complexity stories, whether everyday or literary, serve us as means of mass transportation, as *metaphorai.* (115)

De Certeau brings together story and action in his notion of the tactic. Says de Certeau:

> I call a "tactic,"...a calculus which cannot count on a "proper" (a spatial or institutional localization), nor thus on a borderline distinguishing the other as a visible totality. The place of the tactic belongs to the other. A tactic insinuates itself into the other's place, fragmentarily, without taking it over in its entirety, without being able to keep it at a distance. It has at its disposal no base where it can capitalize on its advantages, prepare its expansions, and secure independence with respect to circumstances. The "proper" [which de Certeau opposes to the tactic] is a victory of space over time. On the contrary, because it does not have a place, a tactic depends on time—it is always on the watch for opportunities that must be seized "on the wing." (1988:xix)

De Certeau seems to be suggesting that the story, being spatial, opposes the tactic; however, this is not the case. For de Certeau, "spatial practices concern everyday tactics, are part of them" (115). To understand this seeming contradiction we need to consider de Certeau's distinction between "space (*espace*) and place (*lieu*)" (117). A place delimits a field. In place "elements are distributed in relationships of coexistence.... The law of the 'proper' rules in the place" (117). The proper "serves as the basis for generating relations with an exterior distinct from it (competitors, adversaries, 'clientèles,' 'targets,' or objects of research)" (xix). It is a form of capture. In the proper, "The elements taken into consideration are *beside* one another, each situated in its own 'proper' and distinct location, a location it defines.... It implies an indication of stability" (117). The proper derives from what de Certeau refers to as "strategy"; that "calculus of force-relationships which becomes possible when a subject of will and power (a proprietor, an enterprise, a city, a scientific institution) can be isolated from an 'environment'" (1988:xix). De Certeau opposes space to place. Space exists

> when one takes into consideration vectors of direction, velocities, and time variables.[17] Thus space is composed of intersections of mobile elements. It is in a sense actuated by the ensemble of movements deployed within it. Space occurs as the effect produced by the operations that orient it, situate it, temporalize it, and make it function in a polyvalent unity of conflictual programs or contractual proximities. On the view, in relation to place, space is like the word when it is spoken, that is, when it is caught in the ambiguity of an actualization, transformed into a term dependent upon many different conventions, situated as the act of a present (or of a time), and modified by the transformations caused by successive contexts. In contradistinction to the place, it has thus none of the univocity or stability of a "proper." (1988:117)

In short, *space is a practiced place.*

Richard Foreman's prescription for "How to Write a Play," can be successfully compared to de Certeau's notion of *space.* A play is not an alternative environment, nor, we could say, *a place.* Rather, it is "actuated" by movement within a structure—referred to by Foreman as the "nonbeautiful" (in Ulmer, 1994:346). For Foreman, the movement results when one takes into consideration "small points, gaps, unarticulated or unmapped places" within the nonbeautiful.[18] This notion of movement echoes de Certeau's notion of space, which is "composed of intersections of mobile elements" (117). Just as space makes its way across place, then, the literary makes its way across the place of the proper (given the name the "nonbeautiful" by Foreman). The literary, then, is *an action of tactic* and thereby performative. Existing in the interstices of the proper, it is a single articulation before it is doubly articulated or before it is taken in a relationship with an exterior *beside* it.

Map/Tour

De Certeau identifies two determinations in stories, one toward "being-there" and one toward "operations" (1988:118). The *being-there* is of the inert. These *things* adhere to "the law of a 'place' (from the pebble to the cadaver, an inert body always seems, in the West, to found a place and give it the appearance of a tomb)" (118). This kind of determination forms a *map*, for example, "The girl's room is next to the kitchen." On the other hand, "a determination through *operations*" (118) specifies "spaces." Whether the operations are attributed to "a stone, tree or human being,...a movement always seems to condition the production of a space and to associate it with a history" (118). Thus, opposing the map of the first determination, this second determination is said to be "tour"-like. An example of the tour type of determination is given thus: "[y]ou come in through a low door" (119). There is a passage between these two determinations, back and forth, so that stories make active inert places. De Certeau writes: "Stories thus carry out a labor that constantly transforms places into spaces" (118). The reverse also happens. As de Certeau notes, the everyday or ordinary uses of language nevertheless favors the *operations* mode, which de Certeau equates with a performative mode. The stories about the places where people live make up "a first and enormous corpus" and are most often told in terms of an operation. You are told "how to enter each room," which, de Certeau points out, constitutes a speech act (119). The speech act "furnishes a minimal series of paths by which to go into each room" (119), for instance, "if you turn to the left" (119). The paths are made up of a series of units, for instance, " 'to the right,' 'in front of you,' 'if you turn to the left' " (119), etc., which in turn form vectors. For de Certeau the structure of travel stories consists of a "chain of spatializing operations" punctuated by what the performance produces, "(a representation of places) or to what it implies (a local order)" (120).

De Certeau notes that over time (since the birth of modern scientific discourse, from the fifteenth to the seventeenth centuries) the "interlacing" of the performatives and *maps* have been "slowly dissociated in *literary* and scientific representations of space" (120, my italics). De Certeau uses a literal example of early medieval maps, noting that these included

"itineraries (performative indications chiefly concerning pilgrimages)....
Each of these maps is a memorandum prescribing actions. The tour to be
made is predominant in them" (120). However, in time (with Euclidean
geometry and descriptive geometry), the map superseded its inclusion of
pictorial figures, which indicated the journeys made on the maps. These
figures include a boat on the seas, which indicated the means by which
the travelers made it to the shores. The map thus pushed "into the wings,"
"off stage" (interestingly, atlases used to be called "theatre"), "the operations of which it is the result" (120). De Certeau describes the map as
a "totalizing stage on which the elements of diverse origin are brought
together to form the tableau of a 'state' of geographical knowledge" (121).
For de Certeau, both maps and tours are practices, but maps are "constituted as proper places in which to *exhibit the products* of knowledge," that
is, they "form tables of *legible* results" (121). For de Certeau, "Stories about
space exhibit on the contrary the operations that allow it...to mingle its
elements anyway" (121), thus making it a non-"proper" place. De Certeau
gives the example of the apartment-dweller's story of space when he says
of the rooms in his flat: "One can mix them up." For de Certeau, everyday
stories tell us of the possibilities of use of a certain geography, including
what we can make out of it. "They are treatments of space" (122). It is
important to note, here, that these treatments of space are not being put
forward as unmediated spaces. Disciplines, aesthetics, rhetorical figures,
and plot are the determinations of the proper (of place), which the *operations* mode of the story must pass through. In this sense, the performative
is not innately liberatory but has always already been captured by various
regimes of place. Ulmer's Mirandas are also not given here as alternative
realities, in *existence*, but as the beginning of an approach to writing that
places more emphasis upon the compositional, upon the *tour* mode. Such
an emphasis, as de Certeau demonstrates, makes way for the treatment of
space and is thereby micropolitical.

De Certeau's notion, that everyday stories provides us with a treatment
of space, becomes a most important attribute of the literary. It may explain
a mode of resistance belonging to the literary. TV drama, drama, and the
novel, approached with a theory of performativity, may be thought of as
sites of resistance—in ways media theory that does not take account of the
performative cannot anticipate. Serials, those of TV, prose fiction etc.,[19]
may be particularly "tactical" since the same geography is repeatedly
returned to in varying ways, and the moves undertaken upon the proper/
geographical space are "mixed up." (Interestingly, Bakhtin's notion of
the dialogic may also be considered as a topography of nonproper space.)
Space is the predominant figure in the writing of the American author
Paul Auster. It is inhabited, given itineraries, and involves "performative

indications chiefly concerning pilgrimages." (This is a common literary topoi and mirrors the literary function.) In *Timbuktu*, the entire ontology of the two main characters (a dog named "Mr. Bones" who narrates the story and his owner, Willy Christmas, a schizophrenic) is spatial and tour like. Their lives are marked by journeys *through* (they never stay in one place) different American states, family life, and an array of institutions. In other words, Mr. Bones and Willy Christmas inhabit places as spaces. The drama begins when Mr. Bones has run out of space. Willy Christmas is about to die and leave Mr. Bones to the *proper* institutions in charge of stray dogs. Auster's writing of space, then, becomes a leitmotif for the metaspatiality belonging to the literary, which produces space in its acts of detournement, that is, in its tour-like use of proper place/language.

De Certeau as much as says, then, that performative, tour-like language is literary, and that the performative/literary mode constitutes a tactical space. The literary could be defined here as acts of enunciation furnishing pathways of escape through the forming of vectors, or, if we take Deleuze and Guattari's description, through the forming of "a statistical order of connections and successions" (1987:40–41). For de Certeau, then, the book or the literary is *closer to the ground* than the map in that it includes history (the act), as the old maps used to (1988:120).

Foucault's Cartography, the Literary Function, and Potentialities

So far, this chapter has elaborated an idea of performative mapping in relation to the literary function. A comparison has been made between representative cartography and performative cartography, also referred to as "pathic knowledge." Pathic knowledge and performative mapping is said to constitute potentiality. This section will bring a focus to literary/performative mapping and *potentialities*, an emphasis (perhaps) best found in the work of Foucault. Foucault's early work on cartography (in his archaeology phase) involves an arche-cartography. In exploring this, we can examine the *conditions* of cartography and its relationship to the literary and to potentiality.

As mentioned earlier, according to Deleuze, Foucault's writing shows a "passion" for description (Deleuze, 1988); Deleuze recalls Foucault's depiction of the scene of the prison and the little prison van, the chain gang, and the asylum, the "descriptions of *Las Meninas*, Manet and Magritte" (80). Deleuze makes a link between this descriptive prose and Foucault's interest in literary texts, in particular, in the work of *Raymond Roussel* (1963). Deleuze puts Foucault's "affinity...with the new novel and with Raymond Roussel" down to the importance of describing scenes (80). In what follows, we shall consider the significance of description to Foucault's cartography and the link between description, the literary function, and potentiality.

In considering the role of description in Foucault's cartography, it is necessary to consider his distinction between the visible and the sayable.[20] (While I am not proffering here an equation between the spatial of de Certeau and the visible of Foucault, both have in common a direct and important relationship to the literary function and its performative nature.) For Foucault, knowledge comprises the seeable (or visible) and sayable—which are further articulated as scene and curve, and again, as descriptions and statements. Both the seeable and the sayable have form and substance. An example of form belonging to the sayable is penal law, its substance, by corollary, is "delinquency," "in so far as it is the object of statements" (Deleuze, 1988:47). An example of seeable form is prison; its substance, those imprisoned. The seeable and the sayable are designated content and expression, respectively, but both have form and substance. The form and substance of the seeable and sayable is vital to understanding Deleuze and Foucault's notion that there is a being of language. The seeable and sayable form two strata—bands of visibility and fields of readability, and hence they make up historical formation (47). For Deleuze and Foucault, "language is offered in its entirety, or not at all" (55). "What...are the conditions of the statement?" Deleuze asks, then gives his own answer: "It is offered up by the 'there is language,' 'the being of language' or the language-being, that is to say by the dimension involved, which is not to be confused with any of the directions to which language refers" (55–56).

Of great importance to Foucault's literary-type cartography, according to Deleuze, is the notion that the seeable and sayable are two different and irreducible forces. Statements, or the sayable,

> are kinds of curves or graphs.... Statements cannot be reduced either to phrases or to propositions.... The statement is not at all defined by what it designates or signifies. It seems to us that what we must understand is this: a statement is the curve joining individual points. (Deleuze, 1988:78–79)

Visibilities form scenes (80):

> Visibilities are not forms of objects, nor even forms that would show up under light, but rather forms of luminosity which are created by the light itself and allow a thing or object to exist only as a flash, sparkle or shimmer (52)...Visibilities, in the light of historical formations, form scenes. (1988:80)

Scenes, then, "are to the visible element what a statement is to the sayable or readable.... In the most exact sense, the description-scene and statement curve are two heterogeneous forces of formalization and integration" (80). In Deleuze's *Foucault*, knowledge is affected by a dualism between seeing and speaking—between the visual and the articulable (82). Seeing and speaking constitute opposing forces of power—one acting upon the other. The power involved in these clashing, opposing forces is seen to have primacy in the final outcome, knowledge. "If there is primacy," writes Deleuze, "it is because the two heterogeneous forms of knowledge are constituted by...conditions pertaining only to forces" (82). It is power that makes us speak: "Seeing and Speaking are always already completely caught up within power relations which they presuppose and actualise" (82).

Although Foucault's theory of knowledge and power is seemingly a dualism, this dualism "involves a preliminary distribution operating at the heart of pluralism" (83). By way of explicating the use of dualism in Foucault, Deleuze refers to Syberberg, who "once said that dividing something into two is an attempt to distribute a multiplicity which cannot be represented by a single form" (84). Before they operate as a pair, Seeing and Saying are utterly discrete and make up two types of multiplicities (83). "Between the two," says Deleuze, "there is no isomorphism or conformity" (161).

These discrete multiplicities are in fact what is needed for knowledge to form. However, Deleuze explains that, "[t]hroughout the entire range of Foucault's work, visibilities...remain irreducible to statements" (49). (It is the irreducibility of visibilities that is important to Foucault's cartography, and we shall soon see why.) Visibilities are said to be determinable, while the articulable is referred to as determination (this is why there is a primacy of the statement in Foucault); however, the determinable/visible is said to not be impeded by the statement because it is irreducible to it. This is important since the statement needs "something irreducible" (50) to function. Deleuze explains:

> the visible has its own laws, an autonomy that links it to the dominant, the heautonomy [*sic*] of the statement. It is because the articulable has primacy that the visible contests it with its own form, which allows itself to be determined without being reduced. In Foucault, the places of visibility will never have the same rhythm, history or form as the fields of statements, [elsewhere, Deleuze explains that one is a system (the statement) the other a machine (the visible)] and the primacy of the statements will be valuable only in this way, to the extent that it brings itself to bear on something irreducible. (50)

There is, then, a mutual presupposition between the pair. The "gap" between the visible and the articulable is in fact necessary to the function of the pair. Without the gap, the statement could determine the visible ad infinitum. Deleuze puts the problem like this: "[h]ow would the visible not slip away, as something eternally determinable, when statements can determine it ad infinitum?" (68). He shows what occurs when the statement is viewed in isolation to the visible. Citing Roussel's work, he describes it as having run aground due its dependence on language: "Language is arranged in a circle within itself, hiding what it has to show, flowing at a dizzying speed toward an invisible void where things are beyond reach and where it disappears on its mad pursuit of them" (68).

Power, then, is mute and without a form; "[n]o doubt power, if we consider it in the abstract, neither sees nor speaks. It is a mole that only knows its way around its network of tunnels, its multiple hole....[It is] precisely because it doesn't itself speak and see, it makes us see and speak" (82). Importantly, however, power is not simply violence, on the contrary, it is deconstructive. "Power relations designate 'the other thing' to which statements (and also visibilities) refer," due to the machinic and systemic operations of the articulable and seeable—their operation of integration (83). Although seeing and speaking—the result of power—produces truth, it "produces truth as a problem" (83) since it designates "the other thing" to which statements and visibilities refer. Moreover, power is nonviolent in that "it passes in itself through categories that express the relation between two forces (inciting, inducing, producing a useful effect etc.)" (83).

In using a plethora of descriptions, Foucault's cartography evokes the silent, invisible mole of power—which makes us speak. As his descriptions resist the statements that determine them, Foucault's cartography produces truth as a problem. In other words, Foucault's cartography acts deconstructively when the statement does not entirely capture the content—despite its determining nature—of the description-scene. For example, in his description of the prison, Foucault shows the statement of "delinquency" capturing the content of the prisoner.[21] But apart from these deconstructive activities, Foucault is engaging in a positive activity: a singular articulation and pathic knowledge, also employed by literature and painting. Such singular articulation brings about potentiality. Potentiality is the result of the "differential relations between forces" (79) that make up Statement-curves and visibilities alike. Differential relations between forces produce intensities and affects. These affects are, for Deleuze, "the particular feature of power," which he also refers to as potentialities (79). When visibilities are emphasized, so too is the "differential relations between forces" (79), and this silent, invisible mole of power, these intensities, make us speak—and paint.

The emphasis on the description-scene and potentiality belongs to Foucault's "new solution," that is, to his nonanalytic philosophy and to what I am calling "performative philosophy." Furthermore, the "new solution" can be viewed as a philosophy of the performative. Literary and visual arts have always urged writers and painters to speak (find their own voice, a voice that shows), not to analyze the spoken (as an end in itself).

Added to a definition of the literary, then, is an emphasis on visibilities, on the description-scene. The literary function is not restricted to the book or linguistic forms. For instance, in speaking about Foucault's description of *Las Meninas* by Velásquez, Deleuze refers to the painting as a poem. It is said to be a poem because it brings about "a series of flashes and reflections of light within a complete 'cycle' of representation" (80). For Deleuze, the scene makes the poem a poem of receptivity (81), and what the poem of receptivity brings about are "the particular features of a relation between forces, which in this case is the relation between the painter and the sovereign such that they 'alternate in a never-ending flicker'" (81). Says Deleuze, "Descriptions may be verbal, but they are nonetheless different from statements" (81). Deleuze affirms the literary as a regime of signs, with an emphasis upon visibilities, when he notes that, "a strictly literary analysis...is likely to rediscover the difference between scenes and curves" (81).

A Lesson from Literature

For the theorists of performative cartographies, the literary provides a lesson in ethics: a way of being. For the historians, Foucault and de Certeau, the literary is the description given to modern man. The literary performs modern man, no less. For de Certeau, modern man (dawning around the sixteenth century) is Everyman, she appears with the death of God—she is thereby identified with death itself, with the other, with destiny. And modern man is anonymous since she is identified with the "common." Modern man, writes de Certeau, is "organized by the community" and is due to the "erosion and denigration of the singular or the extraordinary" (1988:1).[22] Modern man is produced when "ironical literature" produces a certain "anonymous laughter." "[B]y producing a certain kind of anonymous laugher [*sic*] a literature defines its own status: because it is only a simulacrum, it is the truth of a world of honors and glamor destined to die" (de Certeau, 1988:2). Everyman is "a name that betrays the absence of a name," and thus "this anti-hero is...also Nobody," that is, as with the character of literature, Everyman is nobody—mere simulacra (de Certeau, 2). Everyman is without his own responsibilities ("it's not my fault, it's the other: destiny"), and this makes for a "'common' madness and death," doubled in literature:

> The role of this general character (everyman and nobody) is to formulate a universal connection between illusory and frivolous scriptural productions and death, the law of the other. He plays out on the stage the very definition of literature as a world and of the world as literature. Rather than being merely represented in it, the ordinary man acts out the text itself. (2)[23]

De Certeau presses home the deconstructive attribute of the literary. Ordinary man

> makes plausible the universal character of the particular place in which the mad discourse of a knowing wisdom is pronounced. He is both the nightmare or philosophical dream of humanist irony and an apparent referentiality (a common history) that makes credible a writing that turns "everyone" into the teller of his ridiculous misfortune. But when elitist writing uses the "vulgar" speaker as a disguise for a metalanguage about itself, it also allows us to see what dislodges it from its privilege and draws it outside of itself: an Other who is no longer God or the Muse, but the anonymous. (1988:2)

In other words, literary discourse, through the "vulgar speaker," and through an emphasis on the "description-scene," produces truth as a problem. The literary discourse "allows us to see what dislodges it from its privilege" (de Certeau, 2). The vulgar speaker and descriptive-scene draw the discourse "outside of itself: an Other who is no longer God or the Muse." Thus, literary discourse denies a realist epistemology. In the absence of a name (Everyman is also Nobody), is the absence of a thought that involves "a line...drawn between subject and object.... Rather, thinking takes place in the relationship of territory to earth" (Bosteels, 1998:145). Another way to consider this is to say that Everyman acts out the performative nature of knowledge. Ulmer's Miranda is an embracing of a Godless language. The Miranda is a territory, the database, earth. The performed knowledge is a discourse outside of itself. It "allows us to see what dislodges it from its privilege" (de Certeau, 2).

Like de Certeau, Foucault considers modern man to be the effect of literature although Foucault dates this phenomenon in language from the beginning of the nineteenth century. For Foucault, from the classical to the modern age, literature develops a new function. In the classical age, it has a representative function, it had buried "itself within its own destiny as an object and allow[ed] itself to be traversed through and through by knowledge" (Foucault, 1973:300). But by the nineteenth century, it had lost its unifying function only "to rediscover it elsewhere,…in literature which acts as a new function," and this new function is the production of "man" who became the "'figure occurring between two modes of language'" (Deleuze, quoting Foucault, 1988:56). Writes Foucault:

> Man has been a figure occurring between two modes of language; or, rather, he was constituted only when language, having been situated within representation and, as it were, dissolved in it, freed itself from that situation at the cost of its own fragmentation: man composed his own figure in the interstices of that fragmented language. (1973:386)

It is modern literature, then, which produces these "gaps" (the gaps caused by fragmented language, but also, gaps between the seeable and the sayable) from which modern man emerges, and from which a general ethics may emerge. Writes Foucault:

> From the nineteenth century, literature began to bring language back to light once more in its own being: though not as it had still appeared at the end of the Renaissance. For now we no longer have that primary, that absolutely initial, word upon which the infinite movement of discourse was founded and by which it was limited; henceforth, language was to grow with no point of departure, no end, and no promise. It is the traversal of this futile yet fundamental space that the text of literature traces from day to day. (1973:44)

(This "futile yet fundamental space" resonates with de Certeau's notion of tactical space.) For Foucault, although we have had literature "since Dante, since Homer" (300), it is only referred to as "literary" when it establishes an "isolation of a particular language" (300), around the nineteenth century, which then has the effect of producing "man" due to having established the "imperious being of words." At the beginning of the nineteenth century, language became an "independent form, difficult of access, folded back upon the enigma of its own origin and existing wholly in reference to the pure act of writing" (Foucault, 300). For Foucault, it was the function of literature in the nineteenth century—the "literary" function—to produce the being of language (300) from which man arose. De Certeau expresses a similar idea:

> The straying of writing outside of its own place is traced by this ordinary man, the metaphor and drift of the doubt which haunts writing, the

phantom of its "vanity," the enigmatic figure of the relation that writing entertains with all people, with the loss of its exemption, and with its death. (1988:2)

What is important is Foucault's notion that because literature has made "the being of language shine…once more on the frontiers of Western Culture" (1973:44), more and more, it is "that which must be thought." Importantly, of course, it cannot "be thought in accordance with a theory of signification" (44).

4

The Literary Function and Society I: Affirmation of Immanent Aesthetics

In raising the question of the aesthetic, the aim is not to reclaim or arrive at a vocabulary specific to the literary, in order to define it, but to consider the *relationship* of the literary to other domains, to rethink the problem of the relationship between text and society, including the manner in which it is expressed across certain instances of postmodern cultural criticism.[1]

The move from literary to cultural studies can be seen, in part, as a move to further articulate the relationship between literature (taken up under the term "text") and society. However, the articulation of the relationship between literature and society, by postmodern cultural criticism, results in a *capture* of the literary. For Deleuze and Guattari, apparatuses of capture are instruments of State societies and the tool of capitalism (1987:435): the "State as apparatus of capture has a *power of appropriation*" (437). Diverse formations (matter defined as *phylum*, by Deleuze and Guattari, 437) are captured by the State (and all social formations) and "form an axiomatic of decoded flows" (434). This axiomatic produces an isomorphism between parts. Deleuze and Guattari use the example of the capitalist axiomatic: "There is one centered world market, the capitalist one, in which even the so-called socialist countries participate" (436). When capture occurs, it slows down and controls the internal relations of the body it captures. How has the literary machine been captured, and what are the consequences of this capture? For Deleuze and Guattari, the Western States become "models of realization for an axiomatic of decoded flows" (434). Models of realization, analyzed in depth by Guattari in "Schizoanalytic Metamodelization," *Chaosmosis: An Ethico-aesthetic Paradigm* (1995), function by way of structures and systems, to which Guattari opposes his concept of the machine (58). For Guattari, structures are "associated with a feeling of eternity" (58) and fixity (59) while machines are associated with "an awareness of finitude, precariousness, destruction and death" (58). Structures and systems function beneath the diversity of beings and realize beings instead within their models, such as "religious, metaphysical, scientific, psychoanalytic, animistic, neurotic" (60). Opposed to the world of structures is the world of "machinic interfaces. Being crystallizes through an infinity of enunciative assemblages," that is, through the actualized association of both discursive and "non-discursive, virtual components" (58). The result is a "singular point of view on being, with...precariousness, uncertainly and creative aspects" (59). For Guattari, models of realization "nearly always skirt around the problem of self-referential enunciation" (60). The postmodern cultural-critical turn has resulted in a "model of realization" as it has resisted an immanent approach to the literary, opposing key terms such as "literature" and "aesthetic" for their association with transcendence and elitism. This chapter will revisit these terms and construct them as immanent and as tools with which models of realization can be critiqued. It is with these terms that the relationship between text and society will also be explored.

In the past, theories of performativity have been used to explain the relationship between text and society, but these models, too, have served as a model of realization. J. L. Austin's notion of the performative utterance, for example, is that of the coincidence of language and an act, the moment of language's realization. Other approaches tie performance to competence (see Lyotard, 1984). However, here, the performative is rethought as an immanent act. Drawing upon Mikhail Bakhtin's theory of the act, the performative is considered in terms of a once-occurrent event, and as an act of becoming ("something-yet-to-be-determined") (1993:33). Culture sits upon such an event, or rather, lies within its folds. This notion of the performative is a crucial component to the rethinking of the literary function, immanently. The literary, it is argued, has a particular relationship to performance that ensures that it is a virtual, immanent, regime of signs.

As was discussed in the introduction of this book, within Deleuze and Guattari's empiricism, the concept is the expressed of an event—which is "immaterial and unpresentable" (Cook, 1998:28). Cook distinguishes between an expressive utterance in Deleuzeoguattarian empiricism and the descriptive utterance of the abstract concept. In what follows, the literary function is portrayed as an expression of the literary/performative event and in so doing the capture of the literary by models of realization and their abstraction is overturned.

In continuing to explore the literary function and society, this book ultimately turns toward Deleuze and Guattari's notion of "primitive" regimes. They oppose these to capturing regimes. The literary function is a primitive regime, affecting transformation and, to use Deleuze and Guattari's expression, a line of flight. The connection of the literary function to this type of regime, which also belongs to certain social formations, means that the concept of the literary function is immanent to itself.

But before turning to the notion of the performative as it applies to the literary function, we must first turn to that which eliminates an immanent approach to the literary, that being apparatuses of capture.

Apparatuses of Capture

This section considers the notion of capture in order to rethink terms from political economy. It does so for two reasons: first, in order to consider the literary function in relation to political economy, and thus, in relation to society; and second, in order to critique current approaches to the literary.

For Deleuze and Guattari, capture is primarily of the earth, and what captures the earth is "overcoding, or the Signifier" (1987:428). The State overcodes when it makes (diverse) points resonate, which is what it does primarily. Deleuze and Guattari call the State "a phenomenon of intraconsistency"(433). While making diverse points resonate— for example, "town, geographic, ethnic, linguistic, moral, economic, technological"—the State retains some of the elements of the diverse points, and thus "it necessarily cuts off their relationship with other elements" (433). It causes them to become exterior, slowed down, and controls those relations (433). In other words, it captures them. The State thus produces a circuit unto itself, it isolates itself, and this leads to a second point of importance: it has a unified interiority. This "interior essence or…unity of the State" (427) is what Deleuze and Guattari refer to as "capture." The zone of resonance then "operates by stratification"; the State forms "vertical, hierarchized aggregate(s) that span…horizontal lines in a dimension of depth" (433). Such a regime is thus referred to by Deleuze and Guattari as "the paradigm of the bond, the knot" (428). It is an *apparatus* of capture. Deleuze and Guattari give three primary regimes of overcoding of the earth, these being: Rent, Profit (labor), and Taxation. Deleuze and Guattari's account deals in great depth with these mechanisms of capture; however, suffice it to say that these three regimes introduce capital, which is the ultimate device of equivalence, and of resonance. For example, Deleuze and Guattari's point concerning taxation is that taxation makes money a general equivalent (442). When both the rich and poor were taxed, say Deleuze and Guattari, "the poor in goods or services, the rich in money,...an equivalence money-goods and services was established" (442). "It is taxation that monetarizes the economy; it is taxation that creates money" (443), and, "it is through taxation that goods and services come to be like commodities, and the commodity comes to be measured and equalized by money"(443). The apparatuses of capture, then, function by way of a "general space of comparison and a mobile center of appropriation" (444). These converge to form a monopolistic regime. For Deleuze and Guattari, the regimes of overcoding belonging to the State are capitalism's *models of realization*, they "coincide...in an agency of overcoding (or significance)" (444). Apparatuses of capture, say Deleuze and Guattari, are "the semiological operation par excellence" (445). The three agencies of overcoding are "like three capitalizations of power, or three articulations of 'capital'" (444).

For Deleuze and Guattari, "there have been States always and everywhere" (429). Even writing, speech, and language presuppose the State. The State "appears as preaccomplished and self-presupposing." It is, then, a "magic capture" (427). However, Deleuze and Guattari make the highly significant point that, contrary to evolutionism (430), *everything is not of the State since there have always been States, everywhere*. There is, then, another regime that coexists with the State and that both wards off and anticipates the formation of (its) central power, and this regime belongs to collective mechanisms (431). We have seen that the State deterritorializes codes but in so doing it releases "decoded flows" (448) that escape from it and these are multiple or collective in nature. For example, in the archaic State, which created large-scale works, there also escaped a flow of independent labor (notably in the mines and metallurgy) (449). The "decoded *flow*" is multiple since, even if it enumerates only one, for the time being, it cannot be assimilated by the *unifying* apparatus of capture—in which equivalence reduces everyone and thing to the Same, to One.

As mentioned, however, capitalism "seeks" these flows in order to deterritorialize them, "It is their abstract conjunction in a single stroke that constitutes capitalism" (453). In fact, capitalism itself "forms with *a general axiomatic of decoded flows*" (453). For example, capitalism takes the flows and "processes of subjectification" and capitalizes them into "a single unqualified and global Subjectivity" (452) when it conjugates "the flow of unqualified wealth" with the "flow of unqualified labor" (453). The Subject is thus produced by and subjugated to capitalism. In short, it is "alienated"—it belongs to the paradigm of the bond (453). The abstract conjunction formed in a single stroke, of capitalism, or the magic capture of the State, results in the regime of capital appearing as a right, or as Deleuze and Guattari say, "'a relation of production that is manifest as a right.'" The result of this is that the regime is "'independent of the concrete form that it cloaks at each moment of its productive function'" (Deleuze and Guattari quoting Arghiri Emmanuel, 1987:453). Deleuze and Guattari discuss this phenomenon in relation to the Subject; they point out that when Marx begins to define capitalism he begins by noting:

> the advent of a single unqualified and global Subjectivity, which capitalizes... "all activities without distinction"... now expresses itself in an Object in general, no longer in this or that qualitative state: "Along with the abstract universality of wealth-creating activity we have now the universality of the object as wealth." (452)

It is in the context of the abstracting and equalizing nature of the overcoding apparatuses, then, that Deleuze and Guattari refer to the figure of the Outsider as collective (449): collective mechanisms keep points and "formations of power" from "resonating together" and thus being captured by "a higher point"—the overcoding State apparatus—"and from becoming polarized at a common point" (433).

One of the most significant aspects of Deleuze and Guattari's notions of capture—for the purposes of the literary function—is their notion that capture entails *models of realization*. The recent "sociological turn" in literary and cultural studies has seen the critical vocabulary become a "model of realization." The immanent field of the literary has been overcoded and thereby captured by "the sociological," "the cultural," by "semiology" and by "the text." This capture circumvents an exploration of the literary function in relation to society and, moreover, as a possible "collective mechanism," capable of warding off State or centralized power. It is, however, the literary function's performative quality that makes it a collective mechanism. It is the elimination of the performative potential from the literary function that has enabled its capture. The performative in this book is an *aesthetic* category, which is to say that it involves an irreversible, autonomous terrain, and to these ends, the literary is also an aesthetic category (see chapter 1). The literary, as with aesthetics, has been captured by cultural criticism, perhaps inadvertently, while such criticism has sought to sidestep the undesirable transcendental uses of these terms. In *The Ideology of the Aesthetic* (1990), Terry Eagleton explains the problem with the aesthetic category within literary studies:

> The emergence of the aesthetic as a theoretical category is closely bound up with the material process by which cultural production, at an early stage of bourgeois society, becomes "autonomous"—autonomous, that

is, of the various social functions which it has traditionally served. Once artifacts become commodities in the market place, they exist for nothing and nobody in particular, and can consequently be rationalized, ideologically speaking, as existing entirely and gloriously for themselves. It is this notion of autonomy or self-referentiality which the new discourse of aesthetics is centrally concerned to elaborate; and it is clear enough, from a radical political viewpoint, just how disabling any such idea of aesthetic autonomy must be. It is not only, as radical thought has familiarly insisted, that art is thereby conveniently sequestered from all other social practices, to become an isolated enclave within which the dominant social order can find an idealized refuge from its own actual values of competitiveness, exploitation and material possessiveness. It is also, rather more subtly, that the idea of autonomy—of a mode of being which is entirely self-regulating and self-determining—provides the middle class with just the ideological model of subjectivity it requires for its material operations. (1990:9)

Cultural Criticism against the Aesthetic

Michel Foucault's geneological approach to literature is arguably the principal influence upon cultural criticism's antiaesthetic trend. In some cases, it has resulted in a shunning of the term "literary" altogether. For example, the cultural critic Ben Agger constructs a traditional literary studies/cultural studies divide (1992:11).[2] For Foucault it was necessary to go beyond the idea of autonomy. Foucault concedes that it was probably necessary to "pose the great principle that literature is concerned only with itself" (1988:309) for literature to lose its expressive character—"the idea that literature was the locus of every kind of traffic, or the point at which all traffic came to an end, the expression of totalites" (309).[3] However, for Foucault it was necessary to go beyond even this notion—of "literature as a structure of language capable of being analyzed in itself and on its own terms"—since it ran the risk of continuing the "sacralization" of literature. The sacralization of literature, for Foucault, begins with the connection between the two institutions, the university and literature. He states that "literature functions as literature through an interplay of selection, sacralization, and institutional validation, of which the university is both the operator and the receiver" (309).

Fred Pfeil, *Another Tale to Tell: Politics and the Linguistic Sign* (1990), is an early literary-turned-cultural critic who positions himself in opposition to the aesthetic. Like other such critics, he introduces his tale with the literary fallacy.[4] In so doing, he begins a uniform attack on the aesthetic as a transcendent term. For Pfeil, the literary fallacy consists of taking imaginative writing as an end in itself, a "closed, autonomous, self-referential body" (21) and (as he notes in the case of Walter Pater) imagining that it

" 'aspire(s) to the condition of music' " (Pfeil quoting Pater, 1990:21)—that is, to beauty rather than to meaning. For Pfeil, the literary fallacy has lead to obscure writing, rendering writing irrelevant.[5] Pfeil uses an expression of W. H. Auden to describe such literature: " 'a plane over Wyoming at night' " (Pfeil quoting Auden, 21). The implication is that such literature is distant and irrelevant just as the people of Wyoming are a long way from the plane and few (compared to the whole of America). The term "at night" may imply such writing is off in its own *dream* world, as are the people of Wyoming at night. Pound and Mallarmé are also derided by Pfeil for contending that "it is the purpose of poetry 'to purify the language of the tribe' " (Pfeil quoting Pound and Mallarmé, 21). Pfeil condones the Leavisites for their anthropological activities and in seeking to know the reading habits of the people of England, but condemns them for their close readings of texts.

In all, some cultural criticism seems to have followed in Foucault's footsteps in preferring to focus upon the external rather than internal life of the text. Foucault put it like this:

> In order to know what literature is, I would not want to study its internal structures. I would rather grasp the movement, the little process, by which a type of non-literary discourse, neglected, forgotten as soon as it was made, enters the literary field (1988:311).

Foucault wishes to know of the sociological and institutional shifts that have taken place that allow for a different aesthetic within literature.[6] This external consideration of literature is also the approach of the sociologist Pierre Bourdieu. For Bourdieu, art, including literature, is viewed entirely from factors external to it, which, for Bourdieu, are the *institutions* of art (1993). For Bourdieu there is no art outside of these institutions.

Within cultural-oriented criticism, then, which emphasize the external life of the text, there is a capture of the literary aesthetic. Literature is overcoded (and thereby captured) when it is of interest only as a trace of social and historical movements. And it is overcoded when it is equated with the *institutions* of art and the university. As with the State, in cultural criticism, diverse points of order are made to resonate: the subject, institutions, class, history, the social, the economic, literature, the aesthetic, etc. For Deleuze and Guattari, such an operation is an operation of stratification (1987:433). The unifying body (as mentioned earlier, in relation to the State) "forms a vertical, hierarchical aggregate that spans the horizontal lines in a dimension of depth" (433). Moreover, a unifying body, in "retaining given elements...cuts off their relation with other elements, which become exterior, it inhibits, slows down, or controls those relations"

(433). Foucault shows some reservation about this capture. When asked: "[a]re there criteria internal to texts, or is it simply a matter of sacralization by the university institution?," Foucault states: "I don't know" (1988:309). However, other cultural criticism is less reserved. Discourses, such as Pfeil's, which call for nonobscurity in art and literature, capture the literary totally. Literature is expected to have an *intraconsistency* with other accessible discourses. "Writing should demand we see. Seeing should demand we change" (1990:28), writes Pfeil.[7] In Pfeil and throughout cultural criticism, popular culture is vehemently opposed to the opacity of modernism, high art, and literature. The worst case for Pfeil being that of Joyce, as when "his separation from the world approaches infinity as the reality or perception explored in his work approaches zero" (29). However, as Guattari says of modernism's technological innovations (and here I include the modern aesthetics), "[it] is impossible to judge such machinic evolution either positively or negatively: everything depends on its articulation within collective assemblages of enunciation" (1995:5).

Pfeil's own collective assemblage of enunciation is worth exploring in order to view further the capturing qualities of that discourse. Pfeil's concern is that arcane writing won't reach a society/audience conditioned to absorb it unreflectively into its fold. However, Pfeil approaches this problem with old tools and paradigms. Pfeil's criticism could be seen to echo the Marxist literary critic, Georg Lukács's, for example: a "formal aesthetics" (modernism) is placed in binary opposition to an "honest" (non-Literary) discourse.[8] Pfeil speaks at length about the lie of Literary discourse. He tells of the American writing establishment at that time, mostly men, who gather to see who can write the best sentence. In doing this, for Pfeil, they turn writing into a kind of arm-wrestling match. Writing, then, becomes the long arm of the foul mask of machismo, and thus, a lie. The problem with this prescriptive criticism of Pfeil's is that it is metadiscursive and thereby belongs to the metanarrative mode of modernism. Moreover, Pfeil's prescriptive criticism, based upon the moral imperative that writing isn't merely a form of onanism, belongs to the "model of realization" of postmodern cultural-critical turn, and is, thereby, another capture.

In more recent criticism, for example, that found in Lance Olsen's chapter, "Pragmatism, Politics and Postmodernism, or: Leaving the White Hotel" (1990), there continues a move toward the cultural model of realization. I chose someone like Olsen because, like me, he is attempting to consider the relationship between text and society beyond the confines of linguistic-based postmodern criticism and literary history. The type of literary history Olsen refers to is an *intrinsic* history of literature, described by Lee Patterson as a narrative account of either literature as a whole or of specific modes (poetry, drama, fiction), genres (epic, comedy, pastoral, or forms (complaint, sonnet, ode), that covers either a broad sweep of historical time or confines itself to one of the chronological periods into which the cultural past has been typically divided. (1990:250)[9]

Such approaches capture the literary and/or inhibit an exploration of the relationship between the aesthetic and society, as is the case with some formalist and postmodern criticism. However, I am critical of Olsen's methodology, believing that it does not take us beyond literary history, as he claims.

In Olsen, both postmodernism and deconstruction come under attack for being, in short, merely academic. Olsen uses a story by David Lodge, *Small World: An American Romance,* to make his point about deconstruction. Upon being released

[a] kidnapped academic comes to realize that he has lost his faith in deconstruction because "death is the one concept you can't deconstruct. Work back from there and you end up with the old idea of an autonomous self. I can die, therefore I am".... There is nothing like a good dose of death to bring one out of the realm of theory and verbal games, and to cement one firmly to the realm of fact, experience, and action. (Olsen, 1990:119)

And:

There is nothing like a good dose of death to force one to reexamine the important practical questions about life and understand that freeplay is never completely free, that there is an eternity between presence and absence. (119)

Olsen has this to say about postmodern criticism:

The moment the critics articulated the presence of absence, an antisystem began to turn into a merely negative system. To say that postmodernity explores the impossibility of imposing a single meaning on a text through both minimalism of degree zero writing (Kafka, Borges, and Handke) and the maximalism of plurisignification (Sorrentino, Pynchon, and Melville) is of course, to impose a meaning on a text, to create a menu, and the rest is a move toward the past, toward literary history. (121–122)

I agree with Olsen's general dissatisfaction with the capture of the "text" by postmodern criticism—and the subsequent turning toward literary history (except I exchange "the text" for "the literary"). However, Olsen does not escape the very tradition he critiques. Olsen puts forward, in the place of postmodern theory and deconstruction, a Jamesian-type pragmatics, a pragmatics that "seeks meaning in praxis, in the concrete, in nitty-gritty facts" (117). Olsen quotes the following passage from William James:

> "A pragmatist turns his back resolutely and once and for all upon a lot of inveterate habits dear to professional philosophers...[The pragmatist] turns away from abstraction and insufficiency, from verbal solutions, from bad *a priori* reasons, from fixed principles, closed systems, and pretended absolutes and origins. He turns towards concreteness and adequacy, towards facts, towards action and towards power." (Olsen quoting James, 1990:118)

For James, writes Olsen, "there can be no more purified professional philosophers than the postmoderns, who have raised self-consciousness and theory to a paralytic level" (118). Pragmatics, for Olsen, brings about a return to meaning through the process of praxis itself, overriding the "destabilized" world of the postmodern. Says Olsen:

> The more one experiences a postmodern text, the less postmodern it becomes for the simple reason that humans need to make meaning in the texts around them, even if that meaning is in some way informed by the knowledge that the text cannot be *wholly* knowable. (121)

In Olsen's pragmatics, meaning is made according to our needs, not according to this closed (aesthetic) system or that: ideas are true, "'*just in so far as they help us to get satisfactory relations with other parts of our experience*'" (Olsen quoting James, 118, italics in the original James). Convinced that humans make meaning come what may, overriding the notion in postmodern theory of fundamental meaninglessness of the text, Olsen concludes that there is a contradiction "in the idea of the postmodern at the levels of ontology, politics, and aesthetics" (121). In other words, the aesthetic differs from the ontological and political reality of postmodernism. (Postmodern) criticism, then, for Olsen, comes down to *mere* aesthetics and it is these "ideas" that are typically "airy play toys to fool with freely" (118), as opposed to ideas in pragmatics that "are things that become relatively true...just in so far as they help us get along in our day-to-day world" (118).

Aesthetics is the enemy for Olsen since postmodernism has culminated in the end of meaning, and has consequently divorced itself from the social.[10] Olsen cites the novel *The White Hotel* (1981) by D. M. Thomas, as a kind of case study and analogy of what happens when society is divorced from its stories—and by implication its politics and ethics—by closed systems such as aesthetics. The story is of a Jewish woman who visits Freud after World War I with prophetic "symptoms" of Nazi atrocities. She suffers pain in her left breast and ovary and shortness of breath. The story of the White Hotel eventually contextualizes these symptoms as being prophetic of her brutal death at Babi Yar, the site of a massacre during World War II in which 33,000 people are killed. This fictionalized massacre parallels the documentary novel by Anatoli Kuznetsov called *Babi Yar*. For Olsen, it is Freud's scientific, closed, aesthetic system that fails in addressing the actual history in which he and his patients live. For instance, there is no scope within the confines of his science to cope with Elizabeth's Jewishness. Says Olsen, "Freudian analysis is impotent in the face of utter political menace.... Committed... to the psychological it cannot understand the realm of the political" (131). And, "We come to realize that the battle between the death instinct and the life instinct in our century has been raised to a cultural level" (131). It is for this reason that Olsen pillories so-called aesthetic, closed systems, referring to them as narcissistic fantasies. Into this category he includes political fantasies, occult investigations, and psychoanalytic systems. He joins Thomas, who quotes W. B. Yeats, in condemning such "fantasies," for instance, the "nineteenth century fantasies of revolution and freedom (that) have given way to twentieth century visions of brutality and ruin" (124). The Yeats quote Thomas uses is: "We had fed the heart on fantasies, / The heart's grown brutal from the fare." For Olsen, Thomas's use of Yeats line "seems to indicate that being fed on *any* fantasies, any systems whatsoever, can contribute to violence" (124). At the end of the story, Elizabeth identifies with her cultural self and an ethical and political statement is achieved. The story as a whole marks a passage of awareness from the narcissistic (postmodern/psychoanalytic) self-awareness to "the practical morality of praxis, and the final connection between personal and collective tragedy" (134). Olsen opposes the aesthetic to "the practical power of praxis," the "concrete," the "nitty gritty facts" (117). Aesthetic inquiry is cast with a range of negative descriptions: decadent, uncommitted (postmodernism), frivolous (postmodernism), self-reflexive, and intellectual gaming. It is damned by its "belief in the universe as joke" (124) (this he compares to "a belief in the universe as horror" [124]) and for being self-fulfilling and a closed system.

I argue that Olsen is wrong to make aesthetics the enemy. In so doing, in opposing pragmatics to aesthetics, Olsen marks a return to literary history and not a move away from it. Olsen, as mentioned, is opposed to literary history—of the kind discussed above. However, he works an alternative literary history, which, I will argue, ultimately does not depart from the type to which he objects. Olsen's critical practice is concerned "with the relations of literature...to history, as a series of events" (Patterson, 1990:250).[11] In Olsen, the function of literature is to provide us with the facts through "the practical power of praxis." This is literature as History[12]. Olsen's wish for literature's role departs little from that of Lukács's, who considers it attendant upon the novel to include "an artistically faithful image of a concrete historical epoch" (1989:19). The literary, at this point, is understood as genre—that of the historical novel—and at such a point it is returned to literary history of the kind Olsen opposes, the kind that defines literature by genre and other such categories.

Moreover, in shunning the aesthetic, Olsen is left with no alternative but to evoke a metaphysical sign. In the case of the "Lodge" example, it is the metaphysical sign of death and the subsequent autonomous self that is invoked. In both of the scenarios above, literature takes on a mimetic role; it is a useful *object* of reflection for the autonomous self and for history. It is also interesting to consider Olsen's construction of literary mimesis in relation to metaphysical thought. Olsen's discourse uses figures consistent with binary (and thereby metaphysical) thought, such as realism/experimentalism, horror/joke (paralleling the Aristotelian tragedy/comedy, and the rhetoric/nonrhetoric distinction), aesthetic/nonaesthetic, and system/nonsystem.

Olsen, then, is opposed to, but also caught up in, the paradigm of intrinsic literary history. In establishing the worth of praxis by opposing its virtue to an "evil" aesthetic, he casts his critical practice on the paradigm of intrinsic literary history. In speaking of the Thomas novel, Olsen says that, "[i]nto the midst of frivolous self-reflexivity and intellectual gaming thunders the dread practical power of praxis" (124). In an implicit way, even Olsen admits that these binaries are convenient distinctions of the academy and as categories are not as ubiquitous as these linear arguments perforce make out. However, instead of choosing to focus on the somewhat glib observation that there is an eternity between presence and absence, as Olsen does, Olsen could have equally explored the notion that there is an eternity between death and life—the latter always involving precisely verbal games and "theory." However, Olsen opposes the aesthetic to "the practical power of praxis," the "concrete," the "nitty gritty facts" (117). In Olsen, and elsewhere, life (death), the facts, the serious, the nitty gritty, are opposed to freeplay. Freeplay, and its home in aesthetics, consists of intellectual gaming. Olsen's pragmatics, then, captures the literary in a model of realization of a varying complexity. The act (the power of praxis) becomes—as with Austin's notion of the performative speech act—a *realization*. Added to this intraconsistency of praxis, culture, and the literary (aesthetic), is intrinsic literary history.

What is needed, then, is a move away from the (implicit) Arcadian notion of "free" found in Olsen (to which he opposes his own work as though it were somehow *free* of the academy, of intrinsic literary history). Olsen follows a somewhat tired paradigm along which literary criticism with its internal pole, liberalism (associated with the aesthetic) and socialism (associated with fact), have long traveled. To avoid a return to this binary and to avoid the capture of aesthetics by such a paradigm, a reserve should be placed around such spiraling frames as aesthetics and history (or praxis). Instead, aesthetics itself could be productively explored in relationship to, for example, subjectification and community, to which I will turn shortly. The aesthetic does not have to mean a (postmodernist) end to ethics. What is needed is not to attempt to describe epochs by genres (modern, postmodern) or the reverse, genres by epochs (history), and thereby capturing both, but an attempt to describe genres by themselves, immanently, a constructivist aesthetics.[13] The question must be not how close or far away a discourse is from "reality," from "culture," from the "nitty gritty," but—how does it work? What are its (aesthetic) conditions of production?[14]

Guattari's discussion of the aesthetic in the context of his psychotherapeutic practice is useful as an example of how aesthetics may work in practice. Far from seeing simulacra as a negative, Guattari puts it to use in family therapy. Rather than fixing "lived scenes as actually embodied in family structures" (1995:8), a "realist" attitude, to quote Guattari, "the therapists improvise psychodramatic scenes" (8), themselves getting involved. This points to the "artificial and creative character of the production of subjectivity" (8):

> [T]he scene implies a layering of enunciation: a vision of oneself as concrete embodiment; a subject of enunciation which doubles the subject of the statement and the distribution of roles; a collective management of the game; an interlocution with observers commenting on the scene; and finally, video which through *feedback* restores the totality of these superposed [sic] levels. (Guattari, 1995:8)

It is in fact in the freeplay (or "playful freedom," as Guattari puts it,) with the simulacra that the subject is able to observe certain semiotic manifestations that effect subjectivity. The result is an ethico-aesthetic paradigm. An ethico-aesthetic paradigm, when applied to literature, will locate the aesthetic in an ethical and social struggle while not collapsing this into History, into an epoch. In other words, rather than fixing the "lived scenes" of the text as actually being embodied in Historical structures, which, to recall Guattari, is a "realist" attitude, an ethico-aesthetics approach involves an immanent study. For such an immanent study, the development of a vocabulary is necessary, for without it the literary is captured by a "higher" regime of signs, such as History. An immanent concept would not be a totalizing account of the literary but would, instead, be self-specific.

An Immanent Literary Pragmatics and the Aesthetic

A common tracing of the history of literary theory and criticism by the then-new cultural critics (ca. 1990) was that of intrinsic literary history, autotelicism, and hermeneutics, involving traditional aesthetics, Author Criticism, Formalism, New Criticism, and American Deconstruction. However, a different critical history could be mapped involving the aesthetic. This other line involves the pragmatic implications of the aesthetic, and it is most fully realized in the work of Deleuze and Guattari, for example, in their combined work, *A Thousand Plateaus: Capitalism and Schizophrenia,* Deleuze's work, *The Logic of Sense,* and Guattari's concept of the "ethico-aesthetics."[15] A moralism has struck up around the aesthetic—as we have just alluded to. It is deemed "guilty" of being a scientific vocabulary and by this is meant a discourse studied in isolation.[16] Tony Bennett in *Formalism and Marxism* points out that the two formalist groups, the Moscow Linguistic Circle and the *Opoyaz* group, "were united to establish the study of literature on a scientific footing, to constitute it as an autonomous science using methods and procedures of its own" (1979:19). However, Bennett also notes that what is overlooked in this assessment of Formalism is that "literariness"—a literary text's "ability to "defamiliarize" (50)—was not an attribute of the literary text's "purely formal, intrinsic properties," but "the inherently *relational* nature of the concept of defamiliarization"(50). To quote Bennett in full:

> Whether or not a given text can be said to embody the attribute of defamiliarization thus depends not on its intrinsic properties in isolation but on the relationship which those properties establish with other cultural and ideological forms.... The accusation that the Formalists tended to fetishize the literary device is similarly misconceived. For the effect of defamiliarization depends not on the device itself but on the use to which it is put.... Literary language is distinguished from prosaic language, for example, not by the presence of metaphors in the former and their absence

from the latter, but by the different use to which the device of metaphor is put as between the two cases. (1979:50–51)

Formalism, then, identified different "literary systems" and the functions they fulfilled. The "function and meaning" of texts were determined not by their origin but by their "relationship to other such units of meaning" (74). This structuralism within Formalism did result in similar limitations as those found in Saussure's linguistics, that being one could not account for the changes that took place within the different "literary systems," or, in the case of Saussure's linguitics, "the means by which *la langue* moves from one synchronic state to another" (74).

Generally, when the story of Russian Formalism is told, it is told along lines of "Formalism and Beyond"—the name given to Bennett's chapter from which I have been quoting. The "beyond" refers to Volosinov and Bakhtin's introduction of the concept of the dialogic. The dialogic considers the word as it is "oriented to and takes account of the use of words in the utterances to which it is a response or in the utterances which it seeks to solicit as a response" (76). "Dialogism" has become a significant concept in cultural criticism as it concerns the utterance in its social and historical context. Writes Bakhtin:

> At any given time, in any given place, there will be a set of conditions—social, historical, meteorological, physiological—that will insure that a word uttered in that place and at that time will have a meaning different than it would have under any other conditions. (1981:428)

For Bakhtin, utterances are "heteroglot in that they are functions of a matrix of forces practically impossible to recoup, and therefore impossible to resolve" (428). It is the condition of heteroglossia "which insures the primacy of context over text" (428). However, what is lost in cultural criticism, with its emphasis upon context, is due consideration given to the aesthetic. Thinking such as Deleuze and Guattari's, on the other hand, does not dismiss the aesthetic, and in this respect they mark a different pathway from the literary theory and criticism inheritance as that taken by much of cultural criticism. In this other pathway, the aesthetic is considered as a necessary attribute of content and context. It is thus often their foregrounded object of study and/or discursive frame. The point to be made from the notion that the aesthetic is a necessary attribute of content and context is that the aesthetic is therefore political, social, and is concerned with questions of ethics. The inclusion of the aesthetic in both Deleuze and Guattari's work involves borrowing from Louis Hjelmslev, a linguist at the forefront of Copenhagen structuralism, and Bakhtin.

The Significance of the Aesthetic to
Content and Context

Deleuze and Guattari (1987) begin with Hjelmslev when most directly addressing the question of the relationship between the aesthetic and content.[17] In particular, Guattari is interested in Hjelmslev's formulation, Expression/Content, and its potential reversibility. This potential reversibility (still not entirely realized in Hjelmslev's formulation) Guattari opposes to structuralisms signifier/signified couplet. He takes from Hjelmslev the notion that "the connection between Expression and Content is realized at the level of *form* of Expression and *form* of Content" (1995:23, my italics). For Guattari, Hjelmslev's notion of a form of expression and a form of content was intuitive of a formal machine, which Guattari suggests is not at the root of language (23) (Chomsky's abstract machine, on the other hand, is linguistic-based), but of what Deleuze and Guattari call *the enunciative assemblage*. The *enunciative assemblage* is, in Guattari's words, "a machinic assemblage of enunciation" (1995:24).

Deleuze and Guattari, as mentioned, redress Hjelmslev. Hjelmslev addressed the issue of Expression and Content with a tripartite division between matter, substance, and form. Form was like a net that when cast over matter resulted in substance of expression and substance of content. Such a notion, however, for Deleuze and Guattari, only unifies substance, the signifier reducing it to abstraction and equivalence. Thus, Hjelmslev, along with Saussure, maintains a reversible signifier/signified, Expression/Content couplet. For Deleuze and Guattari, this couplet is, in the final analysis, inadequate because it is too linguistic. (The linguistic leads to postmodern noncommitment,[18] as we have seen in chapter 2). Overriding Expression and Content, then, is a "formal machine, transversal to every modality of Expression and Content" (Guattari, 1995:23). In the place of the Expression/Content opposition of Hjelmslev-Saussure, Guattari puts forward a "multiplicity of expressive instances" or "an indefinite number of substances of Expression" (1995:24), "whether they be of the order of Expression or Content" (1995:23). The expressive instances may be semiotic or linguistic but they may also be " 'non-semiotically formed matter' " (Guattari quoting Hjelmslev 1995:24), such as "biological codings or organizational forms belonging to the socius," or "extra-linguistic, non-human,...technological, aesthetic, etc." (1995:24). *It is the machinic assemblage of enunciation that "agglomerates these different partial enunciations"* (1995:24, my italics)[19]. Guattari, thus, moves away from Hjelmslev's linguistic model so that substance is seen to belong equally to "non-semiotically formed matter" as well as to the semiotic. Form is not imaged as it is in Hjelmslev—as a net cast over matter—engendering substance of Expression and Content. For Deleuze and Guattari, there is never Expression or Content prior to form. Both Content and Expression already have form and substance. Thus, we arrive at an immanent, or, what is also referred to as irreversible, autonomous, nonlinguistic, and pragmatic machine.

This understanding explains the way in which "literary systems" and synchronic formations, in general, change over time, since they are always at one with substance and matter and belonging to the formal machine— the multiplicity of expressive instances. Moreover, such an understanding of form and substance clearly erodes the power given to the signifier by postmodern criticism in which the signifier is equivalent to a net cast over matter, resulting in equivalence. The signifier, for Deleuze and Guattari, is "a sign of the sign" (1983:206), an overcoding, a "deterritorialized sign"; it has displaced what they refer to as a "territorial representation." For Jean-François Lyotard,[20] Jean Baudrillard,[21] Deleuze and Guattari, and others, the sign before it is deterritorialized is determined by its use and function value—rather than exchange value. For Baudrillard, prior to exchange value, signs exist within a complex system of symbolic exchange. For Deleuze and Guattari, territorial representation is "the order of connotation...in which the word (*le mot*) as a vocal sign designates something, but...the thing designated is no less a sign, because it is furrowed by a graphism that is connoted in conjunction with the voice" (1983:203). "What becomes a sign is rather the thing or body designated as such, insofar as it reveals an unknown facet described on it, traced by the graphism that responds to the word" (Deleuze and Guattari, 204). For Deleuze and Guattari, territorial representation consists of three elements, voice, graphism, and eye (203–204). The eye functions as a bridge between the vocal and graphic elements. The eye sees the word rather than reads it, "inasmuch as it appraises the pain emanating from the graphism applied to the flesh itself: the eye jumps" (204). For Deleuze and Guattari, this connoting system—connecting words, graphic traces, and eyes—is a polyvocal usage and "*a way of jumping* that cannot be contained within an order of meaning, still less within a signifier" (204). Rather, this is a "system of cruelty where the word has an essentially designating function,...the eye goes from one to the other, extracting and measuring the visibility of the one against the pain of the other. Everything in this system is active, en-acted *(agi),* or reacting; everything is a matter of use and function" (204).

Where the signifier is concerned, "problems of exegesis prevail over problems of use and efficacy" (Deleuze and Guattari, 206). Exegesis requires a linear flow of writing, in other words, a system. This system is introduced with the advent of the "despotic machines and imperial representation" (205). Emperors require a *new alliance* (to replace the existing alliances within the social). The new alliance is brought about by a *direct filiation* between god and emperor. This in turn brings about a *flow* of writing, from transcendent god to emperor. According to Deleuze and Guattari, the two fundamental despotic categories, new alliance and direct filiation, bring about "a fictitious voice from beyond that expresses itself in the flow of writing as *direct filiation*" (205). The transcendent origin brings about the exegetical question, What does it mean? and the flow continues from there. At this point, write Deleuze and Guattari: "Graphism aligns itself on the voice, falls back on the voice, and becomes writing" (205). For Deleuze and Guattari, territorial representation is a "polyvocal graphism, flush with the real" (206), and it is replaced with a "biunivocalism forming the transcendent dimension that gives rise to linearity" (206). Biunivocalism is "a sign of a sign," which in turn is sign as signifier. Write Deleuze and Guattari, this is "the sign made *letter*" (206). Thus, the signifier makes matter equivalent (and not polyvocal) since signifiers refer to other signifiers within a system of meaning. For linguistics-based postmodern theory, the signifier saturates space. It is the net of form, of a system, cast over matter, and as a result the real is lost (see also Baudrillard, 1983). However, within Deleuze and Guattari's materialist theory (of desire), the "magic triangle" (205) of the eye, voice, and graphism, "subsists as a base and as a brick, insofar as the territorial machine continues to function in the framework of the new machine" (205). For Guattari, postmodernists have hardly anything innovative to say about the "idea that the socius [*sic*] is reducible to the facts of language, and that these facts are in turn reducible to binarizable 'digitalizable' signifying chains" (1996:111). It is for this reason that postmodernism does not escape "the modernist tradition of structuralism."

Territorial machines are important to an immanent understanding of the aesthetic and to the place of the aesthetic in society. In chapter 2, I have discussed the aesthetic in relation to the refrain, but here it is important to note that refrains are also territorial machines. Refrains are the "freeing…of matters of expression in the movement of territoriality" (Deleuze and Guattari, 1987:316). For Deleuze and Guattari, this is "the base or ground of art" (316). The refrain, like the territorial machine, does not have a system, the refrain only has lines and movements (350). They are both autonomous; Deleuze and Guattari refer to territorial representation as detachable partial objects (1983:204). And both are pragmatic machines; with territorial machines "everything is a matter of use and function" (Deleuze and Guattari, 1983:204).

An immanent approach to the aesthetic, such as Deleuze and Guattari's notion of territorial representation is needed, then, in order to approach the question of the relationship between art and society, or between literature and society. *Where a signifier/signified, Expression/Content couplet is used, no importance can be given to the aesthetic and its counterpoint to equivalence. It is due to the formal machine that content is contextual but also in a state of becoming and thereby virtual.* Consideration given to the relationship between text and society must, then, include the aesthetic and its *processual nature.* Artistic pursuit, for Deleuze and Guattari, brings "about a development of Form" (1987:349–350) that is at once both a deterritorialization (of form) and also a reterritorialization—because the sign is one of territorial representation, even if that territory is the Cosmos (350).

If we read the aesthetic through the developments of Deleuze and Guattari, we can see that it has helped us understand the relationship between text and society, and not, as it is more generally thought, foreclosed on this problematic. Roman Jakobson's notion of the plane of combination and the plane of selection is precursive of a machinic assemblage of enunciation, just as the notion that in poetry the plane of selection is raised to the plane of combination[22] is precursive of the "multiplicity of expressive instances." The plane of selection and combination are entirely linguistically based and therefore cannot account for the way in which synchronic formations in general change over time; it cannot account for a relationship between text and society. However, Deleuze and Guattari's pragmatic understanding of language, in which language is always already bound with substance—substances of expression and content—changes this. What we can now say of poetry is that it brings our attention not to language and the signifier (as deconstruction and postmodern theory suggest) but to the activeness of language, that is, to its form as *substances* of expression and or content, what Deleuze and Guattari refer to as "a becoming of Forces" (1987:350). Importantly, then, this pragmatic understanding of the aesthetic is a nonrepresentational approach to the text (and in this respect, the word "text" is not adequate). Deleuze and Guattari's pragmatic understanding of the aesthetic is fundamentally an expression of the *relationship* between text and society. This includes the way in which the aesthetic, as territorial refrain, functions as an alternative force to the signifier as a regime of equivalence. In this light, we can further understand Guattari's statement: "Poetry today might have more to teach us than economic science, the human sciences and psychoanalysis combined" (1996:21).

The Literary Function and Society II: Community and Subjectification

The aesthetic power of feeling, although equal in principle with the other powers of thinking philosophically, knowing scientifically, acting politically, seems on the verge of occupying a privileged position within the collective Assemblage of enunciation of our era.

(*Félix Guattari*, Chaosmosis: An Ethico-aesthetic Paradigm)

The Aesthetic, Ethics and Subjectification

For Guattari it is aesthetics that provides an ethics that enables a "transgressive" machine in the form of subjectivity or singularization.[1] The "aesthetic mode," for Guattari, is a way to ward off the alienation and fragmentation resulting from a postmodern world. "The devaluation of the meaning of life provokes the fragmentation of the self-image" (Guattari, 1995:12). Guattari attempts to "grasp [subjectivity] in the dimension of its processual creativity" (1995:13), the result is an ethico-aesthetics. His notion of a processual subjectivity is that in *creating* a subjectivity one is "geared" toward the future and not the past, that is, not "'readymade' dimensions of subjectivity crystallized into structural complexes" (1995:7). What role does the literary function play in the subjectivity born of processual creativity? How does such a subjectivity unpack from, and fold back into, territory, community, society, and so on? What are its *affects*—in our prior use of the term, meaning a body that is the result of an action and that does not precede the action?

Subjectification is important to Deleuze and Guattari's notion of aesthetics and transgressive ethics since it is also in subjectification that dominant reality and power resides—making subjectification a double-edged sword. In discussing "ready-made" dimensions of subjectivity, Deleuze and Guattari begin with the notion of subjectification. Subjectification can be anything, but it must "display the following characteristic traits of the subjective semiotic: the double turning away, betrayal, and existence under reprieve" (1987:129). An example of subjectification is of the Jews who turned away from empires: "God withdraws his face, becoming a point of subjectification for the drawing of a line of flight or deterritorialization" (128). There is a modern/Christian philosophy that is a turning away. Nineteenth-century psychiatry is "subjective delusion separated from ideational delusions" (128). There are endless points of subjectification; for anorexics, food becomes a point of subjectification as they turn away from it.

Subjectification replaces transcendent and centralized power. Points of subjectification operate through normalization (130) and "power is instead immanent and melds with the 'real'" (130). Deleuze and Guattari explain subjectification's relationship to dominant reality, thus:

> [f]rom the point of subjectification issues a subject of enunciation, as a function of a mental reality determined by that point. Then from the subject of enunciation issues a subject of the statement, in other words, a subject bound to statements in conformity with a dominant reality.... The subject of the statement has become the "respondent" or guarantor of the subject of enunciation, through a kind of reductive echolalia.... This relation, this recoiling, is also that of mental reality into the dominant reality." (1987:129)

Deleuze and Guattari refer to subjectification as "passional," postsignifying, and a "strange invention: as if in one form the doubled subject were the cause of the statements of which, in its other form, it itself is a part" (130). Deleuze and Guattari point out that "the more you obey the statements of the dominant reality, the more in command you are as subject of enunciation in mental reality, for in the end you are only obeying yourself!" (130). They see this as a new form of slavery, "namely, being slave to oneself, or to pure 'reason'" (130). This passional regime of signs (Deleuze and Guattari point out that it is just one regime of signs among many [130]) is also, quite obviously, dangerous in the constitution of an unreflective, fundamental mentality.

Subjectivity thus brings about a uniformity in the substance of enunciation (129). Guattari turns to the aesthetic to counter this, to focus upon that which is "auto-enriching," making the aesthetic a political and ethical end in itself. It is thus not captured by a signifying order. (Guattari points out that Freudian psychoanalysis has increasingly become adapted "to society, and its conformity with a signifying order" [Guattari, 1995:10].)

Processual Subjectivity and the Act

Guattari's ideas about processual creativity draw upon the thinking of Mikhail Bakhtin.[2] It is useful, however, to explore the ideas of Bakhtin in isolation from those of Guattari since they give an account of the psychological motivation behind the *act* of processual creativity—which results in subjectivity. In other words, Bakhtin is important for the emphasis he places upon the function of the *act* (of process) itself in the production of subjectivity, even before it is thought in terms of aesthetics. (In Bakhtin the act is also referred to as " 'the world of human action'—'the world of event' [*mir sobutiia*], 'the world of the performed act' [*mir postupka*]" [1993:xxii].) Processual subjectivity is at the heart of Bakhtin's posthumously published work, *Towards a Philosophy of the Act*. In this work, Bakhtin writes about the relationship between not "the now familiar gap between the order of signs and the order of things" (x), but the gap between the act and its account, between our deeds and words. For Bakhtin, it is the relationship between our acts and our words that is responsible for subjectivity. The subject weaves a relation to the deed by accounting for it, and this produces his/her "own radical uniqueness"(xii), or subjectivity. Because of our "own unique, never-repeatable 'place' in Being" (xxii), we lack an alibi, and this causes us to feel guilt, which in turn prompts "a unique 'answerability' " (xxii). Bakhtin introduces the concept of a " 'non-alibi' in Being" (xxii) to account for the verbal response to the deed. For Bakhtin, the act is a deed, and not a matter of "one damned thing after another" (xii), and because of this responsibility we have to account for it. The relationship between the act and its meaning, then, is not a priori, it is not grounded in a preexisting structure, as it is for Kant, for instance (xii), but "must always and everywhere be *achieved*" (xii). In other words, the *act* is a creative process (just as Guattari's (ethico)aesthetics is a creative process) and a performative pragmatics. In both Bakhtin and Guattari, the result is a production of singularities, autonomy, and subjectivation[3] (Guattari)/*subiectum* (Bakhtin).

For Bakhtin, the relationship between our deeds and words results in an *authentic experience* and self. Subjective experience is for Bakthin, authentic (he uses the expression, actual), because it occurs when the subject *experiences* an object *actually*, which he or she does when he or she carries out something in relation to it (1993:32). When the subject engages with an object in an effort to understand their ought in relation to it (the attitude or position I ought to take in relation to it), this presupposes their answerable participation, and not an abstracting from themselves. This performed act,

> [t]he actually performed act—not from the aspect of its content, but in its very performance...sees more than just a unitary context; it also sees a unique, concrete context, an ultimate context, into which it refers both its own sense and its own factuality, and within which it attempts to actualize answerably the unique truth [*pravda*] of both the fact and the sense in their concrete unity. (1993:28)

The Aesthetic and Virtual Content and Subjectivity

For Bakhtin, however, the object that *I* engage with is not "totally finished" (32). The totally finished object "cannot be something one becomes actually conscious of, something one experiences actually" (32). Bakhtin writes: "Insofar as I am actually experiencing an object, even if I do so by thinking of it, it becomes a changing moment in the ongoing event of my experiencing (thinking) it, i.e., it assumes the character of something-yet-to-be-achieved" (32). Bakhtin points out that the word too,

> the living word, the full word, does not know an object as something totally given: the mere fact that I have begun speaking about it means that I have already assumed a certain attitude toward it—not an indifferent attitude, but an interested-effective attitude. (32)

Experiencing the act, actuality, then, belongs to processual subjectivity, or rather subjectivity belongs to experiencing, to the processual. This truthful subjectivity or "once-occurrent Being," as Bakhtin also refers to it, is opposed to the world abstracted in closed or "totally finished" (32), meaning, in "theoretical cognition" (9), in which *I* do not exist. Writes Bakhtin:

> Any kind of *practical* orientation of my life within the theoretical world is impossible: it is impossible to live in it, impossible to perform answerable deeds. In that world I am unnecessary; I am essentially and fundamentally non-existent in it. The theoretical world is obtained through an essential and fundamental abstraction from the fact of my unique being and from the moral sense of that fact—"as if I did not exist." (9)

For Bakhtin, Kant's notion of Being is indifferent to "unique being," it cannot in principle add anything to it or subtract anything from it, for it remains equal to itself and identical in its sense and significance, regardless of whether I exist or not; it cannot determine my life as an answerable performing of deeds, it cannot provide any criteria for the life of practice, the life of the deed, for it is *not* the Being *in which I live,* and, if it were the only Being, *I* would not exist. (9)

Bringing together Guattari's notion of processual subjectivity (subjectivation) and Bakhtin's notion of once-occurrent Being, *we can say that the aesthetic is the expressed of subjectivity.*[4] Guattari's emphasis on processual creativity, the bringing together of differing "enunciations" to create a subjectivation, is complemented by Bakhtin's emphasis on once-occurrent Being. *Once-occurrent Being fully explains the aesthetic as "once-occurrent-event," as irreversible autonomous singularity.* For Bakhtin, in once-occurrent Being, the utterance is intonated with my emotional-volitional tone (due to my personal responsibility to the object obtainable only in the act). To quote Bakhtin:

Everything that is actually experienced is experienced as something given and as something-yet-to-be-determined, is intonated, has an emotional-volitional tone, and enters into an effective relationship to me within the unity of the ongoing event encompassing us. (1993:33)

Guattari notes that, for Bakhtin, there is a transference of subjectivation operating between author and contemplator of a work of art. The aesthetic form achieves an "isolating or separating function of such a kind that the expressive material becomes formally creative. The content of the work of art detaches itself from its connotations that are as much cognitive as aesthetic" (1995:14).[5] The example Bakhtin gives is, in music

isolation and invention cannot be axiologically related to the material: "It is not the sound of acoustics that is isolated, and not the mathematical number of the compositional order that is made up. *What is detached and fictively irreversible is the event of striving,* the axiological tension, which actualizes itself thanks to that without any impediment, and becomes consummated." (Guattari quoting Bakhtin, my italics, 1995:14)

It is the creative work, then, that engenders creative subjectivity since the aesthetic frees content enabling it to be "inserted into a living *subiectum*" (Bakhtin, 1993:14). "The world of aesthetic seeing, obtained in abstraction from the actual *subiectum* of seeing, is not the actual world in which I live," however, "its content aspect is inserted into a living *subiectum*" (1993:14).[6] It is important to emphasize the notion that the isolated content does not relate to the material or the work as a thing but " 'is freed from certain necessary connections with the unity of nature and the unity of the ethical event of being' " (Guattari quoting Bakhtin, 1995:14). As a result, the aesthetic regime of signs does not pertain to significance as that pertains to a uniformity in the substance of enunciation and a doubly articulated subjectivity. The aesthetic/act is an ongoing event (of my experiencing) and something yet to be determined (unfinished). It is therefore, virtual. For Guattari, the virtuality of the aesthetic results in a "virtual ecology" engendering "the conditions for the creation and development of unprecedented formations of subjectivity that have never been seen and never felt" (1995:91). Models of realization do not pertain to such a virtual ecology.

The aesthetic/act, then, is not a signifying regime of signs. As a result of the personal "investment" (to the ongoing event of my singularity), the act provides an "inalienable moment" (1993:33).[7] To quote Bakhtin:

[a]n emotional-volitional tone is an inalienable moment of the actually performed act, even of the most abstract thought, insofar as I am actually thinking it, i.e., insofar as it is really actualized in Being, becomes a participant in the ongoing event. (1993:33)

Here, context and content are deterritorialized and made virtual, bound to the yet-to-be-determined regime of signs and the once-occurrent-event. In other words, they cease to be Historical and captured within the signifying regime of signs.

In light of an ongoing critique, here, of aspects of postmodern cultural criticism, at this point it is worthwhile considering these ideas of Guattari's and Bakhtin's with respect to the category of the author. The literary author does not merely transpose (parody) a priori literary systems—genre, narrative, discourse, etc.—as postmodern theorists tirelessly argue,[8] but rather produces a once-occurrent-event from the author's[9] own Being/experience.[10] This experience would no doubt include aesthetic experience. In addition, Deleuze and Guattari's notion of territorial representation and Bakhtin's notion of the act are useful in enabling us to rethink the author function. Because the aesthetic regime of signs belongs to territorial representation—they are also detached and fictively irreversible—the author (its function) becomes the body of the sign. To return to an earlier quote from Deleuze and Guattari: "What becomes a sign (in territorial representation) is rather the thing or body designated as such, insofar as it reveals an unknown facet described on it, traced by the graphism that responds to the word" (1983:205). The body of the author becomes a sign when the graphism of the author's

answerable act "reveals an unknown facet described on it" /
author, then, becomes the sign of their answerable act or deed in a way
that the authors of nonaesthetic answerable acts cannot be. The aesthetic
sign/body, then, is a politics of the one, which is also a politics of the
multiple. The Bakhtin quote here emphasizes the multiple nature of the
answerable act:

> [t]he answerable act or deed alone surmounts anything hypothetical, for
> the answerable act is, after all, the actualization of a decision—inescap-
> able, irremediably, and irrevocably. The answerably performed act is a
> final result or summation, an all-round definitive conclusion. The per-
> formed act concentrates, correlates, and resolves within a unitary and
> unique and, this time, *final context* both the sense and the fact, the univer-
> sal and the individual, the real and the ideal, for everything enters into the
> composition of its answerable motivation. The performed act constitutes
> a going out *once and for all* from within possibility as such into *what is
> once-occurrent*. (1993:28–29)

I would like to now add to Foucault's famous phrase, "What matter who's
speaking?" (1977:138), the notion that the body/sign of the author performs subjectification and multiplicity. In the irreducible utterance, which
is also the *sign* of the author, content and context are deterritorialized
and made virtual. This response to Foucault's phrase is an ironic one and
opposed to the view of many postmodern cultural critics who have taken
the phrase as an invitation to dismiss the category of the author, outright,
as an unwanted transcendental sign. My point here is not that the job of
dismissing a transcendental signifier (i.e., the author) is an unsound job,
but that, as Foucault's open question begs, dismissing it outright closes
the text in a way that bespeaks of master-narrativization.

Subjectification and Social Apparatuses

Throughout Deleuze and Guattari's work, the theme of ethico-aesthetics
is persistent and central, and yet for some time it was largely ignored by
the various interpreters of their work. This could be because two of the
areas it evokes, aesthetics and subjectification, are in fact out of favor in
the current postmodern climate. Deleuze and Guattari oppose subjectification to the State Subject and the regime of Capitalism. For Guattari,
in arming against the division of labor and "its modes of valorization
and finalities," one needs to accept as the only finality of human activity, the "production of subjectivity that is auto-enriching" (1996:21).
Subjectification needs to be explored, then, within the context of the

social apparatus in order to move beyond the postmodern impasse that critics like Olsen rightfully point to.

For Deleuze and Guattari, a subjectification is produced within social apparatuses: processual subjectification is a style (of life), created from within existing social apparatuses.[11] "We are not confronted with a subjectivity given as in-itself, but with processes of the realization of autonomy" (Guattari, 1995:7). The processual, Guattari claims, provides "an authentic relation with the other" (1995:7). For both Deleuze and Guattari, then, subjectification is a production of "a line of flight"; it is an escape from the "bond of the Subject," and subsequent alienation, produced by Capitalist apparatuses of capture. Deleuze, in "What Is a Dispositif?" draws upon Foucault's notion of the dispositif (social apparatus)[12] in exploring the relationship between the social apparatuses and the self.[13] The dispositif consists of *lines of force* that come about as the result of the relationship of one point with another. In subjectification the line of force "bypasses itself." It bypasses itself when it

> turns on itself, meanders, grows obscure and goes underground, or…instead of entering into a linear relationship with another force, (the force) turns back on itself, works on itself or affects itself. (Deleuze, 1992:161)[14]

The lines of force are the dimension of power, which Deleuze refers to as "the third dimension of space, internal to the apparatus" (160). They are formed out of knowledge. However, subjectification or the "[s]elf is neither knowledge nor power.…[It is] subtracted from the power relations which are established as constituting forms of knowledge [*savoirs*]" (161). Subjectification is then, "a sort of surplus value" (161).

Furthermore, for Deleuze, a subjectification produced within social apparatuses may enable the apparatus to transform from one social apparatus into another. Deleuze ponders on whether or not the lines of subjectification "form the extreme boundary of social apparatus and if perhaps they sketch the movement of one apparatus to another, in this sense preparing for lines of fracture" (1992:163). Guattari adds to this theme when he says that "the aesthetic paradigm has become the paradigm for every possible form of liberation, expropriating the old scientific paradigms to which, for example, historical materialism or Freudianism were referred" (1995:91). We can now say that the literary-subjectification, as a regime of signs, is *transformative*, a mode of becoming.[15]

It is important to note that this notion of the transformative marks a shift from many prior critical frameworks, including postmodernist—which identifies the aesthetic with self-reflexivity—and many instances of cultural criticism that claim that "'material effects depend on their cultural encompassment'" (Patterson quoting Sahlins, 1990:261).[16] Such views are opposed to Bakhtin's view, mentioned above, which claims that the content of a work of art detaches itself from its symbolic connotations and becomes formally creative. Deleuze and Guattari's pragmatics is twofold: generative and transformational. The generative involves tracing the mixed semiotics that form from a machinic assemblage of enunciation. The means by which these mixed semiotics can be measured is by observing "the *transformational component* that accounts for the originality of a regime as well as for the novelty of the mixes it enters at a given moment in a given domain" (Deleuze and Guattari, 1987:139). The transformational component, thus, is the more profound component. "It is the only means of measuring the elements of the first component" (139). The transformational component involves the literary function and vice versa.

For Guattari, then, aesthetic subjectivities are singularities that are "a rupture of sense, a cut, a fragmentation, the detachment of a semiotic content…[which] can originate mutant nuclei of subjectivation" (1995:18). Guattari uses the word "mutant" to indicate the notion that aesthetic subjectivities "have no prior existence" in that they are a complete break or bifurcation of existence (pp. 18 and 91). These aesthetic subjectivities become "resingularized Universes of subjectivation" (19), which act in "catalysing existential operations capable of acquiring consistence and persistence" (19). For Guattari, this is the "task of the poetic function."[17] Universes of subjectivation are a counterpoint to a contemporary society that has lost its "old existential Territorialities" (19) to mechanically engendered information fluxes.

The Collective Utterance of Aesthetic Subjectification

An important final attribute of resingularized Universes is their collective nature. Says Deleuze, subjectification "bears on groups and on people" (Deleuze, 1992:161). Or, as Guattari says, "subjectivity is collective" (1995:9). Elsewhere, Deleuze and Guattari attribute subjectification to a *collective of partial* enunciations, agglomerated by the machinic assemblage of enunciation. Subjectivity, then, is partial, polyphonic, collective, and machinic.

Bakhtin's concept of *dialogism* makes it clear that verbal art is a machinic assemblage of enunciation that agglomerates collective assemblages of enunciation and performs "creative subjectivity" (Guattari, 1995:14). For Bakhtin, the aesthetic form is neither the expression of the life of a character nor an arbitrary form given to the life of the character by the writer, but the result of the relationship between the writer and characters:

> Aesthetic form cannot be founded and validated from within the hero, out of his own directedness to objects and meaning, i.e., on the basis of that which has validity only for his own lived life. Aesthetic form is founded and validated from within the *other*—the author, as the author's creative reaction to the hero and his life. (Bakhtin, 1990:89–90)

Further to the notion of the dialogic and to the collective nature of the aesthetic, Bakhtin defines the novel "as a diversity of social speech types (sometimes even diversity of languages) and a diversity of individual voices, artistically organized" (1981:262). To quote Bakhtin more fully:

> The language of a novel is the system of its "languages."...The novel orchestrates all its themes, the totality of the world of objects and ideas depicted and expressed in it, by means of the social diversity of speech types [*raznorecie*] and by the differing individual voices that flourish under such conditions. (263)

For Bakhtin, the novel as a genre has a "stylistic uniqueness" (262), which is due to the system of its "languages"; the internal stratification given to the languages by the author. Stylistic uniqueness, in Guattari's development of Bakhtin, constitutes resingularized Universes. Poetry also produces stylistic uniqueness—which is also referred to as "autonomization" (1995:14). Where the novel creates a system of its languages, poetry creates a system of its words by seizing upon "the sonority of the word, its musical aspect; its material significations with their nuances and variants; its verbal connections; [and] its emotional, intonational and volitional aspects..." (15). In other words, the system of languages and system of words belonging to the aesthetic/literary utterance are responsible for stylistic uniqueness and thereby, the irreversible, fragment of content. It is the collective nature of the literary utterance that makes its content mutational (detached) and thereby belonging to processual subjectivity.

The collective utterance has, reflexively, been the form of content of much recent drama and the novel focusing on community. This focus on verbal art has been in place at least since the historical novel and the plays of Brecht,[18] however, the central theme of community is particularly popular in the TV serial, for example, *Coronation Street, Shortland Street,* and more recently in dramas whose focus is small-town communities, such as Atom Egoyan's film *The Sweet Hereafter* (1997) (of which there is a reading in the following chapter). Other examples include the Irish television production *Hamish McBeth* (1995), the Australian television production *Sea Change* (1991–2001), the film *The Full Monty* (1997), Douglas Coupland's novel *Generation X* (1994), Ian McEwan's *Amsterdam* (1998), and many more. Within these dramas about community, communities are produced and defined by their collective utterance. Each member of the community is so by dint of the fact that they contribute to the collective. Their utterance is thereby partial. And because the collective utterance is polyphonic and thus decentered, it does not add up to a whole, complete utterance. For example, in *Generation X*, the narrator's story is one of many stories related (each character speaks for him or herself, tells of her or his own experience).[19] Beyond the event of this collective utterance, there is nothing told, no *one* story.

Being partial, the collective assemblage of enunciation does not constitute knowledge, nor, thereby, power and is not therefore a linear force that can form a linear relationship with another force (for instance, one community joining another). Such a linear relationship of forces results in a logic of equivalence and the members of the community, in such a scenario, being "alienated"—to return to Guattari's theme of the division of labor. On the other hand, the community formed by a collective of partial enunciation is directed against the alienation of the individual. (Guattari notes that the decentered enunciation is "decentred in relation to that of human individuation" [1996:22].) Rather than making sense, then, there is in fact a resistance to completion on the part of individual utterances within the collective.

The collective utterance thus constitutes a plane of consistency (a body without completion or arrival). A zero intensity. This plane of consistency is the surplus value of subjectification, mentioned earlier. To quote Deleuze in more depth on this issue:

> The line of subjectification ... is neither knowledge or power. It is a process of individuation which bears on groups and on people, and is subtracted from the power relations which are established as constituting forms of knowledge [*savoirs*]: a sort of surplus value. (1992:161)

The plane of consistency, then, as a kind of surplus value, is the nonatomization of space, or the deatomization of space. The groups that it comes to bear upon are produced by the subjectification of the nonatomization of space—the group as an irreducible multiplicity. Equally, the collective utterance constitutes a plane of consistency, or individuation, since it is from the social apparatus that the subjectification comes. To quote Deleuze:

> The dimension of the Self is by no means a pre-existing determination which one finds ready-made. Here again, a line of subjectification is a process, a production of subjectivity in a social apparatus [dispositif]: it has to be made in as much as the apparatus allows it to come into being or makes it possible. (1992:161)

While this may sound as though the social is a literary or aesthetic machine, what is important to note is that what is collective is not a group, per se, but their (aesthetic) formal machine. Guattari writes:

> Subjectivity is collective—which does not, however, mean that it becomes exclusively social. The term "collective" should be understood in the sense of a multiplicity that deploys itself as much beyond the individual, on the side of the socius, as before the person, on the side of preverbal intensities, indicating a logic of affects rather than a logic of delimited sets. (1995:9)

The social, then, needs the formal machine belonging to the aesthetic in order to become a multiplicity. The formal machine belonging to the literary is the system of its "languages."[20] Their partial utterances share an intimacy (are proximal and collectives) rather than significance. This enables the collective utterance to be processual and simultaneous with life. It involves an authentic relationship with the other, and the result is the production of a life *style*, to refer to Foucault (see Foucault, 1997, and Deleuze, 1992). The literary *act*—the collective assemblage of enunciation—is, then, an ethics that places the individual on the side of the socius, but at the same time deterritorializes the socius "on the side of preverbal intensities": affects.

In the "realm" of the aesthetic, then, the subject is not alienated. In the place of atomized space and alienation is the incomplete (processual) collective utterance. It is "solidarity"—without the word being mentioned (rather, it is being performed). Michel de Certeau notes that solidarity is precisely what is lacking in nonpoetic speech. The aesthetic, as viewed here, then, is free from the capture of a variety of forms of criticism, but it also puts the social to flight, frees it from apparatuses of power, and thereby capture.[21] Poetic speech for de Certeau describes the "speech" of the collective, of "collective management" (1997:12), of a true democracy. De Certeau compares the speech of the collective to the poetic inasmuch as both are immanent and speak for themselves alone, not as a universalizing modeling. For de Certeau, the breakdown in the social fabric in France that brought about May '68 (a period of civil unrest and protest) was due to the "distance that separated the represented from their representations, the members of society and the modalities of their associations" (1997:9). In talking of the May '68 revolution, de Certeau says that it was in speaking for oneself—"those who spoke in their own name" and not others, in having this right—that the revolution was situated. Thus, for de Certeau, the revolution of May '68 was a symbolic one: "[l]ast May speech was taken the way, in 1789, the Bastille was taken" (11). Speech (of the self) for de Certeau functioned in May '68 as a capturing device. Territory was gained. De Certeau notes the statement on a flyer at the Sorbonne, "The poet has lit the fuse of speech" (13).

De Certeau makes the observation, however, that the speech itself was empty. "What was *positively* experienced" (14) as a collective, based upon "the direct experience of democracy, the permanence of contestation, the need for critical thought, the legitimacy of a creative and responsible participation for everyone" (12), "could only be expressed *negatively*, as a refusal" (14). For de Certeau, "The main problem today is posed by the disparity between a fundamental experience and the deficit of its language, between the 'positivity' of something lived and the 'negativity' of an expression that, in the form of a refusal, resembles more the symptom than the elaboration of the reality being designated" (15). However, de Certeau's account of the poetic speech of May '68 is too linguistic, and this accounts for his despair. The assemblage of the collective utterance is extralinguistic; it is the event itself, which in turn captures (reterritorializes). De Certeau describes the experience of May '68 as an event, but misses, in part, the immanent, extralinguistic nature of the aesthetic utterance. The existential refrain or collective utterance is the immanent (form of expression) of the event. Because being of the *event*, most significantly, the aesthetic or existential refrain is *of a terrain* (albeit a virtual terrain, a point I will soon elaborate). The community needs a terrain and cannot thrive on ideology alone. In fact, as it will be seen, the terrain belongs to the community where ideology does not. This makes ethico-aesthetics also an eco-aesthetics or a bio-aesthetics.[22]

The Aesthetic (Plane of Consistency) versus Models of Realization

Deleuze and Guattari's consideration of the aesthetic (in relation to processual subjectification and a collective subjectivity) marks a departure from the way in which the aesthetic has been thought (in relation to ideology) by Raymond Williams, Antonio Gramsci, and others before them. In general, in these accounts, the aesthetic is considered as the concrete expression of a concept, and not as a kind of surplus value resulting in the production of an autonomous Self, able to be in an authentic relationship with the other. As Terry Eagleton writes, the aesthetic acts "[a]s a kind of concrete thought or sensuous analogue of the concept" (1990:16). Thus, the aesthetic (subject) is captured by the concept. This thinking in respect to the aesthetic is dialectical in nature. Eagleton writes that the task of the aesthetic, as it is generally approached, is to "order (sensational life)...into clear or perfectly determinate representations, in a manner akin to (if relatively autonomous of) the operations of reason proper" (1990:16). The aesthetic is considered an inferior logic, "*ratio inferior*" (by the German philosopher Alexander Baumgarten, referred to by Terry Eagleton, 1990:16), and the "sister" of rational logic that acts as a go-between between the sensational and the rational. Eagleton says that "the aesthetic partakes at once of the rational and the real, suspended between the two somewhat in the manner of the Levi-Straussian myth" (1990:16). The aesthetic is considered crucial, therefore, in achieving the historical relevance of the concept, the concept and the aesthetic being two sides of the same coin. As Eagleton writes, "[r]eason...is not simply a contemplative faculty, but a whole project for the hegemonic reconstruction of subjects—what Seyla Benhabib has called 'the successive transformation and reeducation of inner nature'" (1990:21). The example given in the chapter by Eagleton is the aesthetics of the bourgeois subject that explains or fits entirely with the rational of capitalism—in much the same way as Marx, referred to earlier in this chapter, has explained.

Raymond Williams's notion of cultural materialism explains the relation between art and culture equally as dialectically as the views put forward by Eagleton. For Williams, writes Andrew Milner, all of culture, including art, "is similarly 'material'" (1996:34), and therefore "art and thinking about art" are indistinguishable "'from the social processes within which they are...contained'" (Milner quoting Williams, 1996:34). Culture is the material means of production by which a "'lived dominance and subordination of particular classes'" (33) is made possible. For Williams, then, "The specializing concept of 'literature'...is essentially one of a series of 'evasions,' by which art and thinking about art 'separate themselves...from the social processes within which they are...contained'" (Milner, 34).

Thus, the aesthetic, in such (dialectical) thinking as the above, is immanent *to something* (as discussed in chapter 2)—immanent to rational thought, social process, and "lived dominance." The aesthetic is captured by these models of realization. In addition, it becomes a model of realization, overcoding the real in conjunction (or what Deleuze and

Guattari would call, in a double articulation) with rational thought. Thus, the aesthetic becomes an apparatus of subjugation and capture. Opposed to this is the aesthetic viewed immanently, the incomplete collective utterance of processual subjectification. We can contrast the views of Williams and Eagleton, in which the aesthetic and the rational act dialectically, with Bakhtin's view of the relationship between the performed act and the rational (since we have already established the link between the aesthetic and processual Being).[23] For Bakhtin:

> An act of our activity, of our actual experiencing, is like a two-faced Janus. It looks in two opposite directions: it looks at the objective unity of a domain of culture and at the never repeatable uniqueness of actually lived and experienced life. But there is no unitary and unique plane where both faces would mutually determine each other in relation to a single unique unity. (1993:2)

For Bakhtin "the world in which I live and in which I answerably perform my deeds" and "the theoretical and theoreticized world of culture...do not intercommunicate; there is no principle for including and actively involving the valid world of theory and of theoreticized culture in the once-occurrent Being-event of life" (1993:20). Writes Bakhtin:

> It is only the once-occurrent event of Being in the process of actualization that can constitute this unique unity; all that which is theoretical or aesthetic must be determined as a constituent moment in the once-occurrent event of Being, although no longer, of course, in theoretical or aesthetic terms. An act must acquire a single unitary plane to be able to reflect itself in both directions—in its sense or meaning and in its being. (1993:2)

There are, then, two activities involving the aesthetic, one, "the objective unity of a domain of culture" (Bakhtin, 1993:2), and the other, the incomplete collective utterance of processual subjectification. Importantly, there is no unitary and unique plane where both of these activities "mutually determine each other" (2), as there is for Eagleton and Williams. Instead, Bakhtin's "single unitary plane" has resonances with Deleuze and Guattari's notion of a plane of consistency, that being a body without completion or arrival, the surplus value of subjectification. For Bakhtin, the act is a plane of consistency upon which everything comes to rest, and rather than throwing "light" upon the world, rationality, the law, etc., are but moments of answerability, "'like a glimmer of light before the sun'" (Bakhtin quoting Nietzsche, 1993:29). The act unites subjective and objective moments, "the moment of what is universal (universally valid) and the moment of what is individual (actual)" (29). It creates a "unitary and unique truth [*pravda*]...posited as something-to-be-attained *qua* synthetic truth [*pravda*]" (29). For Bakhtin, only

> an act or deed that is taken from outside as a physiological, biological, or psychological fact may present itself as elemental and blind, like any abstract being. But from within the answerable act, the one who answerably performs the act knows a clear and distinct light, in which he actually orients himself. (1993:30)

Transposed to the aesthetic and to creative subjectivation, Bakhtin's notion of the act tells us that the aesthetic—as a plane of consistency—is not in a dialectical relationship with rational logic, is not, as it is for Eagleton, the "sister" of rational logic, is not the handmaiden of reason in a "whole project for the reconstruction of the subject" (Eagleton quoting Benhabib, 1990:21). Rather, it is a pragmatic truth belonging to the subject alone and more importantly, belonging to the subject's own ethics—as the act involves the subject engaging with an object in an effort to understand their *ought* in relation to it. The act presupposes the subject's answerable participation (as mentioned earlier). "[F]rom within the answerable act, the one who answerably performs the act knows a clear distinct light, in which he actually orients himself" (Bakhtin, 1993:30). To quote Bakhtin in full:

> The ongoing event can be clear and distinct in the act or deed he himself performs. Does this mean that he understands it logically? That is, that what is clear to him are only the universal moments and relations transcribed in the form of concepts? Not at all: he sees clearly *these* individual, unique persons whom he loves, *this* sky and *this* earth and *these* trees...and the time; and what is also given to him simultaneously is the value, the actually and concretely affirmed value of these persons and these objects. He intuits their inner lives as well as desires; he understands both the actual and the ought-to-be sense of the interrelationship between himself and these persons and objects—the truth [*pravda*] of the given state of affairs—and he understands the ought of his performed act, that is, *not* the abstract law of his act, but actual, concrete ought conditioned by his unique place in the context of the ongoing event. All these moments, which make up the event in its totality, are present to him as something given and as something-to-be-achieved in a unitary light, in a unitary and unique answerable consciousness, and they are actualized in a unitary and unique answerable act. And this event as a whole cannot be transcribed in theoretical terms if it is not to lose the very sense of its *being an event*, that is, precisely that which the performed acts knows answerably and with reference to which it orients itself. (1993:30–31, my italics)

The way in which Bakhtin describes the once-occurrent event and being is akin, then, to the way in which the aesthetic (or creative subjectivity, Guattari, 1995:14) is explained by this chapter. The aesthetic is not viewed in a dialectical relationship with rational thought and thereby seen as an extension of culture and ideology, from which there is no outside. The aesthetic may be taken up by culture, by logic, by poetics, and so on, but this is not the aesthetic *act* itself, to which this chapter refers. Rather, the aesthetic is viewed as a fragment of (mutant, irreversible) content and the answerable act that orientates the subject in relation to their "autonomies[ed] self" (Guattari, 1995:14). It is as a fragment that the aesthetic "utterance" sits, both outside culture, and is a plane of consistency upon which culture comes to sit. Bakhtin's theory of the act and my understanding of processual subjectivity (the aesthetic) interpret the aesthetic not as a model of realization, a complement to culture, but as a line of flight and as that which is always in the process of becoming and transformation.[24]

The Virtual and the Aesthetic

In contemporary theory and criticism, a great amount of emphasis has been given to context, to "the facts," but where the aesthetic is concerned it is important to appreciate that context involves the yet-to-be-determined. It is a mode of becoming. For Bakhtin, the event (and thereby the aesthetic event) is virtual because, "when I experience an object actually, I thereby carry out something in relation to it: the object enters into relations with that which is yet to be achieved, grows in it—within my relationship to that object" (1993:32). To quote Bakhtin in full:

> This world-as-event is not a world of being, of that which is given: no object, no relation, is given here as something simply given, as something totally on hand, but is always given in conjunction with another given that is connected with those objects and relations, namely, that which is yet-to-be-achieved or determined: "one ought to..."'" "it is desirable that..." An object that is absolutely indifferent, totally finished, cannot be something one becomes actually conscious of, something one experiences actually. (Bakhtin, 1993:32)

It is this mode of becoming that makes inadequate theorizing the literary as immanent to something else. *When the literary is made immanent to something else—to culture—the world is placed in externality to the (aesthetic) text and a "concrete uniqueness of singularity of the world, is*

lost" (Bakhtin, 1993:13). As is becoming. Bakhtin's theory of the act has been crucial in establishing this idea.

Bakhtin refers to what he calls Real Work, which is the adaptation of a speech genre to a context, involving creativity on the part of the utterer, as each utterance is, because of the context, unique (Michael Holquist, 1990). However, context here, in view of Bakhtin's theory of the act, must now be considered as virtual, in part because of the "becoming" nature of the act, but also in part because of its collective nature. Once again, it is helpful to use Bakhtin's understanding of the event in order to understand the collective nature of the aesthetic. For Bakhtin, "once-occurrent uniqueness or singularity cannot be thought of, it can only be *participatively* experienced or lived through..." (1993:13, my italics). *In this respect, ironically, there is no subject of the act just as for Deleuze and Guattari, there is no subject of enunciation.* Says Bakhtin, "From within the act itself, taken in its undivided wholeness, there is nothing that is subjective and psychological" (1993:29). Furthermore, far from the aesthetic being made visible, as a moment in the metadiscourse of theory, as Williams and Eagleton envisage, it is a plane upon which such discourses are but a "moment." To quote Bakhtin:

> All of theoretical reason in its entirety is only a moment of practical reason, i.e., the reason of the unique *subiectum's* moral orientation within the event of once-occurrent Being. This Being cannot be determined in the categories of non-participant theoretical consciousness—it can be determined only in the categories of actual communion, i.e., of an actually performed act, in the categories of participative-effective experiencing of the concrete uniqueness of singularity of the world. (1993:13)

To make an utterance actual but not virtual is to individuate the statement (and the subject) and place them within an economy of exchange. Thus it is that they are captured. The collective virtual utterance therefore functions as a resistance to context and capture. It is untimely and produces a *surplus value*, in the sense of an excess.

The Literary as Anti-(State) Capturing

Chapter 4 addressed the way in which Capitalist society—through regimes of overcoding (Rent, Profit, and Tax)—create an equivalence and resonance between goods, services, and money. In other words, Capitalist society operates by creating an equivalence, a general space of comparison, between elements. Overcoding, which functions as an apparatus of capture and a mobile center of appropriation, results in a monopolistic regime. The literary function wards off this monopolistic regime. This section explores this relationship of the literary to the State. In this regard, it explores the collective utterance as a performative utterance. As de Certeau points out with his story of May '68: there and then collective speech occupied a terrain, speech "was taken in the way, in 1789, the Bastille was taken" (1997:11). The performative nature of the collective utterance follows a regime of signs belonging to primitive societies, which, for Deleuze and Guattari, are anti-State and anticapturing. The literary also wards off the State through the production of surplus value, to which I now turn.

As we have already discussed, surplus value involves utterances that are partial by dint of the fact that each utterance has folded back on itself, let itself meander along its own line of force, grow obscure, go underground, and bypass itself. And surplus value results from the collective utterance. As my analysis here will suggest, the film *The Full Monty* (1997) tells the story of this production of surplus value. *The Full Monty* is also an allegory for the literary function.

Gaz, played by Robert Carlyle, goes to work on his own enunciations and subjectivity by turning his subjectivity in on itself, allowing it to meander along its own line. At the start of the narrative, Gaz, along with other workmates, has been laid off from the town's steelworks. His ex-wife urges him to take up a £2.50 an hour factory job where she works. Instead, he returns to his past "occupation," that of petty thievery. As a petty criminal, we see Gaz in his element—in his own very particular subjectivity—which is, in the film, quite literally *underground*. However, Gaz finds himself in danger of being made a social outcast and losing custody of his son. At this point, Gaz concocts a plan to form a male strip "troupe," consisting of other workers who have also been laid off from the steelworks. Thus, he brings others in the community into his plan. De Certeau says of the collective utterance, "Our own knowledge has become the language of others and of another experience.... Knowledge [is] 'taken' in a different way, 'occupied'" (1997:23).[25] As a necessary adjunct to his own subjectification, Gaz teams up with a community. Their "knowledge" thus becomes *the "language" of the community* and *of another experience*—it is, thus, an occupying force. The enunciation/event of the strip show that ensues is autoenriching, a singularity, and a subjectification (to recap Guattari's definition of the aesthetic [collective] utterance). This is because it "speaks" for the steelworkers and not for "the context." This knowledge—which is "taken in a different way," "occupied," can be understood as a kind of antiknowledge—or as the kind of surplus value of which Deleuze speaks. As mentioned, such surplus value derives from the process of individuation, which in turn "bears on groups and people" (Deleuze, 1992:161). It is "subtracted from the power relations which are established as constituting forms of knowledge [*savoirs*] (161). For what does it *mean* for these men to perform as strippers? Surplus value results from the plural nature of the collective, performed utterance (i.e., male steelworks, strippers), it is derived from knowledge becoming the "language of others and of another experience."

At this point, "Gaz's line" grows increasingly obscure, his pathway goes underground—this aspect is doubled in the film when the troupe must hide their clandestine operation from the townfolk. The pathway then bypasses itself, Gaz becomes a (good) father, saving the custody of his son, and he becomes community minded, helping save some souls destroyed by redundancy. Within the collective utterance, then, Gaz's subjectification is "taken" in a different way. It is "liberated"—quite literally in the film—from the law and his ex-wife's disapproval. At the same time, it is an "occupying" force, a reterritorialization (outside of the capitalist economy).

The partial fragments of enunciation operate as "shifters" of subjectivation[26] (Guattari 1995:20) making each player within the collective utterance a poet or, more importantly, *making them living poetry*. Play is crucial. We must counter Olsen's rejection of it. Play of the utterance (when one plays around with one's own line to produce a subjectification) is not linguistic play alone—but it is play (and language is itself play*ful*, not least because it belongs to collective assemblages of enunciation). Play is crucial to the untimely aspect of the collective utterance. This is indeed the case in *The Full Monty*—in all, no one expects the town's men to perform as strippers, and in order to do so they have each undergone a process of subjectification. The surplus value thus comes also from the transformative nature of the aesthetic utterance—(ex-steelworkers becoming strippers, etc.). It seems, then, that play is far more cosmological and pragmatic than someone like Olsen sees it as being.

Our decentered enunciations (subjectivity) produce the partial statement necessary for the collective assemblage of enunciation. And our partial enunciations are formed through the collective. We are dependent on its interlocution (though this is far too linguistic a term). It is the *history* of the collective that enfolds our subjectivity. Without the collective we are individuated, made the Same, and subjugated; "I" must say what is *expected* when I *talk* in context.

The criminal, considered revolutionary because of doing things differently, creatively, is not a new idea.[27] Neither is the notion that such a character is responsible for our pleasure of the crime/text. But a Deleuzeoguattarian pragmatics can add to this the relationship between these ethics and aesthetics (the autopoietic). In *The Full Monty*, when Gaz is *in full flight*, performing as a stripper, having given up the "straight and narrow," which his ex-wife desired for him, she returns to see him. In the film *Out of Sight* (1998), there is a similar tale to tell. Here, the Law (an FBI agent) falls in love with the criminal (a subjectification). The criminal in *Out Of Sight*, John Michael "Jack" Foley, played by George Clooney, chooses crime over what, in his eyes, is the demeaning job of security guard. (Security guard is also the job the character Dave runs away from, literally, in *The Full Monty*.) The word "demeaning" takes on the double sense here; "to lower in dignity or standing"[28] but also, to suffer loss of meaning (de-meaning). The line of subjectification the criminal instead chooses offers him or her Self meaning. (Bakhtin's notion of "unitary and unique truth" is helpful here [1993:29] as is de Certeau's notion of the inalienable collective utterance.) Deleuze and Guattari speak about the surveyor as being the original artist,[29] staking out a map on an existing *geography*. In these films, the criminal/artist *stakes* out a territory upon the existing territory (of the 9–5 job), their subjectification coming from the existing social apparatuses—a complex assemblage including political, economic, ethical, and aesthetic formations. In *The Full Monty* this "reterritorialising" happens when Gaz takes over the institution of "male stripping," reterritorializing it, *making* it "speak" for himself and his friends—not body-beautifuls but a straggly bunch of local guys.[30] At this point, we can see just how extralinguistic the partial enunciation/subjectification (or existential refrain) is, and how continuous it is with life—its study, geological.[31]

The virtual collective assemblage of enunciation is counter to an economy of equivalence and exchange, and models of realization. It is a weapon, a magic carpet (rather than a magic capture)—a line of flight. To have produced such a weapon, such a "flight," is to have created a new Earth.[32] It is, seemingly, contrary to its transitory body, real, not imaginary (which is where Olsen situates play).

Brian Massumi says that all utterances are collective (1992:43). However, I would add to this that not all regimes of signs *act* collectively. Collective utterances belonging to the literary operate according to Deleuze and Guattari's notion of the regime of primitive societies. In this way, they ward off the State. In summarizing Pierre Clastre's theses on the nonevolutionary nature of the State, Deleuze and Guattari note that "societies termed primitive are not societies without a State, in the sense that they failed to reach a certain stage, but are counter-State societies organizing mechanisms that ward off the State-form, which make its crystallization impossible" (1987:429). It is in the chapter, "700 B.C. Apparatus of Capture" (1987), that Deleuze and Guattari make a distinction between regimes of signs within State and Primitive societies. The State operates as a network, it is a connector with other States in turn, enabling things to flow along a stable network. The State is then a formation of power—two points connecting to produce a line of force. These connecting points make it an apparatus of capture: "In retaining given elements it necessarily cuts off their relations with other elements, which become exterior, it inhibits, slows down, or controls those relations" (1987:433). The two points that meet in a line of force anticipate an external point on another line, the State; this external point is a central point and thereby productive of a hierarchy. Hence, a *collective* (utterance) may not be formed. By contrast, in the Primitive society there is a mechanism that prevents the points or centers of power from crystallizing. There are indeed formations of power in Primitive societies; Deleuze and Guattari note Primitive societies have a central point common to horizontal segments and a central point external to a straight line. However, the points do not operate as concentric circles (as they do with the State) and "require a third segment through which to communicate" (1987:433). Deleuze and Guattari note that this is the sense in which primitive societies have never crossed the threshold into Statehood.

The literary, as a regime of signs of the collective utterance, can be thought of as a primitive regime of signs, which wards off the State. This is allegorized in the film *The Full Monty*. In *The Full Monty* the collective utterance involves three segments, as with primitive societies: The Boy, Gaz, and the rest of the Troupe. All three segments are necessary to the utterance—Gaz, while in the middle is not on top. As segments, these three cannot communicate with one another without each other. At the eleventh hour, it is in fact Gaz's son who insists Gaz strip, in a way giving him permission (detracting from the father figure as central authority). This collective quality of the utterance operates according to Deleuze and Guattari's notion of primitive societies; its structure is horizontal, on the one plane, and antihierarchical. Its enunciations are multiple, collective, and it is not a regime of signs governed by the Signifier, a central point (in the form of the Father) that acts on behalf of the State to overcode and capture. In the place of the Signifier and capture is the performed act, the event, allegorized in the strip show. This regime of signs is thereby immanent and thereby anti-State and anticapture. The primitive enunciation, then, is collective *and* a performed act.

The performative is referred to by Deleuze and Guattari and Brian Massumi, as "the order word." When I say, "Speaking in context I must say what is expected," I am describing the order word. When I say, "I do," and I mouth the rest of the marriage vows I am placing myself within a preexisting structure. I am obeying, with these words, that structure. But the order word is also said to house an antiorder word[33] (something subversive). The antiorder word involves "continual variation" (Massumi, 1992:41), which in turn means that it relinquishes unheard and implicit presuppositions in (my) lines—making my lines "superlinear." The literary function performs such continual variation in the order word.[34] Where lines of force are the result of a connection between seeing and saying (producing the order word) and where the postmodern points to a gap between seeing and saying, *the literary function performs something else: continual variation and implicit presupposition.* This is allegorized in *The Full Monty* in the variation, steelworkers becoming strippers. The implicit presupposition "released" from this variation is that townfolk might not be typically sexy, but being townsfolk they are something like "sexy." The presupposition produces an intensity. Something unsayable. (For what is sayable about what is sexy! And what is sayable about what it is to be townfolk?) The implicit presupposition—this superlinearity—is then, precisely as it says, implicit, virtual, and it cannot be spoken. Rather the implicit presupposition "exists" within the collective utterance (male strippers, steelworkers, a petty criminal, morality, the law, ethics, place, etc.) *and must be performed.*

The implicit presupposition, then, resists the overcoding of the Signifier (of being spoken *for,* and thereby captured). Importantly, the implicit presupposition cannot exist without the collective utterance being performed. It is an event. The collective utterance is performed because it cannot be said (in a single utterance/line) but only performed. In *The Full Monty*, what is important to the steelworkers becoming strippers/sexy, is their action—the event of stripping. This theme of performance is allegorizedd by *The Full Monty* when the performance (the striptease) of the steelworkers—and whether or not they will perform—becomes the central motif of the film. The performative replaces the use of a negative expression in the form of a refusal (to return to de Certeau's complaint with the event of May '68). The collective enunciative performance of the literary act subverts overcoding regimes (belonging to the State) in a way linguistic acts (of refusal) cannot. The performative, here, produces an antiorder word because of the assemblage and the extralinguistic expression (remembering, the order word comes before me and when I repeat it I uphold its particular social architecture). Superlinearity, the virtual, plurality, becoming, transformativity, and it being untimely, are all due to the performance of a collective utterance. The performative (antiorder word) is here not understood as the Law of language, to which "I" belong and by whose linear force "I" am moved. In fact, one does not "speak" (for oneself) in the antiorder performative utterance at all. There is no subject of enunciation in the collective utterance. Instead, the collective utterance is of territory, of the Earth, multiple. My community.[35] (The pronoun "my" in French, *Moi,* is not singular, like the pronoun "I," but plural. It includes myself as everyone and thing.) Moreover, it is of the earth, territory, because it is plural. The plurality of the performative (collective utterance) means it is entirely immanent and pragmatic. It is not a matter of doing what language says, as with the order word, but rather, as an "existential refrain," you are outside the law, in a performance all your own, "affecting your Self"—a subjectification. Something is being performed by the collective utterance, something real. Real, but not actual.[36] It is the virtual quality of the collective performative—which does not belong to language but to Earth, and is immanent and pragmatic—that is crucial to its subversive nature. The collective performative, then, is utterance as action because it is extralinguistic, untimely, and without use (exchange). It is therefore, utterly pragmatic, a terrain is made, a new Earth, a line of flight is hewn. It is the utterance as geological because it is continuous with life—"of continual variation." A plane of consistency.

*   *   *

Furthering the debate in literary and cultural studies concerning the relationship between text and society, it is more fruitful to consider the relationship between the literary aesthetic and society. The term "literary aesthetic" in fact replaces the term "text" and indicates a change in concept and theorization of the issues. The "literary aesthetic" is used over Barthes's term and notion of "text" as it involves a theory of pragmatics where the Barthes's term does not. And as the literary aesthetic refers to a process, the term "text," indicating an object, is also obviously unsuited. The literary aesthetic has a pragmatic role in the formation of terrain, subjectivation, and community. It is counterproductive, then, to position the literary and or aesthetic in binary opposition to the "concrete," to "the power of praxis," to "the nitty gritty facts." Equally, a model of realization in relation to the literary aesthetic overlooks its performative function. When the literary is taken as a mediation between the sensible and the theoretical, the particular pragmatic belonging to the literary regime of signs is captured and lost. In such theorizing, the literary becomes indistinguishable from social processes, which are " 'the lived dominance and subordination of particular classes' " (Milner quoting Williams, 1996:33). Rather, the literary aesthetic is taken here, as a pragmatics, as a function, which is transformative and enables social apparatuses to be put to flight.

The literary aesthetic, then, is a performative, collective assemblage of enunciation (without a subject of enunciation), virtual not actual, and a horizontal formation. It is in this way that the literary function is autopoietic, autonomous, irreversible, and event-centered. It is also, thereby, without significance (overcoding) and is not a model of realization. Overcoding involves a doubling and a repetition of the same as diverse points are made to resonate. The literary is captured by theories that imply doubling when the literary is thought to be immanent *to* something, be that rational thought and or social processes (lived dominance). If the literary appears to double, it is, however, not a repetition of the Same. For Deleuze, in "aesthetic repetition" (1994:11), there is "nothing repeated which may be isolated or abstracted from the repetition in which it was formed" (17). Deleuze criticizes Freud's notion of repetition, which maintains a "bare, brute repetition (repetition of the Same) [16]" in referring to dreams, condensation, displacement, and dramatization. For Deleuze, these occasions of doubling, which he also refers to as disguises, variations, masks, and costumes (16–17), "do not come 'over and above': they are, on the contrary, the internal genetic elements of repetition itself, its integral and constituent parts" (17).

The literary function is not, then, a model of realization since it produces implicit presuppositions, becomings, and works the assemblage and not the Signifier. It is a performed, collective utterance and is immanent. To say these things is also to say that the aesthetic object is communal, contrary to the "model of realization view" that envisages the literary as doubling a hierarchical structure. It is at this point that the literary function comes closer to the condition of music. The state of continual variation is the state of play between lines (of knowledge). Language is here used as geographical marker, as refrain, and, thereby, territory. The case of Walter Pater, imagining that literature "aspire(s) to the condition of music," rather than to meaning, does not now sound as unlikely as it did to pragmatists like Pfeil.

6

The Reader and the Event of Fiction

There has been a whole so-called ecological movement—a very ancient one, by the way, that did not just start in the twentieth century—that was often in opposition, as it were, to a science or, at least, to a technology underwritten by claims to truth. But this same ecology articulated its own discourse of truth: criticism was authorized in the name of a knowledge of nature, the balance of life processes, and so on.

(Michel Foucault, Ethics: Subjectivity and Truth; Essential Works of Foucault 1954–1984)

In the above quote, Foucault notes that ancient criticism was "authorized in the name of a knowledge of nature," it was an ecological discourse concerned with "the balance of life processes" (1997:295). For Foucault, at the center of this ecological discourse was an ethics for a concern for the self. Says Foucault: "Philosophy's most important preoccupation centered around the self, with knowledge [*connaissance*] of the world coming after and serving, most often, to support the care of the self" (294). Guattari's thinking in *Chaosmosis* also brings together criticism and a concern for self, evident in the idea that one needs to accept as the only finality of human activity the "production of subjectivity that is auto-enriching" (1996:21). Following on from the previous two chapters, here I explore the literary function with respect to an ethics for a concern for the self, and in doing so situate this form of criticism within an ecological discourse. However, where the previous chapter considered the question of the literary function in relation to society, this chapter considers the literary function in relation to the activity of the reader. In examining the "role" of the reader, further implications of the literary function—as an ethics for a concern for self and as an ecological discourse—can be explored.

This approach to criticism, as a discourse upon ethics and ecology, marks a paradigmatic shift away from the West's long dependence upon scientism—in philosophy, psychoanalysis, and criticism. For Foucault, this shift enables a discussion of self, freed of the institutions of law. Foucault puts the problem like this: if you analyze the subject on the basis of structures of truth or institutions of truth, including psychoanalysis, "you can only conceive of the subject as a subject of law" (1997:300). Foucault, therefore, rejects "a priori theories of the subject" (290) when attempting to analyze an ethics for a concern for the self. Guattari's ethico-aesthetics is an exploration of the subject outside the law, free of a priori theories. Guattari's notion, as outlined by Bosteels, of signifying semiotics, explains the subject of the law. Signification and interpretation (forming a priori theories) "go hand in hand with an individuation of subjectivity, split into the subject of enunciation (*je*) and the subject of the enounced (*moi*)," which are both subjugated to the signifying chain (Bosteels, 1995:353). For Foucault, in order to analyze a subject outside the law, it is necessary to critique power on the basis of "freedom, strategies, and governmentality" (1997:300). How can reading—and the fictional Reader—pose a *strategy* for a concern for the self? What becomes of the category of the fictional thought through the literary function? The previous chapter considered Guattari's ethico-aesthetics as an approach to aesthetics that avoids scientism. In this chapter, Foucault's thoughts concerning an ethics for a concern for the self are explored in relation to the "role" of the reader of literary texts in order to further steer this discourse away from a scientific paradigm and toward a paradigm of ethics.

This analysis of the fictional regime of signs results in a conceptualization of the subject outside the law. This approach to the fictional, as a reading practice and strategy for a concern for the self, is viewed against a psychoanalytic and structuralist-type modeling of the fictional reading practice, which, it is argued, is a scientism and positions the subject within the law. Marie MacLean's *Narrative as Performance* (1988) is a work that is an example of such scientism but is of particular interest in that is has a shared interest in questions of performativity in relation to the literary text.

In exploring the formation of self (outside the law), Foucault turns to the games of truth played by the subject as "a practice of the self" (1997:282). For Foucault, games of truth vary; there are those of science or those of institutions. These are "coercive practices" (282) or "practices of control" (281) that result in "the states of domination that people ordinarily call "power" (299). However, these are not the only games of truth, and power is not always negative. For Foucault, for power to be positive what is needed is "power relations," what he describes as "strategic games between liberties" (298). Power relations result in freedom. But in order to play these positive power relations, practices of the self and of freedom are necessary. Says Foucault, "[t]he problem...is to acquire the rules of law, the management techniques, and also the morality, the *ethos*, the practice of self, that will allow us to play these games of power with as little domination as possible" (298).[1] This chapter explores the fictional as a game of truth involving a "practice of the self" (Foucault, 1997:282).

MacLean's analysis of fictional narrative is as a game of truth. For MacLean the interaction between the two bodies, that of the narrator and the narratee, results in a game of truth. MacLean refers to the configuration of narrator and narratee as a *scene of performance*. This exploration by MacLean, of the scene of performance, moves beyond the formal conditions of reception, and her work edges toward questions of the subject and ethics. However, due to the narratological and structuralist paradigms she employs, MacLean's subject does not, ultimately, escape the law—and neither does it escape its dominating, coercive practices. Opposed to MacLean's vision of the fictional as a law-abiding discourse, the fictional is capable of providing the reader with an ethos, "a way of being and of behavior" (Foucault, 1997:286), which is auto or self-enriching—that is, it creates a self outside the law. Such a self is deemed necessary in the pursuit of nondominating games of power and truth.

MacLean's work *Narrative as Performance* is an attempt to theorize the effect of narrative upon the reader and the effect of the reader upon the narrative. It is an attempt to move away from a structuralist analysis of narrative in which the analysis is centered on the text as object (1988:xi). MacLean's notion is that since "every performance is unique" (xii) a structural framework is overcome. However, due to MacLean's narratological approach to fictional discourse, her "scene of performance" ultimately functions as a structuring principle, rendering the subject a subject of the law. Emphasis is given by MacLean to the category of the fictional, for her it is a mode of narrative that is "golden" in its capacity to create a critical, self-aware subjectivity. However, by subsuming the fictional within the narratological, a structural mapping of the fictional is maintained and a subject of the law is the result. Contrary to this is an idea of fictional reading practice providing an ethics, a way of being and of behavior, which is *a practice of self contra to the law.*

For MacLean, the fictional is of particular significance with respect to the scene of performance on account of its emphasis, as a regime of signs, upon doubling. For instance, in seeing their own narratives doubled in the text—or by "reading between the lines"—the reader is able to act as (self) analyst. I concur with Mary Louise Pratt, quoted by MacLean, when she states that the doubling of experience is the "major benefit provided by fiction" (MacLean 1988:76). However, the role of doubling does not involve a doubling of the Same, as is envisaged by Pratt and MacLean. Doubling, a return—to visit Nietzsche's now common idea—is always a return of difference. And so the process is one in which the self reaches beyond "self"-analysis into a *practice of self*. Here, reading involves an ethos and a way of being and behavior that goes beyond games of truth that are coercive practices.

MacLean and Performance

MacLean turns to performance to explain the relationship between reader and narrative text—including the fictional narrative text. For MacLean, there is an interaction between text and viewer/reader, and this interface constitutes the scene of performance. For MacLean, this interaction is dynamic and unique (and hence a performance) because each interaction varies. Performance is also entirely pragmatic; "Performance is not subjected to the criterion of truth or falsehood, but judged on success or failure" (MacLean, 1988:xi). MacLean follows Roger Caillois who refers to the interaction in narrative (performance) as an "'arena of play'" (MacLean quoting Caillois, 1) in which narrative is determined by the demands of the audience—the social and cultural situation and audience context[2]—as much as it is determined by the inclusive and/or exclusory codes the teller employs. For example, gender may be the governing factor brought to bear upon a narrative audience, excluding from the narrative either men or women.

MacLean draws upon a variety of interactive instances to explain the scene of (narrative) performance. For MacLean the "arena of play" can in part be attributed to narrative oral storytelling traditions that she sees as the basis for written narrative and staged drama.[3] The development of the scene of performance from oral storytelling traditions, for MacLean, is largely due to the fact that the audience is close at hand. The teller can adjust the story where necessary in order to keep the listener's attention, thus it has been said that, "the teller is as much in the control of the hearer as the hearer is in that of the teller" (1988:3). Ultimately, the hearer may even leave the scene, controlling entirely the flow of the narrative. MacLean considers other interferences brought to bear on the telling of the narrative by the listener/reader. She refers to "noise," which includes factors such as the hearer's/receiver's "ignorance, incompetence, or unwillingness as well as for example their physical discomfort" (1988:3). MacLean borrows from Michel Serres's work *The Parasite* (1982) in order to discuss transformations to the narrative as a result of the scene of performance. For MacLean, the readers' anarchic input, including "noise," can "stimulate the mutation and the new growth of narrative forms and their evolution within the wider interplay of social force" (1988:4). Orally performed narratives were also restricted by "the memory capacity of the teller and the attention span of the hearers" (8).

Oral narrative, says MacLean, has moved into the dramatic form, and the narrator has become one with the voices of his characters. As a result, for MacLean, drama continues to provide an ideal model for the exploration of narrative and reader. Drama is also important in understanding the reader and narrative because it continues the tradition of audience involvement. It does so by engaging the audiences' senses with sound and image; it does and can include feedback, and being in "real" time, drama puts an "emphasis on the situational aspects of narrative" (9) (unlike the written text where narrative is reduced to textual space). The connection MacLean makes between the spoken and written narrative text, then, is at the level of the *énonciation* of the text, that is, the telling or narrative, as opposed to story or tale. MacLean notes that the énonciation is a *fabrication* (of narrator and narratee) which "only becomes itself an act when read, that is when interacting with an actual audience" (10).

MacLean points out that "[d]ramatic models, and indeed theatrical models, are constantly used within written narrative" (11). She mentions dialogue, found in both forms, and "*embedding*," which she borrows from Todorov. Embedding as a device "stresses the iconic value of the portrayal of selected moments.... It functions as microcosm to the macrocosm of the text" (12). In drama, embedding may take the form of tableau scenes. It is *en abyme,* a reflexive device. For instance, when used as a play within a play within drama, the audience may see themselves "reflected in another audience" (13). Embedding compares to Bakhtin's notion of chronotope and the novel. MacLean points out that the chronotope is first discussed by Bakhtin in the context of the theater—the "'chronotope of the theatre'" (13)—and it refers to "off" spaces. "Off" spaces may include historic and geographic illusions, but also "fictional and mythological spaces" (12). When used in the novel, multilayering results. Narrators are also common to both dramatic and written narrative.

Adding to the dramatic model of narrative-reader interaction, and to further theorize the narrative-reader dynamic, MacLean turns to Austin's notion of the performative speech act. For MacLean, speech-act theory is "the most promising development in the study of verbal performance in general" (22) and when considered in the light of the narrative utterance the performative speech act has enabled critics to theorize the narrative/reader or viewer dynamic. Says MacLean, "[Austin's] analysis of the performative not only showed language in action, but made it clear that this action was only possible because of an interaction between sender and receiver of verbal messages" (22).

Austin's notion of the performative speech act, ironically, does not initially extend to the theatrical, since, for Austin, it is a felicitous discourse; it "produces no effect in actuality" (MacLean, 1988:23). However, MacLean argues that since all language is "sign-based, symbolic and therefore fabricated,...natural discourse, as a semiotic system, is in no way distinguishable from fictional discourse" (24). The distinction is made, for MacLean, at a cultural level when we, in some manner, "ask" whether something is fiction or not; "'[d]id that really happen or is it a story?'" (24). For instance, in seeking a book from the "Australian Literature" section of a bookshop, we have already asked this question, in kind. This view of fictional discourse as equally symbolic and therefore fabricated does not, however, rescue the fictional from its nonperformance-based status. As a way out of the invalid/valid distinction and in order to bring to fictional discourse the status of the performative speech act MacLean posits two orders of speech act:

> The first order would operate in natural discourse and in direct speech, and would correspond to the Austinian criteria for "serious" performatives, (these include; promising, requesting, congratulating, asserting, questioning, thanking, advising, warning, greeting,) the second would operate in fictional discourse and everyday narratives. This would acknowledge that narration changes the status of the speech act included in it. (1988:24)

For MacLean, what makes narratives illocutionary—acts produced in the saying, together with the illocutionary categories John Searle cites: "'representatives,' 'directives,' 'commissives,' 'expressives,' and 'declaratives'" (MacLean quoting Searle, 25)—is that they *create* an audience. For MacLean, because narrative is inevitably a mediation of reality, "subject to the whims and selections of the teller," it is "valid only within the framework of the narrative" (24–25), and this is what makes it a second-order speech act. In addition, a narrative tells of a time different from its own (time of telling) and thereby tells of "alternative worlds" (25), which is also what makes it a second-order speech act. However, for MacLean, the narrative is performative because it contractualizes the reader/receiver, "as all true speech acts do," with its "'*Listen,* and I will tell you *a* story'" (25). That is, it is in the directive, "listen," and in the unique version of the events, the *énonciation* of the performance scene, that the listener is contractualized. The narrative performative, then, is a double contract. MacLean, thus, falls back on the instructive aspect of the performative to claim narrative as a performative utterance. She counters John Searle's statement that fictional discourse is not performative since it employs "'a set of conventions which suspend the normal operation of rules relating illocutionary acts and the world'" (MacLean quoting Searle, 25). For MacLean, it is precisely the set of conventions that makes narrative performative since it "instructs one to differentiate between *énonciation* and *énoncé*, and more particularly, between speaking and telling" (25). For MacLean, it is the performative belonging to narrative that enlists the reader's interaction.

MacLean also names five different performance models in showing different aspects of narrative. Three of these are taken from Shoshana Felman's *The Literary Speech Act* (1983) and they are: "the erotic, the theatrical, and the linguistic." To these, MacLean adds "the physical or energetic, and the ludic" (1988:14–15). MacLean adds these last two categories since the scene of performance is a game and "a struggle for power" (14–15) between sender and receiver. She configures the structure, sender-receiver (sender), or narrator-narratee (and narratee turned writer). The erotic model is a negotiation of the "authority" of the narrator over the narratee and is compared to negotiation in erotic interplay. MacLean compares the sexual contract to the narrative contract in quoting Louis Marin, "'[t]he cogito of the writer is "'You are, therefore I exist'"" (129). In the linguistic model the reader negotiates with the multiple voices and previous performances of the text, the social and ideological forces inherent in language, etc. In the "ludic model" the textual strategies—"the rules of the game"—are used in the narrative to advance positions of authority (and control) over the reader. Says MacLean, "Narrative may be seen as a delicate interplay of power in which the narratee submits to the control of a narrator, while the narrator must scheme to overcome the power of the narratee" (17–18). For instance, the narratee gives power to the narrator to shock, offend, and outrage, while "he or she yields to the power of judgment, of acceptance or rejection" (126).

In developing the "energetic" performance model, MacLean uses Deleuze and Guattari's notion of *agencement machinique*, which becomes a kind of meta sender-receiver model. For MacLean, it "enables an appreciation of narrative in terms of a dynamics of performance" (1988:21). In MacLean's use of the *agencement machinique*

> [t]he interplay of the text is comparable to that of a human body, an infinite interlocking of parts, each of which has its own vitality and its own energy. The running down of these energies, the forces of diffusion and stasis, is countered by the constant subversion of the pattern. The points of control and the points of escape are always shifting within the system. (21)

The interplay, for MacLean, is between the telling and hearing, making narrative not a matter of ownership but of *negotiation* (19). In MacLean's "energy" model, the text is viewed as a conduit for force (a kind of thermodynamics), its graphemic shape being a common point shared by two acceptations (sender and receiver). MacLean further abstracts this situation in saying that the narrative text and force are pure performance. We could diagram this notion thus (fig. 6.1):

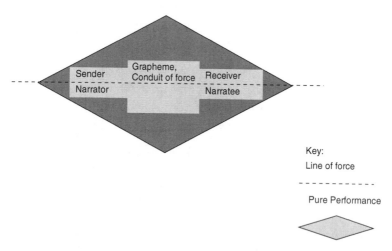

Figure 6.1   Grapheme as conduit of force, thermodynamic model.

MacLean discusses allegory and the ancient rhetorical notion of syllepsis to further explain the thermodynamic model. In allegory and syllepsis "the one phonetic or graphemic shape is shared by two acceptations" (MacLean quoting Michel Riffaterre, 1988:172). In other words, allegory and syllepsis have a double meaning, that of meaning and significance.

This shared grapheme underpins the idea of text as a conduit and line of force. A diagram of MacLean's double-acceptation grapheme might look like this (fig. 6.2):

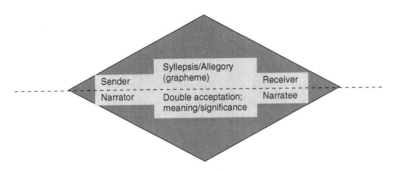

Figure 6.2   Thermodynamic model showing force and pure performance due to double meaning of grapheme.

Narrative, Knowledge, and Power

For MacLean the destination of performance is in a will to knowledge ultimately resulting in a will to power:

> There is a more general meaning to performance: an implementation, and where possible a successful implementation, of a certain set of conditions of knowledge, skills, techniques, rules, or vocabulary. The classic distinction drawn by Chomsky is between the knowledge of vocabulary and of syntax, the paradigmatic and syntagmatic structures of language, which is competence, and the use of those structures to produce a particular discourse, which is performance (MacLean, 1988:41).

The theme of knowledge and power returns frequently in MacLean's writing. Narrative is viewed as a form of control: "the basic problem of narrative is one of control, and one of control by signs" (MacLean, 126). MacLean describes telling as "one of the earliest creative formal skills we acquire" (2). She relays the story of researchers listening in on two-year-olds who, while in bed, constructed narratives that already contained "the three basics of critical situation, complication, and resolution" (2). For MacLean, "[i]n narrative, as in rhetoric or philosophy, texts are the weapons in the 'fight for life'" (127). Performance is grounded in "a verbomotor life style…a society in which 'the sounded word was power'" (8). She describes the narratee's interplay as the *power* "to co-operate or not to co-operate" (3). She sees "noise" not so much as an encumbrance upon the teller but a "challenge of winning the battle for control" (3). Writes MacLean, "[n]arrative…involves negentropy, a marshalling of the resources of language against the seemingly random dispersion of our experience" (2). If the result of negentropy is a "rigid framework of ideologies and preconceptions" and the teller engages in an anarchic energy to counter these, the release of energy is "channeled negentropically in renewed creativity" (2–3).

For MacLean, then, knowledge and power, aided by the structure of narrative, become the destination of fictional narrative. MacLean renders narrative a structuring principle in the way Levi-Strauss renders myth a structuring principle and a means of social organization. Children learn the conventions of narrative so that they might operate negentropy, "marshalling…the resources of language against the seemingly random dispersion of our experience" (2). For MacLean, the fictional is embedded within the narrative contract that is equal to a *power* play between sender and receiver (a point I will be returning to).

Narrative as Currency and the Question of Equivalence and Immanence in MacLean's Scene of Performance

As mentioned earlier, MacLean's consideration of the scene of performance is of interest since it is an exploration of the subject in relation to fictional narrative. In what follows, however, I will consider various problems with MacLean's scene of performance, the subject that is envisaged there, and her treatment of the category of the fictional. MacLean's subject will be seen to be a subject of the law, and the fictional will ultimately not be able to be differentiated from all other forms of narrative. By contrast, the fictional will be explored as a regime of signs that involves an ethos of self, or to use Foucault's phrase, "a practice of self-formation of the subject" (1997:282).

In continuing her theme of reader empowerment, MacLean puts forward the notion that the (narrative) text functions as a currency upon which the reader may capitalize. Narrative is a currency because it involves exchange, and the reader may gain power by dealing in it. Says MacLean, it is in exchange that worth is generated: "The teller is expected to ensure that his or her tale is 'worth' the audience's attention, and that the hearers or readers expect the tale to be 'worth-while'" (1988:85). Says MacLean: the narrator "assumes a certain perlocutionary effect of his story on his narrative audience, an effect dependent on shared conventions" (87). Furthermore, for MacLean, fictional narrative affords the most perlocutionary effect because it most outlines its conventions (87), stresses the interpretation of the message, and is the most self-reflexive. Self-reflexivity is said to speak the "true" that MacLean opposed to speaking the real, something she reserves for first-order speech acts. MacLean describes the fictional as a counterfeit currency but no less effective for that. For Maclean, the fictional "speaks" of its counterfeit nature and this becomes its truth. When self-reflexivity foregrounds "the special status of the narrative act, [it] is one device which maintains the 'gold standard' of literature" (MacLean, 87). By gold standard is meant a very good currency indeed, one which may produce the utmost perlocutionary effect.

MacLean's postmodern reading of narrative fiction, as self-reflexive (counterfeit), and thereby a (golden) currency, renders the fictional act a sign *of equivalence* the function of which is that of exchange. For MacLean, it is in exchange that experience resides. Writes MacLean:

> This relationship of the...receiver to the sender is the same as in that illocutionary contract we all know from the playground: "Open you mouth and shut your eyes / And Johnny will give you a big surprise." Sometimes we got a sweet and sometimes we got a sheep dropping, thus learning in one swift lesson the contractual ambiguities. Baudelaire would say, and shows it amply in the prose poems which play obsessively with the notion of *contract*, that either result is a valid experience. (1988:85)

For MacLean the various exchanges in the narrative contract, the exchange of money, exchange of value, exchange of words, and exchange of pleasure, ensure experience (87). For experience to take place the contract must be fulfilled, that is, the reader must take part in shared conventions of narrative, its codes and signs. This is MacLean's thermodynamic model in action. Experience for, MacLean, is in the *exchange* of signs, in the *contract*. The signs themselves are arbitrary (it could be a sheep's dropping or a sweet), and thereby equivalent. In MacLean, fiction—the most narrative of narratives because of its high degree of self-reflexivity—is reduced to narrative *and exchange*. As with her thoughts on narrative as a means of social organization, MacLean's emphasis on exchange adds to her structural-type understanding of narrative/fiction. Added to this, in MacLean, fiction, as the narrative of narratives, is equated with narrative, which in turn gives a structural orientation to her approach to fiction.

MacLean's rendition of the fictional is thus within a linguistic semiotics.[4] As discussed in chapter 4, linguistic semiotics language is seen to have an abstract machine internal to it. Such a machine takes the flux of the lived and makes it "immanent to the subject and individualized in that which belongs to the self" (Deleuze and Guattari, 1994:47). MacLean's narrative fiction operates in this manner. The destination of the fictional is in the self, expressed in MacLean as "experience." Narrative functions to imbue position A (the senders of the message) and position B (the receiver) as an end in itself. Opposed to linguistic semiotics is mixed semiotics that forms an abstract machine that provides a language with a particular collective assemblage of enunciation. In other words, there is no subject of enunciation in mixed semiotics. Because of MacLean's particular choice of semiotic, then, the fictional is made *immanent to something else*—an a priori subject. The result of MacLean's semiotic, in which the fictional is made immanent to something else (see chapter 2 earlier) is that the fictional is made equivalent as a sign, a signifier, within the abstract machine of language. It thus cannot be explored as an immanent *regime of signs* that might be understood as a practice of self-formation or an ethics of a concern for the self. (According to Foucault, in order to conceive of a practice of self-formation—outside the law—it is necessary to "reject a priori theories of the subject" [1997:290].) Understood as a practice of self-formation, outside the law, the fictional must be understood as a singularity and not a sign of equivalence. I will return to and elaborate the fictional, singularity and an ethics of a concern for the self, but will now turn to MacLean's scene of performance in order to further elaborate the subject in MacLean.

The Scene of Performance and MacLean's Subject

MacLean has attempted to open narratology to questions of the subject and not just the reader, compared to say David Bordwell who limits the spectator to "the formal conditions under which we comprehend a (filmic) text.[5] In considering the subject in MacLean it is necessary to look at the variety of theoretical tools she uses in theorizing the scene of performance: these include theories of oral performance, Austin's notion of performance, and a discussion of the fictional in respect to the abstract machine internal to language, that is, the signifier.

In discussing Austin's notion of the speech act, MacLean attributes to fictional narrative that which Austin preserves for nonfictional speech acts, that being, the status of "serious":

> [o]ur speech "acts" derive their validity only from a long history of accepting the convention of speech acts.... Thus, rather than making a distinction between the natural and the unnatural, the valid and the invalid, we should be seeing each as "serious" within its appropriate context; we

should rather refer to parallel linguistic transactions, some actual, some virtual. (1988:75–76)

For MacLean, fictional narrative (a so-called virtual linguistic transaction) demands an awareness of the doubling of experience, the "representation of a representation" (74). For MacLean, our awareness of the doubling of experience "makes us aware that the fictional speaks not the real but the true" (101). If "the true" is the result of linguistic doubling, "true" must be assumed to mean transcendental Signifier. The excerpt given here, in which MacLean discusses prose by Baudelaire, paints a vivid picture of MacLean's understanding of narrative fiction as the domain par excellence of doubling and thereby the signifier:

> [t]he concrete setting of the café is described in terms of the utmost theatricality, in lighting, decoration, painting, hangings, statuary. Even the food is described as a representation, a *prop* rather than a comestible. The very brilliance of the gas lighting seems to permit penetration, to shed light into every corner. But this is a mere illusion. Just as a stage set permits only visual penetration by the audience and otherwise sets up an impervious barrier, so the café is seen here through the glass, from the outside. It is a feast for the eyes, offering itself to the spectator as a stage set offers itself to the audience. It is from this narratorial perspective that the whole picture of the café is drawn. This is a tableau of consumption, a purely pictorial world where the gold, the gluttony, and the laughter have all been transferred to the walls in a series of figural and mythological representations. The stasis of this tableau scene stands in sharp contrast to the anticipated narrative momentum. (1988:116–117)

Maclean further adds:

> There is nothing human, nothing moving. The depicted women and the boys, the Hebes and the Ganymedes, are themselves objects of consumption to the eyes, frozen as they endlessly proffer their wares. They are the equivalent of the fruit, the pâtés and game, the mouse and the ices. This setting of fictional profusion, the second form of narrative space, is iconically coupled with the fifth form of space, the proliferation of the textual signifiers. The single long sentence from "Even the gaslight" to "gluttony" is a syntactic and rhetorical *tour de force,* where the cumulative effect of the elaborated binary and ternary patterns, an architecture of primary signifiers, parallels the semantic content. Both signifiers and signifieds accumulate in a build-up to the devastating final sign, "gluttony," which sums up the whole space. (117)

Here, "the proliferation of the textual signifiers" conspire in their accumulative effect to produce the *true* sign (gluttony). In other words, the chain of signifiers produces "the fifth form of space," which is the transcendental signifier, "the true" in a system of equivalence.

MacLean states that we should see both first- and second-order performative speech acts as serious "within [their] appropriate context[s]" (76). The "appropriate context" belonging to the second-order speech act is that of the Signifier. However, in her use of Austin, MacLean does not heed Derrida's criticism (Derrida, 1988) of Austin's notion of performance and its dependence on *context* and therefore presence.[6] In MacLean, the "context" of the signifier becomes a transcendentalism. Deleuze and Guattari note that when immanence is made immanent to something (i.e., the signifier), it is automatically a transcendentalism. In making the scene of performance immanent to the transcendental signifier, MacLean's subject is therefore the a priori subject of the law.

MacLean also turns to oral narrative in theorizing the scene of performance. Analyzing this is important to understanding the subject in MacLean's scene of performance. For MacLean, in oral narrative the sender-receiver relationship is at its most poignant—to the point whereby the sender receives the receiver's response. However, for Derrida, where the sender-receiver is considered there is a metaphysical construction of thought. Writes Derrida:

> The conscious presence of the speakers or receivers participating in the accomplishment of a performative, their conscious and intentional presence in the totality of the operation, implies teleologically that no residue [*reste*] escapes the present totalization. (Derrida, 1988:14)

In other words, in the construction of receiver and sender, presence is implied—in the form of a totalization of meaning. For MacLean, the teller/performer brings to the narrative what can only be interpreted as presence:

> [u]nlike the writer, restricted by choice of voice and of person in the narrator, the teller/performer can truly be a microcosm of the creative divinity in his or her work of "subcreations" as Tolkien calls it. She … has the privilege of speaking at the same time in the omniscient voice of the authoritative narrator through which the text imposes itself, and also in her own physical voice and body, the I present and performing the text, an I whose context and territory include the text itself and the license to perform it. (MacLean, 1988:7)

For MacLean, the performer is a microcosom, and his or her work a subcreation, of the "creative divinity" because of a seeming omni*presence,* resulting from a ubiquitous voice, in the form of the narrator, but also the voice of the performer and the performer's physical body. In other words, for MacLean, the performer sends to the receiver, presence (creative divinity). This, once again, makes narrative immanent to something else, a divinity, presence. MacLean does state that the "I" to which she refers is "an I whose context and territory include the text itself and the license to perform it." However, the metaphysics is furthered when MacLean writes: "[o]ral performance is not just an act of saying something. What is said is less important than the *saying*, an interaction which...involves purpose, energy, and effect as well as the message conveyed" (1988:7, my italics).

Here, "saying" is the culmination of the "omniscient voice of the authoritative narrator" and the physical voice and body of the performer, "the I *present* and performing the text" (my italics). It is this collection of communication modes that for MacLean guarantees the message. However, this idea of communication seems to echo the approaches to communication Derrida criticizes. Such approaches see communication beginning with "the language of action" (Derrida, 1988:4), being continued in sound and written language and having "a line that is direct, simple, and continuous" (4). It is this continuous line that guarantees the message to be homogenous (4) and thereby full, which is what MacLean intimates with her notion of a divine subcreation. Derrida criticizes theories of communication that depend upon the presence of the receiver. For Derrida all communication involves writing, which he defines as "*difference* [difference and deferral, *trans.*]" (7) For Derrida, "*difference*... as writing could no longer (be) an (ontological) modification of presence" (7) since writing depends upon the "absoluteness of absence if the structure of writing...is to constitute itself" (7). MacLean's notion of performance that sits within Austin's theory of the performative, is, however, communication dependent upon the presence of the receiver—as she implies with her notion of "interaction" involving purpose, energy, and effect. As Derrida comments, however, such a notion of the performative—which involves "the conscious presence of the speakers or receivers—implies teleologically that no residue [*reste*] escapes the present totalization" (Derrida, 1988:14). This is brought home with MacLean's notion of *the message conveyed* resulting from the *interaction*. The subject in MacLean's "scene of performance," then, is an empirically determinable subject (which Derrida says must be absolutely absent from a theory of writing and communication [1988:7]). And because the communication "scene" is one of full meaning, this bestows upon the receiver, metaphysical presence. The "subject" of the narrative, then, is an a priori subject, in this case, the subject of metaphysical thought.

MacLean notes that the instability of linguistic conventions makes the speech act dynamic and inherently fluid (1988:23). She states that in

> the multiple voices of the telling and its multiple reception...is heard not just the voice of the teller but the voices of language, of narrative tradition, of ideology, of the whole social context. In the spoken subject, we have the whole range of voices of the tale itself and its various actors. Different voices speak in what is said, sometimes in the form of dialogue, sometimes in the form of quotation in, for example, the formulaic utterance or oral narrative. (1988:6–7)

However, while making these claims, MacLean does not consider the emphasis she has placed upon the (transcendental) signifier, upon presence, and upon exchange—which all capture multiplicity. Instead, the a priori subject (reader) becomes the destination of MacLean's narrative fiction, taking the place of the objectified text by more formal studies of narrative.

MacLean's reader/subject is, then, an a priori subject, according to a priori theories and thought—to return to Foucault's point canvassed earlier, concerning the inappropriate nature of a priori theories when analyzing the subject outside the law, and in respect to an ethics for a concern for the self. MacLean's reader is a subject of the law, affected by the structure of narrative. For example, MacLean compares the sexual contract to the narrative contract, " 'The cogito of the writer is 'You are, therefore I exist' " (MacLean quoting Louis Marin, 1988:129). Presumably the reverse also applies with respect to the cogito of the reader. The subject is also affected by the "true" of the signifier. And as with the regime of the signifier in general this is a scene of tyranny,[7] as MacLean's quote indicates, "[f]ictional narrative is a game, but a game for high stakes, in which nothing less than the power of the text over the players is involved" (1988:17). Thus, the uniqueness of the scene of performance—and the subject that results—is lost to the structure of narrative. If we compare Lacanian theories of the subject and language, the I is a reduction of self, of multiplicity. Of utmost importance is that what is lost in MacLean is the chance for the fictional to be explored as a practice of self-formation and a line of flight from the tyranny of the signifier. A practice of self-formation is the way in which Foucault refers to the ethics of the concern for self. It is to the elaboration of these concerns that I now turn.

The Game of Truth of Foucault

MacLean explores narrative in relation to power and the empowerment of the reader. Her implication is that the reader has power because narratives are powerful. However, the value of power is not questioned. Contrary to this, Foucault distinguishes between good and bad power. For Foucault, negative power is "the states of domination that people ordinarily call 'power'" (1997:299). However, power is not "evil" when it is what Foucault calls "power relations." Power relations are to be "understood as strategic games between liberties—in which some try to control the conduct of others, who in turn try to avoid allowing their conduct to be controlled or try to control the conduct of others" (298). For Foucault, power relation results in freedom. (MacLean's conception of power play between narrator and reader could be seen as "strategic games between liberties" but I shall soon point out that this is not the case.) For Foucault, in order to engage in positive power relations, practices of the self and of freedom are necessary. To repeat Foucault's words, "[t]he problem...is to acquire the rules of law, the management techniques, and also the morality, the *ethos*, the practice of self, that will allow us to play these games of power with as little domination as possible" (1997:298).[8] For Foucault, there has been a shift in the "games of truth" from those of science and those of institutions, what he calls "coercive practices" (282)[9] or "practices of control" (281), to "a practice of self-formation of the subject" (282). Foucault describes his project at the Collège de France, 1981–1982, as an attempt to grasp the relationship between the subject and games of truth as "a practice of the self" (282). As discussed, Foucault is interested in the "games of truth, practices of power and so on," in relation to the historical constitution of the subject (290–291). Says Foucault:

> It is what one could call an ascetic practice, taking asceticism in a very general sense—in other words, not in the sense of a morality of renunciation but as an exercise of the self on the self by which one attempts to develop and transform oneself, and to attain a certain mode of being. (1997:282)

For Foucault, in order to achieve his project it was necessary to "reject a priori theories of the subject" (290).

MacLean's conception of power, involving the reader and the games of narrative, fall short of a game between liberties since the destination of the game is toward an a priori subject. Thus, in MacLean, narrative becomes a game of truth of institutions, such as psychoanalysis, that Foucault associates with "coercive practices" (1997:282) or "practices of control" (281). They are not "a practice of self-formation of the subject" (282). In MacLean, reading is not viewed as an ethics for a practice of self "by which one attempts to develop and transform oneself" (Foucault, 282). Rather, there is no indication of a move away from the "games of truth" that are "coercive practices" (Foucault, 1997:282) or "practices of control" (281). For MacLean, the text is significant for its "force" and here force must be interpreted as power that is a state of domination: for MacLean the best the reader can do is take over the reign of the writer and "knock out the next set of readers" (1988:174–175). In MacLean, it is the *structure* of narrative as a conduit of force—it matters little what the message is—which results in a subject of the law.

Rather than a self that attains a certain mode of being, MacLean's subject has resonance with Plato's notion of the subject, which Foucault criticizes. Plato's subject is based upon self-reflexivity. Writes Foucault: "In the Platonic current of thought, at least at the end of the *Alcibiades,* the problem for the subject or the individual soul is to turn its gaze upon itself, to recognize itself in what it is and, recognizing itself in what it is, to recall the truths that issue from it and that it has been able to contemplate" (1997:285). MacLean's emphasis on the self-reflexivity of narrative repeats this theme. In MacLean, narrative, when it is "golden," reflects its discursivity, this is its "game of truth." In contrast to these reflective models of truth, Foucault puts forward the thinking of Stoicism. Here, one learns through the teaching of "a number of truths and doctrines, some of which are fundamental principles while others are rules of conduct" (1997:285–286). This is a pragmatic kind of truth. Further on in this chapter, I discuss the fictional as a mode of reading that is also a rule of conduct—which subsequently results in a practice of self-formation. The fictional is examined as a teaching of various truths or fundamental principles. The film *The Sweet Hereafter* by Atom Egoyan, is analyzed as a story about these functions for fiction. At this point the fictional becomes irreducible to a structure—to the structure of narrative. Rather, it is multiple because it may only be "told" within an immanent *assemblage.* Thus the critical frame is shifted from the scientific to a pragmatic one.

The context in which Foucault discusses Stoicism is around the question of an ethics of the concern for the self. Foucault notes that, "from the first Platonic dialogues up to the major texts of late Stoicism...you will see that the theme of the care of the self thoroughly permeated moral reflection" (1997:284). For the Greeks, says Foucault, freedom was centered upon the ethics of self, of the individual. Significantly, the "Greeks problematized their freedom, and the freedom of the individual, as an ethical problem" (286). The Greeks' sense of the ethical was that of *ethos* that was "a way of being and of behavior" (Foucault, 286).[10]

As mentioned, Foucault links the care of the self to an ecological movement (294) that he says is very ancient and while this movement has been "often in opposition...to science or, at least, to a technology underwritten by claims of truth" it "articulated its own discourse of truth" (295). To this ecological discourse of truth Foucault gives the name, criticism:

> Criticism was authorized in the name of a knowledge [*connaissance*] of nature, the balance of life processes, and so on. Thus, one escaped from a domination of truth not by playing a game that was totally different from the game of truth but by playing the same game differently, or playing another game, another hand, with other trump cards. (Foucault, 1997:295)

For Foucault the concern for the truth is "*the* question for the West. Foucault asks, "How did it come about that all of Western culture began to revolve around this obligation of truth which has taken a lot of different forms?"(295) The answer Foucault gives is:

> Things being as they are, nothing so far has shown that it is possible to define a strategy outside of this concern. It is within the field of the obligation to truth that it is possible to move about in one way or another, sometimes against effects of domination which may be linked to structures of truth or institutions entrusted with truth. (1997:295)

In other words, the care of the self must occur through the concern for the truth. Since this concern is the only way known to define a strategy, it is within this obligation to the truth that it is possible to resist dominant structures of truth.

MacLean's project may be described as an interest in the reader/subject in relation to the games of truth of fiction and thus be considered a similar problematic to Foucault's. And like Foucault, MacLean views power not as necessarily negative but as a power *play*. However, as mentioned, for Foucault there is a distinction to be made between good and bad power, and this is not found in MacLean. MacLean's scene of performance forecloses on an analysis of this power based on *ethos, on practices of the self,* since the subject in the scene pertains to a priori theories of the subject. As Foucault says, "if you try to analyze power not on the basis of freedom, strategies, and governmentality, but on the basis of the political institutions, you can only conceive of the subject as a subject of law" (1997:300). MacLean's subject is a subject of law since it is dependent upon the "institutions" of psychoanalysis and the structures of narrative. This also raises a political issue if we consider Guattari's notion that any production of subjectivity is inseparable from technical and institutional apparatuses promoting it (1995:11). In order to escape producing a subject of law when considering fiction in relation to the subject/reader, it is necessary to consider the way in which the fictional operates in regard to an ethics of *the concern for the self.* It is necessary to ask, what *kind* of *mode of being* does it enable, what *kind* of *ethos*? It is necessary to ask: what is the nature of the "game of truth" of fiction? Such an approach will free fiction from the structuralism of narratology, the conflation of fiction and narrative and the production of a subject of the law.

MacLean's Scene of Performance: Doubling and a Linguistic Modeling for the Subject

Mentioned earlier is the importance of doubling to the fictional. Before commencing a discussion of doubling and its relevance to an ethics of the self, I will outline the significance of doubling in MacLean. For MacLean doubling belongs to the self-reflexivity of the fictional, and it "fore-grounds the arbitrary nature of the fictional world and its transactions and... make(s) us aware of the truth of the virtual world as opposed to its reality" (1988:76). The notion of "true" here is that which "belong(s) to the world of signs and only functions within the realm of discursive proposi-tions" (77). Says MacLean, "[o]ne function of literature is to highlight the distinction between the true, which belongs to the world of signs... and the real, which has reference in the natural world" (77). MacLean gives many examples of doubling, including: the dramatic technique of a play within a play, "the second spectacle," allegory, fable (to which I will be returning), and the use of *mise en abyme.*

For MacLean, self-reflexivity awakens the viewers/readers to their own voyeurism; repetitions mark "the effect of the unconscious drive" (142). The double role of the reader as analyst doubles the narrative when they create their own narrative in the gaps and in following up clues of the narrators' text (145). For MacLean the trajectory of the reader follows the psychoanalytic model in which "the reader's desire is always the desire of the other" (40). That is, it is a doubling. (For Lacan, our desire is the desire of the other [See Lacan, 1977:286].) Says MacLean, the reader

> wants what the other wants as much as it wants what the other is, and can never attain either, it must always involve the transgression implicit in the desire of the other. The extra exclusion of "taboo" thus doubles and rein-forces the barriers of the text, and stimulates reader desire confronted with a double lack. (1988:40)[11]

For MacLean, and Ubersfeld, to whom she refers, doubling juxtaposes two negatives and thereby reveals a positive (1988:76). Thus, it is that the scene of performance is a "scene of" truth—one could add, of the tran-scendental signifier. In MacLean, doubling results in the production of a subject of the law. The reader reads for the other, and the extra/double exclusion by the barriers of the text reinforces this "taboo" and in turn further constitutes me as a subject of the signifier. In other words, the text acts as a barrier, a law, maintaining the subject of the law.

MacLean's also adds to her account of doubling and the scene of performance the double roles of narrator and reader:

> In the narrative contest (between narrator and reader) . . . the double nature of the narrative contract is actualized because each performer is seen in a double role. Apart from explicit judgmental statements, each competitor also gives an implicit opinion of the previous narration by the tale he or she chooses to tell and the manner of telling it. So each is not only actor but audience, and simultaneously both counsel and judge. (1988:126)

In other words, the double nature of the narrative contract creates a critical position the reader comes to occupy. Thus, the reader thereby becomes a narrator. For MacLean, this is the nature of the scene of the second-order performative, the "alternative world" (76), a world that deals solely in the realm of signs and discursive propositions.

MacLean's scene of performance may at first appear to echo Foucault's "ecological discourse of truth" in that both have a link with "criticism." However, MacLean's account of the "game of truth" does not account for the way in which the game is played *differently*, that difference is a necessary part, for Foucault, of an ethos of a concern for the self. In other words, MacLean has explained narrative in general as a game of truth, and as it pertains to the law, but she has not elucidated what actions of reading are specific to a mode that escapes the law, that plays the game otherwise, "with other trump cards," to repeat Foucault (1997:295). For MacLean, doubling ensures that there is no outside the scene (law)—in fact any attempt to ignore the second-order performative, the doubling of experience, of the world of signs, "will produce a debasement of the currency" (1988:76). The second-order status MacLean bestows on the fictional performative (on the scene of performance), as opposed to first-order performatives, means that this utterance is arbitrary and conventional. For MacLean, then, the truth lies with the signifier, the law. The signifier provides a context that in turn provides a "seriousness" to the statement. MacLean states that for both the first- and second-order performatives, "the relation to the context in which they operate" (24) is crucial in making performatives "serious," and since both first- and second-order performatives are language-dependent (24) they are both serious due to the *context* of the signifier. Here, the signifier is supreme. Here, *I* am equal to the signifier, the contract. Embedded within these signs, between two or more linguistic sheets, far from the real, in the negative of all this, *I* appear—or at least to the extent that *I* am involved in the games of truth of narrative doubling.

Beyond the Scene of Performance: The Event of Fiction versus the Position of Narrative

This section puts forward a notion of the fictional that involves "an exercise of the self on the self by which one attempts to develop and transform oneself, and to attain to a certain mode of being" (Foucault, 1997:282). It argues for a self that is constituted beyond the (structural) "scene" of performance but nonetheless through the practice of reading fiction. The constitution of the self will be considered in light of a *concern for the self* and an *ethos*. The film *The Sweet Hereafter* by Atom Egoyan becomes an example of a practice of Self-formation, concern for the self, ethics, and a practice of freedom.

If fiction is to provide an ethos for a concern for the self, the destination of fiction needs to be other than that of the signifier, where the subject remains a subject of law. In other words, the game of truth needs to be played *differently*. We can look for a clue to this different game of truth in Foucault's very brief definition of fiction in an article on the work of Jules Verne, published in 1966:

> [w]hen one speaks in reality, one can very well say "fabulous" things, but the triangle formed by the speaking subject, his discourse, and what he tells is determined from the outside by the situation, so there is no fiction. (1998:135)

Foucault's beguilingly simple definition of fiction is that fiction is non-situation-specific. This raises the question of the *space of fiction* and, moreover, of the *reader* of and in fiction (involving fiction's ethical implications). It counters MacLean's notion of narrative fiction that, like all utterances, is context bound, the signifier being the overarching strategy that determines this.

If the fictional can indeed be seen in terms of an ethos for a concern for the self, Foucault further provides us with a location for the fictional when he tells us that the "ecological discourse of truth"—to which a concern for the self is attached—involves a "knowledge [*connaissance*] of nature." The destination of this discourse, then, is in nature, in "the balance of life processes" (Foucault, 1997:295). In opposition to this, MacLean situates the fictional in a space opposed to the natural world: "One function of literature is to highlight the distinction between the true, which belongs to the world of signs…and the real, which has reference in the natural world" (1988:77).

For Derrida the poetic text is also seen to move beyond its reference "towards the world" (2000:180). The poetic moves toward the world because it is ultimately untranslatable, and it is untranslatable because the poem constitutes its own poetics. Derrida draws this notion from Murray Kreiger. It also has resonance with Guattari's notion of the existential refrain; "a poetics…must also, as if *across* its generality, *become, invent, institute, offer* for reading, in an exemplary way, signing it, both sealing and unsealing it, the possibility of this poem" (Derrida, 2000:180). For Derrida, the poem promises "in the act of its happening, the foundation of a poetics" (180). It is irreversible because it creates its own poetics, just as the existential refrain is irreversible. So, for Derrida, the poetic text is rooted in the event, "in the verbal body of its singularity.… [Its] signature…opens the verbal body onto something other than itself" (180). Further to this, Derrida adds that poetics—"signing, sealing, divulging, unsealing"—is about bearing witness (180). But this is an "untranslatable testimony" (183). What counts, says Derrida,

> is not the fact that the poem names some themes which we know in advance must be at the heart of reflection on responsibility, witnessing, or poetics. What matters most of all is the strange limit between what can and cannot be determined or decreed in *this poem's witnessing to witnessing*. (2000:184)

For Derrida, for the poem to be "assured as testimony, it cannot, it must not be absolutely certain, absolutely sure and certain in the order of knowing as such" (182).

Thus, with the above notions of the poetic and or literary being oriented beyond the text and toward the world, and of the poetic being "not absolutely certain…in the order of knowing", we can see the attribute of multiplicity belonging to the literary or poetic. With this in mind, we can begin to perceive of the possibility of a reader who is also multiple and thereby a singularity, a self and not a subject of the law. In contrast, MacLean's reader is judge and, with his or her implicit opinion, counsel. Doubling results in a doubling of the Same; the verbal body is captured by the signifier and the subject becomes a subject of the law. I will now turn to Atom Egoyan's film *The Sweet Hereafter* (1997) to consider how the poetic is affected by the reader, and how the law is put to flight in an ethos of a concern for the self. Here, the self becomes multiple and of the earth, the world, and nature—as Foucault perceives of nature, as "the balancing of life processes." It is necessary to consider an individual text or "case" since, as Foucault has pointed out, an "ecological discourse" is not founded upon "science or, at least…a technology underwritten by claims of truth" (1997:295). Rather, the Egoyan text is turned toward the search for truths, doctrines, fundamental principles, and rules of conduct. Doubling will indeed be central to the fictional, but not as belonging to the truth of the signifier or to context. Rather, as with Foucault's notion the fictional doubling will result in a virtual world, apart from the subject of law, involving *different* games of truth.

The Sweet Hereafter: An Exegesis

The Sweet Hereafter is a tale about a small isolated community in Canada. The town's crowded school bus is involved in an accident, and there are only two survivors, a girl, Nicole, of thirteen to fifteen years of age, and the bus driver, Delores. A lawyer, Mitchell Stevens, who specializes in class-action litigation, travels to the remote town from the city. He eagerly tries to persuade the locals to file compensation claims. All the locals who have lost loved ones (and this is a large proportion of the population) are initially appalled at the idea of compensation but begin, one by one, to concede, until only one person rejects the idea outright. The lawyer, after patiently sitting out the families' initial rejection of him and his ideas, convinces them of an obligation befalling the bus company. He addresses the responsibility and culpability of the bus company in a complicated discourse that involves an elision of the language of morality and the black-letter legal language of tort law. The love for the community's lost ones becomes entangled in and exploited by this discourse, which is a kind of moral imperative for retribution and a moral obligation concerning the safety of future travelers.

The theme of community is central to *The Sweet Hereafter*. The lawyer interviews the town folk about other members in the community and we find that the people of the town have an intimate knowledge of one another and are very interconnected. Subjectification, and its production through the community (to return to a theme from chapter 5), seems to be another theme the story quickly comes to as the film's focus shifts to the town member, Billy Hansel. Billy's wife has died of cancer two years previously, and each morning Billy follows the school bus in his own vehicle while his two children, who are on the bus, wave from the back window. Subjectification, to recap, is produced when a line of force "turns back on itself, meanders, grows obscure…works on itself or affects itself" (Deleuze, 1992:161). In following the bus, Billy is turning back on the line of force created by the bond of husband and wife (this line also includes their two children). In turning back on the line, Billy makes it grow obscure—it is, after all, an eccentric act that Billy affects.

As with the findings of chapter 5, what is needed for this subjectification is community, not only the small community of Hansel's family but
also the larger community as his wife's memory is also held by the town.
Following the school bus is an indication of this since the man's actions
are overt and belonging to the community. Here, then, is an example of
collective enunciation. In the story of *The Sweet Hereafter*, subjectification, in and by the community, functions to lessen the pain inflicted
by life since subjectification is a mode of becoming and thereby a type
of forgetting. (For example, Billy Hansel gives his dead wife's clothes to
Nicole and when she wears them they will remind him of his wife and
change her memory as well.) To round off the theme of subjectification
and community, all the community members in the small town are portrayed as very individual; there is nothing customary about their actions
or how they reflect on those actions. Moreover, the members of town
have each become who they are (their subjectification) interdependently
of the community.[12]

The Threat of Equivalence

The locals' initial rejection of the lawsuit would have supported and
maintained their community. However, the community comes under
threat as they near the point of compensation. The money the individual
families (effected by the bus crash) might receive should they win the
claim—and again, it should be noted, this is nearly the whole town—will
quantify their (loved ones') worth/self. The quantification of their worth
is a threat to the community since the suit introduces a "valorization and
finality" to the individuals, to repeat Guattari. (Guattari gives the example of the "valorization and finality" brought about by the equivalence,
labor/capital.) Where the community has, in the past, enabled involution,
individual becoming, self transformation, the compensation now threatens the community should each member be rendered down into an economy of exchange and thereby equivalence. If we compare this scenario
of equivalence to that of the labor/capital scenario, also brought about
by equivalence, we can say that the equivalence here is that of subject/
capital. What is at stake here, then, is no less than the community and self
(transformation).

Compensation in the form of capital threatens the community since
it brings signification to the members—destroying the collective, *partial*,
enunciation. Capital causes signification since it is a regime of equivalence and exchange in which diverse points, for example, the community
members, are made to resonate—in this case, in the unity of "victim."[13] In
other words, compensation abstracts the self to the concept, the signified
(of victim), and signification and reduces the members to the Same, to a

mere abstraction. (It is in an economy of equivalence and exchange that a life equates with one, since all numbers are divisible by one.) This connection between capital, signification, and the reduction of the individual is explained by Mark Seltzer in relation to the serial killer. In his book *Serial Killers,* Seltzer describes the psychopathology of the serial killer as being affected by the machine culture belonging to the Second Industrial Revolution. This culture is also known as "the information society" or "digital culture." In this culture

> the unremitting flood of numbers codes and letters is popularly seen as replacing real bodies and real persons.... What it really makes obsolete is the difference between bodies and information. As Norbert Wiener, the founder of cybernetics, put it some time ago, both persons and machines are a "communicative organism." (Seltzer, 1998:17)

The psychopathology of the serial killer is chameleon-like, he or she takes on their surroundings; her killings are literally a voiding of the body by numbers, murder by numbers, as literally befits their cybernetic world. Further on, Seltzer writes, "the serial killer...typifies typicality, the becoming abstract and general of the individuality of the individual" (1988:34). While *The Sweet Hereafter* is not a tale about a serial killer, the legal claim of compensation would result in a similar voiding of the body (of the collective) by numbers. In respect to the notion of the self being replaced by capital and its offspring, digital culture, it is interesting to ponder the gift the lawyer gives Nicole, by way of an enticement to go ahead with a claim: a computer!

The Sweet Hereafter becomes a tale about a struggle against the forces of equivalence that threaten the community and cause the loss of self. The collective body is the resistance to the voiding of the body/self by "digital" culture. The conflation of bodies and information/digitality/equivalence is countered by Guattari's notion that the only finality of human activity that one should accept is the production of a subjectivity that is self-enriching, polyphonic, and collective. It is a subjectification that saves the community in *The Sweet Hereafter.* Moreover, subjectification is seen to be due to a type of reading, a playing of the games of truth, *differently.* Another way to say this is to say that it is the poetic function and its role in the production of subjectification and community that saves the small-town community.

To Return to the Story...

Billy Hansel alone resists the lawyer's argument. He tries to discourage Stevens and the town, in their quest for compensation. It seems that having lost a loved one Billy knows that compensation would only rob the town's folk of what is left to them—their community. But this protest fails. However, Nicole, crippled by the accident, is able to do a lot more. She is at home when Billy calls on her parents, and she overhears him trying to persuade them to drop their claim. Her parents are the most unreserved of the town folk in thinking that compensation is a positive thing. And here the plot thickens—before the accident, Nicole was both Billy Hansel's babysitter and her father's secret lover. The day arrives for the hearing. Being the only surviving witness apart from the bus driver, Nicole's testimony is necessary to clear the driver, Delores, of any fault. However, the unlikely happens. Nicole declares that the driver was driving too fast—well above the limit. She says she could see the speedometer and that this was the cause of the accident. The (lawyer's) claim is thrown out. In playing this card, Nicole has saved the community. "The Sweet Hereafter" of the title song is a place where "everything is strange and new." The girl's move enables the town to continue its own involution, its immanent transfiguration, and to be a place that is always strange and new.

The girl's actions could possibly be interpreted as her taking revenge against her father, but the rest of the tale doesn't support this conclusion. To begin with, the girl's secret meetings with her father are given no more emphasis than her regular babysitting job. And the scenes in which Nicole is caring for Billy Hansel's children situate her in a community. She is akin to Deleuze and Guattari's notion of character in Minor Literature in that her story is that of a community's—rather than the individual (victim) of the bourgeois novel. It is at the babysitting events that we must look in order to see that when Nicole single-handedly scuttles the compensation claims, she does so in order to save the community and self, and not to take revenge against her father. We will also see in what follows that the role of doubling and the literary function bring about these events. Here, we will see the fictional as a process of doubling and an ethos that affects the self—a subjectification.

While babysitting, Nicole reads the children *The Pied Piper of Hamelin*. Nicole appears to have gathered that what happens in *The Pied Piper* is happening in her own life. Away from the babysitting scene, we see Nicole walking with her father to the place of their secret meetings. The story of the Pied Piper doubles the actions of Nicole and her father as we see Nicole remembering words from *The Pied Piper*:

> And came the children, tripping and skipping, running merrily after the wonderful music, the shouting and laughter. When lo! they reached the mountain side a wondrous portal open wide, as if a cavern was suddenly hollowed, and the piper advanced and the children followed. And when all

were in to the very last the door in the mountainside shut fast. Did I say all, no, one was lame and could not dance the whole of the way. And in after years, if you would blame his sadness, he was used to say; it is all dull in my town since my playmates left. I can't forget that I'm bereft of all the pleasant sights they see, which the piper also promised me. For he led he said, to a joyous land joining the town and just at hand were waters that gushed and fruit trees grew and flowers put forth the fairy hew, and everything was strange and new.

Like the pied piper, Nicole's father entices her with music; he is her musical producer and coach.

Further to the issue of doubling, *The Pied Piper* is also a fable about a stranger who comes to town (as with *Rumplestiltskin*) with a promise to fix the occupants' recent dire woes. The strangers, of course, turn out to be perilous. Mitchell Steven doubles as such a character. The other structural similarity is that, as with Rumplestiltskin, the life of the stranger is itself in poor repair: Rumplestiltskin is poor and lives underground and wants to escape, and the stranger in *The Sweet Hereafter* has a daughter with a heavy drug addiction. He is constantly escaping this reality. He also, seemingly, attempts to escape his sense of helplessness in the face of his daughter's addiction by supposedly helping others. It seems Nicole smells a rat when the pied piper's double reappears. The action Nicole takes to counter the two "Pied Pipers," that is, in order to overcome the individuating threat posed by the father and the lawyer, is derived from her reading practice.

Nicole's reading involves a consciousness of the doubling going on between the fable and her own life. This doubling, however, is not a mere doubling of the Same. We need to look at the play on narrative sequence in *The Sweet Hereafter* in order to see that the fable does not merely double Nicole's life. In the "real life" of the film the children have already gone over the cliff (they drown in a lake at the bottom of a hill, beneath ice). The *untimely* event of the pied piper's return, therefore, means the sequence of the story is out. This evokes notions of the eternal return, a return that returns differently. For Friedrich Nietzsche, the eternal return is the being of difference.[14] The *different* sequence of events demands that we read in a superlinear fashion. Superlinearity, to recall chapter 5, involves "continual variation" (Massumi, 1992:41), it is what Massumi calls the antiorder word. The antiorder word is like Nicole's reading, it involves "continual variation" (41). For Massumi, these variations relinquish unheard and implicit presuppositions in (my) lines, making my lines "superlinear." (Superlinear I have taken to be a subjectification, something *I* have invented, a meandering back along a lines of force.) An example of such an implicit presupposition in *The Sweet Hereafter* is that it is the community that are about to "go over the cliff," rather than the children. The *different* sequence of events of the fictional mode, then, as opposed to a doubling of the Same, provides implicit presuppositions that enable superlinearity and subjectification. As Nicole acts, she does so upon an implicit presupposition, thus, her line becomes superlinear; her untimely reading affects, not a subject of the law, but a being of difference, of becoming.

On the issue of doubling and narrative fiction, MacLean states that it is the "doubled-edged *weapon* of quotation" (1988:105) that the writer uses to "snare...his implied reader" (105). For MacLean, the fable is the most poignant example of the scene of performance or narrative contract since its story addresses or speaks to the audience's own circumstances, entrapping them and forcing them to participate (105). MacLean refers to this doubling as an "ironic consciousness" (105) because the reader has been unwittingly entrapped and his or her participation can therefore hardly be called conscious. In some respect this idea of MacLean's contradicts her notion discussed earlier that doubling awakens the reader to his or her unconscious drives. However, both ideas have consistencies with a Lacanian theory of language, and therefore there is a predominance of the signifier. Where MacLean discusses doubling as a form of entrapment, there are resonances with the Lacanian notion of language taking the place (doubling) for an object now lost to our conscious mind, making us dubiously conscious. Language also replaces an authentic body with an inauthentic, repeatable signifier. Doubling, in MacLean, then, is a doubling of the Same/signifier. There is no acknowledgment within this discussion on doubling of the *significance of difference*—between the fable and the narrative. MacLean's emphasis on entrapment indicates that the destination of narrative fiction is the subjugation of the reader by the repeating Letter, the signifier. Such a description of fictional doubling echoes Massumi's definition of the order word—rather than the antiorder word—which "makes me mouth existing words which places me in pre-existing structures" (1992:41). In such an understanding of doubling the subject is one of the law.

It is not, then, at the level of narrative (contract) that the fictional and the literary function reside, but in the realm of the implicit presupposition produced by the return of difference. This implicit presupposition needs in turn to be thought of in terms of subjectification. Subjectification is affected by the *difference* in repetition; *by meandering back along my lines*. It is not merely a matter of the difference between this narrative, as it repeats my narrative, and the narrative I create in the gaps of the existing narrative. But rather, what matters is the *difference* (per se) between the existing tale and the tale as it is retold by the narratee turned narrator.

This *difference* is the fictional. Foucault's distinction between the fable and the fictional is of interest here. In "Behind the Fable" (1998), Foucault states that "[t]he fable is made up of elements placed in a certain order. Fiction is the weaving of established relations, through the discourse itself. Fiction, an 'aspect' of the fable," writes Foucault (1998:136).[15] Here, the fictional is not fables (tales), either that of the narrator or the narratee. Rather, the fictional is an *aspect* of the tale or fable, produced by the weaving of established relations. The fictional is over and above the tale(s). At this point, the fictional may be able to be thought in similar terms to Derrida's notion of a poetics: a poetics is the untranslatable testimony, untranslatable because a poetics is exemplary (2000:180). It is a way of signing, "both sealing and unsealing" the possibility of the poem (or fiction). To recall my previous quote from Derrida: "a poetics...must also, as if across its generality, become, invent, institute, offer for reading, in an exemplary way...the possibility of this poem" (180). In other words, the fictional (like the poem) promises "in the act of its happening, the foundation of a poetics" (180). It, therefore, "cannot, it must not be absolutely certain, absolutely sure and certain in the order of knowing as such" (182).

The fictional, as it is produced by the reader, then, is a multiplicity and does not belong to the signifier. *It is a becoming imperceptible*, rather than a will to knowledge and power. This creation of a poetics by the reader is a subjectification as the reader becomes obscure through meandering back along given lines (to repeat Foucault's point about subjectification, from chapter 5). The act (of becoming imperceptible) is the creation of a line of escape or flight from the law. And because the reader/subjectification is always already a collective body, significantly, *it is within the community that subjectification is situated and toward which the implicit presupposition is directed*. That is, the fictional is not a structure into which *I* am made to fit—a text—as with MacLean's scene of performance, but a pragmatic moment in which the community, multiplicity, is kept afloat, alive. For MacLean, the text is significant for its "force," it is a structure that beats the reader into submission (1988:174–175). The best the reader can do is take the reins off the writer and "knock out the next set of readers" (174–175). In this case, says MacLean, "the donor and recipient of the message have established reciprocity of power" (175). Thus, it is that the text becomes the site of power belonging to tyranny of the signifier and fascistic. Contrary to this, the implicit presupposition breathes new *life* into the order word, as Massumi says (1992:41). (That is, the implicit presupposition belongs to the community, to multiplicity, and not the subject of the law.)

To Return to the Story, Once Again...

It seems Nicole has an eye for the superlinear; in refusing the sequence of events put forward by the law, either as the victim of mechanical negligence or the victim of her father's transgressions, in other words, in escaping signification, Nicole is free to scuttle the lawyer's claim, that is, she is free to transform events—thus, it is that she acts as an agent of subjectification. In not giving herself up to signification and the State, she is not a subject, preexistent, in some text, story, law, or structure, but is created processually, from an "untimely" reading. As a being of difference, Nicole, then, is multiple, she cannot be assimilated by a unifying apparatus. Nicole, as the agent of subjectification, needs only one thing to survive and that is the community, or, life itself, since it is here she can continue to become. And because of her dependence on the community for becoming hers is a partial enunciation, belonging to a collective. (It is no wonder she scuttles the lawyer's claim that threatens the community.) As though to allegorize this figure of becoming, Nicole is a character of action rather than many words—she rarely speaks, and, of course, she does not explain her actions.

In the End, an Ethico-Aesthetics

The Sweet Hereafter is an allegory about subjectification affected by the doubling belonging to the fictional. It is a story of reading in the fictional mode. And it is a story about the fictional as an ethic of a concern for self, for subjectfication. The thesis of this book, then, places fictional reading far from entrapment, from the weapon of the (writer's) text, or a double negative. Rather, here, the implicit presuppositions, difference, doubling, breathes new life into the order word (to briefly translate MacLean's scene of performance), quite literally.

As mentioned earlier, in The Sweet Hereafter, it is Nicole's subjectification that saves the town. Her subjectification is directly connected to her handling of knowledge, the "knowledge" of her secret love affair with her father, the "knowledge" of the bus crash. Deleuze points out that knowledge is the affect of a relationship between one point and another (a capture) that forms a line. This line that is invisible and unsayable, instead, works as a force, as power. Lines form parallel forces that affect one another; they become power and knowledge (the Signifier). Nicole subverts such forces. For example, she deforms the line formed from the points, "mother" and "father." For Deleuze, subjectification occurs when the linear or parallel force is refused by another force. Subjectification is the process whereby, to quote Deleuze: "instead of entering into a linear relationship with another force, (the force) turns back on itself, works on itself or affects itself" (1992:161). When the girl takes the father for a lover, she circumvents the linear forces; mother-daughter, daughter-father. She has, to paraphrase Massumi, not toed the line, not plodded along the straight and narrow path down the aisle—but married the void, become superlinear (41). In taking the father as a lover, a leap has occurred, a superlinearity, that can never be (cash) converted to linearity and thereby knowledge. In the symbolic order, for example, such a move simply doesn't *make sense*. The girl's secret is precisely *not a knowledge*. It is *unknown, antiknowledge*. In this one move, the mother ceases to be a mother, the daughter a daughter, and the father a father. They are now, rather, three subjectifications, outside of the law and of equivalence. In this story "incest" becomes the figure of a line of flight—other figures could be used. It is this unknown aspect, the force of subjectification, city folk often find circumspect in small-town's folk. Across a certain genre, into which we can put the film *Southern Comfort* (1981), it breathes paranoia into the outsiders.

The girl's implicit presupposition (her own unspoken "knowledge"), which she brings to the taking of her disposition in the local school hall, and which she enacts, is: You don't give your*self* up. You don't become a victim, a casualty, that is, you don't become a statement of the State, of legal, medical or psychopathological discourse, a statistic (of knowledge in general), a number, an abstraction; You don't enter equivalence (be it digital or linguistic) and thereby be voided. Instead, to refer to Brian Massumi, you marry the void, you become imperceptible.

Becoming imperceptible is affected, then, in becoming—in the *difference* between my story and the story it doubles. It is in this difference that the self, as imperceptible and multiple, resides. To return (when I meander back along my line) "is the being of becoming" (Deleuze, 1983:189). There are many returns in *The Sweet Hereafter*, many accounts of doubling back, in the fable retold, redoubled, in the man who lost his wife and then his two children, and in the girl who becomes a cripple. (Was she not always a kind of cripple?)[16] In such a return is "the unity of multiplicity," or subjectification.

To return, to repeat, this is the literary function or mode itself. In this way the fictional can be said to be quintessentially literary. The girl's ethics are those of the literary (aesthetic), an ethico-aesthetics. She refuses to reduce the events of her life to the abstractions of incest and cripple, or, moreover, victim. She refuses to tell. Instead she continues in the mode of the literary itself, which is a mode of concatenation, of never stopping to say A equals B (e.g., her father and her equalling incest) and thereby forming concentric circles, an exterior plane to A and B that captures both. But rather she adds another segment according to the existing segments, a meandering along her own line. This is the mode of concatenation, an A+B+C+..., a rhizomic, horizontal plane. In this way the girl does not leave the horizontal plane of the fictional. As a result, she is able to play her hand when the time comes, according to the needs of multiplicity and the community. Thus, she maintains the community, and perhaps more importantly her place in it. In the mode of concatenation she saves the plane of consistency of the community and thus escapes placement within a symbolic order—the order of equivalence. (There is no reason, no teleology pertaining to the community.) Nicole's story—doubled in *The Pied Piper* and *Rumplestiltskin* (Rumplestiltskin wants gold from the straw the girl weaves, and Nicole's father wants money for Nicole's crippled state)—has taught Nicole not to seek justice from above and thus negate your self. Instead of negating her self, of deferring to an exterior line, the State, and thereby abstracting her self (within the category "victim"), Nicole puts her self *into* the story, *enacting* the literary mode. In this mode, Nicole has total power, and she is empowered. She is not alienated—as she would be if she *sold* her story to the State. In the community Nicole is not a cripple or a victim (of incest) but irreducible, multiple, not least because of the latest act (scuttling the insurance claim), which she single-handedly is able to perform! Because of the immanent nature of the aesthetic, there is no way of ultimately knowing its mask. Its disguise is its protection against capture. Nicole seems to know this and uses this mask to optimum effect, she hides behind her mask or, rather, within her mask. In playing the game the way the collective demands, Nicole is able to continue to meander along her own line, continue to grow (obscure), affect her own subjectification, and not deliver the father a sum in place of her *self* and be forever in his *debt*—mere by-product or waste. Play and the notion of the game are crucial here (as MacLean would acknowledge); there is no blueprint for the actions of the collective members. Survival of the community and the self is determined by how well the player can recast the suppositions (order words). In other words, on how well one can *play the game*, winning with a hand of implicit presupposition and superlinearity. To do this, to play the presuppositions, one needs the collective on side for implicit presuppositions belong to the community, they are the "knowledge" of the community, of the collective and horizontal plane. The girl certainly knows this game of presupposition. Instead of telling the "truth," her words don't mean what they say. When she gives her "evidence," she is unconcerned about telling the "truth" because to do so, to be the State's witness, is to obey and thereby be subjugated by the order word—the State literally walking off with her in her words. Instead, she resists this capture with her words: the bus driver was driving too fast. With these words is the implicit presupposition that protects her and the community. Both remain invisible in the mask of performativity, and thereby impervious to the State's capture. Without the community there would be no point to her words.

The community then functions as the machinic assemblage of enunciation. (Deleuze and Guattari point out that all statements are a product of a machinic assemblage, which they also refer to as collective agents of enunciation. By "collective agents" is meant "not peoples or societies but multiplicities" [1987:37]. Elsewhere they write that "*[c]ollective assemblages of enunciation* function directly with *machinic assemblages*" 7.) When the girl plays the card she does, a unique card, available to her as a member of the community, and unavailable to her as a statistic of the State, she performs the community. This is to say that the community is performed, not spoken or known. Its existential refrain is outside the law. Pure performativity. As if to hint at this point, Nicole's role is of someone particularly self-contained, reserved, and nonverbal.

Egoyan's *The Sweet Hereafter,* then, appears as a fable of the fictional mode. The fable is a genre that derives from the imperative speech act, if we accept André Jolles's typological study of literature that based genre types on linguistic forms of everyday speech (Ducrot and Todorov, 1979:155). The fable, therefore, like the order word, is an *imperative duty, a command not to be avoided.* In situating the fictional within the fable, Egoyan tells a story of its pragmatic quality. The kind of action the fictional commands, it turns out, is an ethics for the self. This fable tells us of the importance of the fictional, of being at any one moment at play, in a performance of the Earth, which is always new, always different. To this it opposes us being an audience to an existing world, a world of the Same.

The fictional functions, then, to create a continuum between the sign and life—quite opposed to its reputation as being *just* fiction. Though it is unapologetically of the symbol, of the simulacra, it is, however, contrary to postmodern theory, not of the Signifier, which is a capture of the aesthetic function. The fictional is political and crucial to the community's well-being—to both its existence and its freedom within.

Conclusion: Degrees of Freedom

This book has developed the theorization of the aesthetic of verbal art. The purpose of this theorization has not been to create a formula for creative writing—that is, for artistic practice—but to consider the literary in respect to questions of ethics and politics. Such a theorization, however, might also come to inform pedagogical practice. The theorization of the literary, like Guattari's own theorization, has not been done in order to arrive at stable systems of analysis (of the literary) but to open up the field to an ever-changing and differently focused exploration of the aesthetic. Rather than criticism, the activity of this book has been the analysis and theorization of the literary function for the way in which it has something to teach other fields, including those that theorize subjectivity, community, and pedagogy. The literary has been considered in light of possible ways of being that might set us free or make us freer. In doing so, the literary has been considered in terms of strategies and self-governmentality that result in the formation of subjectification. In what follows, I consider the key aspects of the literary function, in relation to key questions raised by this text, such as the questions of capture and equivalence. In doing so, I briefly consider the work of American writer Bret Easton Ellis and British musician Tricky.

The Literary Function Belongs to Social Production

The literary regime of signs belongs to the literary function once this regime is taken over by a desire of a particular kind. As discussed in the introduction, for Deleuze and Guattari, desire *is* social production, that is, social production is made up of desiring machines. And because reality is invested differently by desire, different regimes result. For Deleuze and Guattari, then, a distinction needs to be made between these *regimes*. It has been the work of this book to distinguish the machinic functioning of the literary regime of signs in order to understand its desire. The literary function has been discussed in terms of the production of self and community. The word "self," as referred to in the course of the discussion in chapter 6, indicates not an individual subjectivity given as in-itself, but rather, *a social production* and a subjectification.[1] Thus, the self in this text is not a figure seen to transcend society—just as the literary machine itself does not—but one that belongs to social production. Such a self is affected by the literary machine's engagement with the various machines it comes into contact with. For example, in the case of novelist Bret Easton Ellis, the capitalist machine is employed, and in the case of the English/Jamaican musician Tricky, the "dub" machine, belonging to Black America, is among many other machines that are employed. As John Marks says, "The writer has 'seen or heard'…events which are collective" (1998:125).

A Line of Flight

But while the literary machine is located in social production, its function is that of the production of a line of flight. Deleuze writes that the line of flight of literature puts "something to flight…a system to flight as one bursts a tube" (Deleuze and Parnet, 1987:26). This conceptualization of the effect of literature is not possible in a linguistically based conceptualization of signs. Here, the (literary) sign is considered in terms of its social value and signs are considered in terms of exchange only—without the possibility of affecting the system in which they circulate. Equally, then, the notion of a line of flight is not possible when there is a link made between the reality of literary expression and representation. Rather, the literary machine's function does something to language itself. Marks paraphrases Deleuze as saying that "[w]riters worthy of attention" employ a "sceptical stance" toward language itself (Marks, 1998:123). "[L]anguage is pushed towards its 'asyntaxic' and 'aggrammatical' limits" (Marks quoting Deleuze, 123). Such writing is said to create a "'new language'" (123), or a foreignness in the existing language. On the one hand this skepticism toward language can be understood in deconstructive terms, as when Barthes says that literary writing (or trans-writing) opposes the idiolect and fights it (1984:168). For Deleuze, as well, literature's enemy is the concealing nature of language itself:

> "[I]t is not only that words are liars; they are so marked with calculations and significations, not to mention with intentions, personal memories and old habits which have cemented, that if a breach does occur in their surface it closes up again immediately. It congeals. It imprisons and suffocates us," (Marks quoting Deleuze, 1998:184).

Literary language functions to dissolve language "so that the void is visible, so that the statement becomes impersonal, indirect" (Marks, 1998:184). In part it does this because it is characterized by " 'the force of the impersonal' freeing us from the first and second person" (Marks quoting Deleuze, 125). It manages to transform the definite into the indefinite. A pure intensity results " 'which pierces the surface' " (Marks quoting Deleuze, 184).

Repetition by the literary also turns the familiar into the impersonal, as with Bret Easton Ellis's repetition—within each work and across his oeuvre—of decadent, late capitalist society. But parody and deconstruction are not the sole purpose of this repetition. This book has worked toward and argued for a more positive outcome resulting from the *line* of flight of literature. In this text literature's line of flight has not merely amounted to an *escape* from language. It is not a fleeing or exit from the world (Deleuze and Parnet, 1987) or a negative expression of the kind de Certeau laments with respect to the actions of May '68. The literary function designates more than a refusal and is more than a symptom of language, as was the action of May '68 for de Certeau. Rather, subjectification ensues.

Subjectification

In the repetition of the writing—over an oeuvre, in each work, as a result of observation itself, or, as a result of the use of similar or slightly changed sounds—the artist produces a line. Or, a line is produced when the artist meanders back along his or her own pathway. The pathway is more than a recounting of personal experience. It is in fact not a recounting at all but an *acting upon* our experience. Our own "never-repeatable 'place' in being" (Bakhtin, 1993:xxii) means we must act upon events according to "a unique answerability' " (Bakhtin, 1993:xxii). That is, we must *carry out something in relation to* the world and objects in order to understand our *unique* relationship to it. This, for Bakhtin, is a once-occurrent event. This relationship between our acts and our accounting of them is responsible for subjectivity. It is the artist who *makes something* of this subjectivity; a subjectification is the result, that is, a cartography, a territory, is the result. Deleuze and Guattari bring the surveyor and the artist together. They ask, is the artist not "the first person to set out a boundary stone, or to make a mark?" (1987:316). But this text has also been interested in the *difference* between the property developer and the artist, and in particular, the literary artist. Deleuze and Guattari point out that territories not only have expressions, they also have functions (315). The "Lullaby...territorializes the child's slumber, the Lover's Refrain...territorializes the sexuality of the loved ones" (Deleuze and Guattari, 1987:327). This text has sought to know what the function of the literary regime of signs—or expression—territorializes. And furthermore, what ethics does the literary expression affect?[2]

Multiplicity

The literary function territorializes multiplicity. Multiplicity and the literary expression can be thought about, in part, with the use of Guattari's notion of pathic knowledge and Bakhtin's notion of the once-occurrent event. Pathic knowledge is the result of what Guattari refers to as the existential function, which, using certain discursive links, "diverts [these discursive links] from their signifying, denotational and propositional incidences" (1995:60). A great amount of attention has been given to the issue of parody in postmodern literature,[3] but this is, in general, a paradigmatic and syntagmatic line of enquiry (which restricts understanding to signifying semiotics) and does not consider the nature of the discursive links, links made across a work, or what Guattari refers to as "transversality." Transversality produces a-signifying semiotics. These are opposed to signifying semiotics that are "the double bind of the horizontal proliferation of signifiers and the vertical interpretation of signified" (Bosteels, 1995:353). Transversality proceeds "along a dimension that is diagonal" (Bosteels, 353). The discursive links of a literary work or oeuvre bring about a consistency of the discursive systems (Guattari, 60), and thus they escape spatiotemporal coordinates. Thus it is that pathic knowledge does not "engender a rational explanation" (61).[4] Instead, pathic knowledge becomes "existential transference" or "non-discursive transitivism" (Guattari, 61). Another way to express this is to say that pathic knowledge is the detournement of discursivity (Guattari, 1995:26), a detournement, not into another discursivity but of discursivity toward matter. An alchemical transformation of the signifying regime of signs takes place. An irreducible, irreversible territory of existential or pathic knowledge replaces the atomization of space—produced by the equivalent and exchange function belonging to the signifier. The result is an ontological crystallization. In this environment, the subject ceases to be a subject of the law—that is, the destination of a (preexisting) order/structure and a unit of equivalence and exchange. Here, language ceases as language, that is, it ceases to function as an ordering system. A subject/object world gives way to a production of Self or once-occurrent Being. Once-occurrent Being is multiple since, as Bakhtin points out, in the once-occurrent event of subjectification, the object is never "totally finished" (1993:32). This is because, "[i]nsofar as I am actually experiencing an object, even if I do so by thinking of it, it becomes a changing moment in the ongoing event of my experiencing it" (32). Pathic knowledge, then, is affected by the once-occurrent event of subjectification; it is the refrain or territoriality of ontological affirmation. Pathic knowledge thus affirms once-occurrent Being, in a way that "theoretical cognition" (Bakhtin, 1993:9) or abstract thought cannot.

Capture and Occupation

Throughout the text I have referred to ways in which the literary function is captured, for example, as a result of a linguistic analysis of the performative, and as a result of a narratological analysis of the fictional. But the literary function also performs its own capture. The two captures are, however, different in kind. The literary function begins its capture by diverting discursive links from their "signifying, denotational and prop-ositional incidences" (Guattari, 1995:60). It does this in a variety of ways. For example, the musician-artist Tricky, takes singing and turns it toward speech; he takes talking and turns it toward whispering; he takes narra-tive and makes it discontinuous, he takes a dub and mixes it with many more music genres to form what is being called Trip Hop. These links are diverted when they are brought together in a "Tricky" assemblage—which has no denotation but rather forms a line of subjectification. (The collective nature of contemporary form is of course well theorized as, and within, postmodern aesthetic; however, the affective attribute of the diagram is far less well understood.) Bret Eason Ellis takes the line of decadent capitalism and meanders back along it, that is, he repeats the theme and incidence of decadent capitalist society to a point of entire saturation. The signs are diverted from their denotational function when they take on this involution. Signification is made up of lines of force formed by the relationship of one point with another, and as mentioned in chapter 5, these lines of force are the dimension of power, which Deleuze refers to as "the third dimension of *space*, internal to the [social] appara-tus" (1992:160, my italics). The involuted line bears no relation to another point, outside it. Thus, such a line becomes rhythmical, a refrain. For what does it *mean* when a statement—such as, "decadent capitalism"—re-peats without variation? In short, a thesis cannot be deducted from such repetition. Such a line is *partial* because it is an utterance folded back on itself. The line has thus grown obscure, gone underground, *bypassed itself*, as Deleuze writes (see chapter 5). Thus it is that the literary function captures signifying "space."

The capture by the literary function is a kind of occupying force but not of a dominating nature, rather, the result is an ethics of a concern for the self—to which I return shortly. The literary function, like de Certeau's notion of "tactic," "insinuates itself into the other's place, fragmentarily, without taking it over in its entirety, without being able to keep it at a distance" (de Certeau, 1988:xix). As a result of its partial nature, the literary function, like de Certeau's tactic, has "no base where it can capitalize on its advantages, prepare its expansions, and secure independence with respect to circumstances" (xix). It does not, thereby, form a "borderline distinguishing the other as a visible totality" (xix) (although the literary expression may certainly be captured by such forces). In other words, the literary function cannot form abstract thought or signification and thereby, like de Certeau's notion of strategy, operate in isolation to its environment. It is this ability of abstract thought that turns thought into a colonizing force, and it is here where thought becomes the official or proper *space*. It is here where the subject is experienced as a function of a structure that replicates across all environments.[5] "The 'proper' is a victory of space over time," writes de Certeau (xix). But equally, we could say that the literary function is the victory of time over space. De Certeau notes that "a tactic depends on time—it is always on the watch for opportunities that must be seized 'on the wing'" (xix). The literary function, as a once-occurrent event, is a seizing "on the wing." The once-occurrent event is the result of the world or object being intonated with one's emotional-volitional tone due to one's personal response to the object obtainable only in the act—or "on the wing." As Bakhtin writes, in the once-occurrent event "[e]verything that is actually experienced is experienced as something given [the proper] and as something-yet-to-be-determined" [in time], (Bakhtin 1993:33)—or, we could say, with one's involution. It is this relationship to time, and not space, that makes the literary expression an assemblage of the Self. As Bakhtin says, in the once-occurrent event everything experienced "enters into an effective relationship to me within the unity of the ongoing event encompassing us" (33). In Deleuze and Guattari's parlance, we could say the literary expression is a Body without Organs (BwO), upon which we lodge ourselves. It is also where we take flight from the order word and all preexisting structures in which we are reduced to a function of that system.

Performativity and Pragmatics

Performativity and pragmatics have been at the heart of the thesis of this book. In revisiting and broadening these terms, we have been able to theorize the literary function in terms of ethics as well as critique existing uses of these terms and their effects upon existing approaches to the category of the literary. The performative, here, has been seen to be more than a matter of subjugation, the subject split by the doubly articulated utterance into the subject of enunciation (*je*) and the subject of the enounced (*moi*). In this book, the literary regime of signs is seen to produce an action (a performative act), an event, which is irreversible, unpresentable. Thus, signs are returned to the flow of the real, the material. Here, the subject escapes subjugation and instead becomes a subjectification, multiple. Here, in the literary function, there is a pragmatics of the multiple, of becoming.

As we are now at a consensus about the paradigmatic shift to the digital apparatus, it is important to restate the fit of the filmic and new media with performative pragmatics and its concomitant affective reterritorialization. The filmic, because of its "extraordinary movement" (Deleuze, 1991:37) and new media because of its " 'remediating,' i.e. translating, refashioning, and reforming other media" (Manovich, 2001:95) *in extremis*, are both in the *business* of the existential refrain! The prevalence of new media and cinema means that we must now consider a world according to electronic and digital literacy where the flow of signs find their destination in the real, the material, and not in strategic operations that enable a sequestering of territory. Julian Assange is himself a living, material, character in such a story; in fact, his is a metastory of the event of digital writing and technology and its ability to perform existential refrains that undermine the stability of space. Hacking, it seems, is the world's newest ethical dilemma. Considering these events there is certainly an urgency for the exploration of aesthetics (the existential refrain) in regard to ethics, asking what transversalities are being made, and why?

An Ethics of Concern for the Self and Becoming

The literary function includes a lesson for a way of being. From this lesson our lives and selves are able to change. Furthermore, from this, our culture and our society are able to change. Our experience, selves, lives, culture, and society are girded by fixed structures, by what de Certeau refers to as strategies, what Foucault refers to as games of truth, housed in science or institutions, by what Massumi, Deleuze and Guattari refer to as the order word, by the Signifier, as theorized by Jacques Lacan (1985). All such structures homogenize, reduce, and, thereby, control our experience, selves, lives, culture, and society.

What is needed in order to escape coercive practices or practices of control, as Foucault, de Certeau and Deleuze and Guattari have said, in one way or another, (see, for example, Foucault, 1997:281–301), is to play the same game differently. Ironically, escape does not come about by ignoring the existing games, the official truths, but by playing them differently. It is the literary function/regime of signs that reemploys/repeats these games, these existent practices, differently. When we play the game differently, from the position of once-occurrent Being—meandering back along one's lines—when we reorder discursive links, we turn the order word into the antiorder word (the antiorder word involves continual variation). Continual variation releases implicit presuppositions in our lines making those lines superlinear and a subjectification. These are no more order words. The literary function *creates* a language according to our Selves. This is an irreversible and irreducible body (a BwO) and it becomes (a place for) the *Self.* Here, the subject has undergone a transformation from being spoken by preexistent structures, the law, the order word, to creating an event *upon which future events may take place.*

There is an example in the literary function of becoming, an example for the practice in life of becoming, the practice of meandering back along one's path. An involution. It is a way of escaping by creating new assemblages (BwO). This is where the Self resides, at the edges of culture, where the social is in a state of becoming. What is important is the relationship between walking back along one's own path and creating a becoming, a different future. These two activities are ironically linked. The literary function, then, is not about remembering but forgetting, creating.

Franz Kafka's parable "Before the Law" (in Derrida, 1992), is a story about a subject and the law. The subject approaches the gates of the law and asks the gatekeeper there if he may enter. The gatekeeper puts the subject off, telling him "he cannot grant admittance at the moment" (183). The subject eventually dies waiting to be granted admittance to the law. But before he dies he draws the gatekeeper near and says to him, " 'Everyone strives to reach the Law so how does it happen that for all these many years no one but myself has ever begged for admittance?' " (Derrida quoting Kafka, 184). The gatekeeper replies, " 'No one else could ever be admitted here, since this gate was made only for you. I am now going to shut it' " (Derrida quoting Kafka, 184). Kafka's subject, it seems, was put off by the many barriers of the law, its architecture, its structures, its gates. He was put off by the law's treatment of him. The subject thus failed to see the potentially subjective nature of the law and the potential, therein, for subjectification. I close now on my own parable of a subject who finds a way of overcoming the gatekeeper and entering the Law.

THE STORY TELLER

There is a girl who is raised in deprivation and isn't taught to read. But she likes to tell stories. She tells stories about the people in her neighbourhood. She embellishes the lives of the people in her neighbourhood, not because she doesn't know about their lives but because she finds in her own stories more fun, more interest. She tells the stories to her mother while her mother prepares the vegetables for the evening meal. The mother likes to listen to the girl's stories but one evening she reveals a concern to the girl. She is afraid that the girl might be developing a habit of lying. The mother says to the girl, "These stories aren't true, are they?" The girl is momentarily confused; she never said the stories were true but she knew her mother's joy in the stories was dependent on them being true stories of the people in her street, and so she always pretended they were true. She had enjoyed her mother's joy in the stories' possible realness. She was disappointed at her mother's apparent and petty concern that she might be in danger of turning into a Liar. The girl thought quickly in order to get back to the story she was telling, and said, "a lady told me." Her mother seemed satisfied with this response and was happy for the girl to continue to tell the story.

Notes

Introduction: The Literary Function

1. Norman Doidge, *The Brain That Changes Itself* (2010).
2. Gilles Deleuze and Felix Guattari, *What Is Philosophy?* (1994:164).
3. The term "affect" has here the inference given to it by Deleuze and Guattari, which is to express a body that is the result of an action and that does not precede the action. The term does not, therefore, correspond to the usual grammatical usage or the current theoretical usage, which may denote either intensity, emotion, or feeling.
4. Gilles Deleuze and Felix Guattari, *What Is Philosophy?* (1994:164).
5. Paul Dawson, "Towards a New Poetics in Creative Writing Pedagogy" (2003).
6. According to D. G. Myers (1993), the genesis of the discipline of creative writing, as it exists in our Anglophone institutions today, began in the mid-1940s with Norman Foerster at the University of Iowa. In Australia, Brian Dibble at the Curtin University offered Australia's first creative writing program, ca. 1974, with an eight-subject major in the undergraduate program.
7. Texts used in such curricula include *Making Stories: How Ten Australian Novels Were Written*, Kate Grenville and Sue Woolfe (1993); *The Creative Writing Handbook*, ed., John Singleton (1996); and *Creative Writing: A Practical Guide*, Julia Casterton (1998).
8. This is evident, for example, in the name of the creative writing degree at the University of Technology, Sydney, which is called the BA in Arts and Communication (Writing and Contemporary Cultures). In the degree description it states: "Great emphasis is placed upon the writer within society." Students are introduced to "knowledge of Australian cultural traditions" and the student learns a "range of strategies for dealing with cultural and social problems" (UTS web page, 2003). The subjects pertaining to this course are listed as: Communication and Information Environments; Media, Information and Society; Contemporary Cultures 1 and 2; Power and Change in Australia; and Colonialism and Modernity
9. For Deleuze and Guattari, a Body without Organs is an experimenting body, one that does not adhere to the "straight" or conventional way of performing or behaving. Write Deleuze and Guattari, the Body without Organs "is where everything is played out" (1987:151), hence, the political nature of the BwO.

10. For instance, as with their coauthored works, *A Thousand Plateaus: Capitalism and Schizophrenia* (1987) and *Kafka, Toward a Minor Literature* (1986).

11. In Deleuzeoguattarian pragmatics, there is no subject of enunciation, rather, there are only collective assemblages of enunciation. In *Dialogues*, both Parnet and Deleuze speak, but they speak the same enunciation as one another. This has made attributing the utterances to any one of these subjects all but impossible. It would be more accurate to say, *"Dialogues* says...," however, this is not the accepted form and so the solving of the issue must remain ambiguous.

12. "Regime" is first used by Deleuze and Guattari in addressing the question of desire, and it is important to visit this connection in order to understand the breadth of the function of the regime in Deleuze and Guattari's work. For Deleuze and Guattari, desire does not belong to a special form of existence such as "a mental or psychic reality" (1983:30). Rather, desire is "one and the same as social production" (30); it produces reality. Write Deleuze and Guattari, "There is never any difference in nature between the desiring machines and the technical social machines" (31). They say that where there is a distinction to be made is in the *regimes* of the desiring machines. (In French, the word *régime* has a number of meanings "including...form of government; a set of laws...speed of operation" (31), and Deleuze and Guattari use the word in a variety of ways.) [Different] regimes, then, replace a conceptualization of existence based upon a split between the psychic realm as fantasy and the social realm as reality. Deleuze and Guattari point out that it is rather the case that reality is invested differently by desire (and different regimes result). For example, "revolutionary desire" (30) may be invested into an existing social field or machine that is repressive (31).

13. In discussing Lyotard's notion of "little narratives," Guattari touches upon the significance of performativity and pragmatics to the study of the literary regime of signs; "[o]nly little narratives of legitimation, in other words, the 'pragmatics of linguistic particles' that are multiple, heterogeneous, and whose performativity would be only limited in time and space, can still save some aspect of justice and freedom" (1996:111).

14. The postmodern cultural-critical turn referred to here is not meant as an entire paradigm of theory but a turn that has had particular figures and instantiations, not necessarily commensurate. The postmodern cultural-critical turn mapped here is found in the contemporary philosophical pragmatism of Richard Rorty as well as a variety of literary and cultural postmodernisms. This text has mapped these instantiations, not in order to give a definitive account of the treatment of the literary in a postmodern context (an impossible task due to the ambiguity of the notion of postmodernism itself), nor to account for the treatment of the literary in all cases of cultural criticism and studies. Rather, the aim in mapping a postmodern cultural-critical turn is in order to establish a symptom relating to the current negation of the exploration of the literary as an immanent regime of signs.

15. For Deleuze and Guattari "[a] book exists only through the outside and on the outside" (1987:4). The important inquiry, for Deleuze and Guattari, is

into the relation between the literary machine and the various machines it plugs into, such as the war machine of Kleist. The aim of this text is to take aesthetics also to the outside, beyond an autonomous or scientific study, and into a political and ethical dimension.

16. The quote from Deleuze is from *Negotiations* (1990:143).

17. Parnet acknowledges that newspapers, radio, the cinema, and TV do have the potential to release Creative functions that no longer pass through the author (1987:28).

18. Throughout the text, there is a proliferation of interconnected terms, such as creative writing, literary expression, literary aesthetic, literary machine, literary function, creative function, literary mode, the performative, pragmatics, and the aesthetic. The meaning of each of these terms is determined by the context of the discussion, and so it is not the case that one term is interchangeable with another. However, they are related; for example, it is the *literary expression* that is responsible for the *literary function*. Together, these terms form a cartography that circumnavigates the text.

19. Cultural critics include Antony Easthope, *Literary into Cultural Studies* (1991), John Docker, *Postmodernism and Popular Culture, A Cultural History* (1994), Catherine Belsey, *Critical Practice* (1991), and Tony Bennett, *Formalism and Marxism* (1979).

20. Milner points out that Leavisite literary criticism, which is taught in Australian schools today, has "institutionalised claims to authoritative cultural judgement" (1996:55). This is the effect of a critical approach based upon opinion. The aesthetic (value), for F. R. Leavis, was "somehow absent rather than present" (8) and therefore there was "no need of any abstract theory of aesthetics" (8). The value of a text was thought by Leavis to be obvious. Leavis shunned "the dead hand of a positivist empiricism" (14) found in sociology, "which would suppress the literary, the critical, the aesthetic" (14). But, for cultural criticism, the "cultivated theoretical inarticulacy of this Leavisite aesthetic" (8) produced a culture singular in nature "predicated on the prior assumption of a white, Anglo-Saxon, middle-class masculinity" (55). Says Milner, "[t]here was no theoretical space at all for the Islamic, the female, the proletarian, even 'the scientific,' in Leavis's famous claim that culture is necessarily singular" (55).

21. Texts that focus on the shift from literary to cultural studies include: Antony Easthope's *Literary into Cultural Studies* (1991), John Docker's *Postmodernism and Popular Culture, A Cultural History* (1994), Terry Eagleton's *Literary Theory, An Introduction* (1985), and Tony Bennett's *Outside Literature* (1990).

22. For example, Milner says, "Williams still accepted an essentially Leavisite notion of literary value and still shared in the alarm at the potentially damaging consequences of commercial culture" (1996:32).

23. In the *Columbia Dictionary of Modern Literary and Cultural Criticism* (1995), the only entry under the keyword "Literary" is "Literary mode of production," which belongs to a cultural-criticism approach to literature. All traces of early aesthetic approaches to the literary have disappeared;

for instance, there is no entry for "Literariness," or for "Literary Function." Recent aesthetic approaches to literature are also absent, for example, that of Deleuze and Guattari's term, "Minor Literature."

24. Richard Hoggart, *The Uses of Literacy* (1958).

25. Deleuze, in *Negotiations*, defends his practice of putting forward "raw concepts," such as multiplicity, difference, and repetition, while others, such as Foucault, work more with mediations. He states "I've never renounced a kind of empiricism, which sets out to present concepts directly. I haven't approached things through structure, or linguistics or psychoanalysis, through science or even through history, because I think philosophy has its own raw material that allows it to enter into more fundamental external relations with these other disciplines" (1990:89).

26. The internal quote in this quote from Milner is from Fredric Jameson, *The Political Unconscious: Narrative as a Socially Symbolic Act* (1981:13).

1   Being Constructivist

1. For Deleuze and Guattari, the geological does not merely provide "historical form with a substance and variable places" (1994:96) but is also mental—a mental landscape.

2. In *Dialogues*, Deleuze again says that the "philosophy-becoming...has nothing to do with the history of philosophy" (1987:2).

3. Deleuze and Guattari's own *A Thousand Plateaus; Capitalism and Schizophrenia* (1987) is exemplary of a philosophy that speaks to nonphilosophers. Perhaps it is for this reason that it is, at times, skirted by those who associate with the discipline of philosophy.

4. The question of the nonreflexivity and metaphysicality of this position is also raised further on in this chapter.

5. See "Conclusion," *Difference and Repetition* (Deleuze, 1994) for a discussion of the paradoxical notion of philosophy's groundless grounds.

6. Importantly, Deleuze and Guattari are not mentioned directly by Rorty as belonging to Philosophy.

7. Lance Olsen, *Circus of the Mind in Motion: Postmodernism and the Comic Vision.* (1990).

8. This, of course, has already taken place where performativity has been deployed further as a field as legal philosophy, literary studies, cultural studies, and contemporary philosophy.

2   Rethinking the Performative in Pragmatics

1. Lyotard's *The Postmodern Condition, A Report of Knowledge* (1984) is an early and significant contribution to the pragmatic nature of knowledge and the place of aesthetic discourse in such a context.

2. Nietzsche's, Hobbes's, and Foucault's notion of knowledge as power, further elaborates this idea.

3. A-signifying semiotics is explained by Bruno Bosteels in his article, "From Text to Diagram: Towards a Semiotics of Cultural Cartography" (1995), as exceeding the signifying semiotics, formed from substances of content and expression, or signifiers and signifieds. The signifying semiotic is the result of a double articulation of the syntagmatic and paradigmatic axes. A-signifying semiotics, on the other hand, adds a third, diagrammatic axis to these existing axes, by proceeding "along a dimension that is diagonal" (1995:353). The a-signifying semiotic works "flush with the real, beneath the relations of signification, representation, and designation, and have a direct purchase on the continuum of material flow" (352). Bosteels points out that signification and interpretation go hand in hand with a "subjectivity, split into the subject of enunciation (*je*) and the subject of the enounced (*moi*), which are both subjugated to the signifying chain" (352–353). This point will gather a greater significance further in the book where we discuss the relationship between the literary function, a-signifying semiotics, and an ethics for a concern for the self.

4. Rorty states that he is not opposing Philosophy on the grounds that Philosophy is wrong and pragmatics is right. Indeed, he adds that pragmatics, as with everything, involves intuition. The reason Rorty gives for opposing Philosophy is that Philosophy's practice of intuition has not paid off.

5. Rorty's pragmatics is about getting things done, and for Rorty good results are the proof of truth (as is getting what we want). This philosophy corresponds to the pragmatism of James, whose primary intuition is the notion that "truth" equates with good. These goals also resonate with moral Philosophy and Utilitarianism (from which Rorty is trying to escape). J. S. Mill, a famous exponent of Utilitarianism, wrote that " '[t]he creed which accepts as the foundation of morals, Utility or the Greatest Happiness Principle, holds that actions are right in proportion as they tend to promote happiness, wrong as they tend to produce the reverse of happiness' " (*A Dictionary of Philosophy*, 1979:361, A Flew, ed.).

6. Writes Gould, "Austin's way of combating the regime of the descriptive and the constative was to use his isolation and mapping of the performative utterance to render first visible, and then salient, the dimension of human utterance that he called the dimension of happiness and unhappiness. His maps and classifications of unhappiness were meant to oppose the philosopher's fixation on their favorite form of utterance, the statement—the linguistic entity capable of being true or (as Austin joked) at least false" (1995:23).

7. Foucault's now famous quote, "[p]erhaps one day this century will be known as Deleuzian" is emblematic of the construction of a condition made possible by conceptualization. (This quote appears on the cover of *Negotiations*, Gilles Deleuze, 1990, New York, Columbia University Press.) For Foucault, it is the " 'task of the history of thought, as against a history of behaviors or representations: *to define the conditions* in which human beings 'problematize' what they are, what they do, and the world in which they live' " (Deleuze quoting Foucault, 1988:vii, my italics).

8. This reference refers to an interview with Deleuze in Foucault's *Language Counter Memory Practice* (1977). Foucault is the interviewer.

9. Roland Barthes says something similar in relation to literary criticism, "The discourse on the Text should be nothing other than text, research, textual activity, since the Text is that *social* space which leaves no language safe, outside, nor, any subject of the enunciation in the position as judge, master, analyst, confessor, decoder" (1984:164).

10. Peter Cook argues that for Deleuze and Guattari, the propositions belonging to philosophy express the event, which is otherwise immaterial and unpresentable (1998:28).

11. Deleuze and Guattari replace the terms "sign" or "signifier" with "regime of signs," and it is for reasons of accuracy that it is used here. The reason for the exchange of the terms is gone into later.

12. Rorty is referred to here as such a philosopher since he fears the deterritorialized sign and in its place evokes a chain of sentences—sentences that link with other sentences.

13. François Recanati states that J. L. Austin "was setting forth on a systematic examination of the relations between signs and sign-users," while his contemporaries, Bar Hillil, and Montague, for example, were not really doing "'pragmatics,' but only semantics incorporating a pragmatic parameter" (1987:8).

14. Ibid.

15. On this account, and in several other instances, there are echoes with Rorty's thinking. However, further in the chapter, Deleuze and Guattari's approach to performativity oppose these linguistic-based approaches.

16. Deleuze and Guattari note that "the sphere of the illocutionary" is a broader sphere than that of the performative (1987:77).

17. Derrida critiques Austin and the performative for being based on the distinction between serious and nonserious speech acts. He sees this distinction as bogus, since, no utterance, for Derrida, is able to be "serious," despite the intention of the speaker, due to the iterability of language and, as a consequence, language's inability to be fully present. For Derrida, then, there is no possibility of context/full meaning and the performative is dismissed as folly. Derrida's position on the performative is addressed further ahead. See Peter Cook, "Thinking the Concept Otherwise: Deleuze and Expression" (1998) for an excellent account of Derrida's critique of Searle's concept of the performative speech act.

18. This is not to say that all transcendentalism is humanist.

19. Deleuze points out that, in Foucault, statements cannot be reduced phrases or propositions (these are the expressed of the statements), rather, "Statements are kinds of curves or graph." Writes Deleuze: "[to] illustrate vividly this point (Foucault) says that the letters which I write at random on a sheet of paper form a statement, 'the statement of an alphabetical series governed by no other laws than those of chance'" (1988:78).

20. See also, *A Thousand Plateaus: Capitalism and Schizophrenia* (1987:86).

21. Deleuze and Guattari's concept of the refrain (1987) and Varela's work on autopoiesis (1980) mark two prior histories of the term, "autopoiesis."

22. "The role of the refrain has often been emphasized: it is territorial, a territorial assemblage. Bird songs: the bird sings to mark its territory. The Greek modes and Hindu rhythms are themselves territorial, provincial, regional. The refrain may assume other functions, amorous, professional or social, liturgical or cosmic: it always carries earth with it; it has a land (sometimes spiritual land) as its concomitant; it has an essential relation to a Natal, a Native" (Deleuze and Guattari 1987:312).

23. Subjectivation needs to be understood here as not belonging to the "subject" or "speaker" but to territory. In a discussion of the refrain Deleuze and Guattari (1987) find that refrains are auto-objective and by this they mean that they "find objectivity in the territory they draw" (317). For Deleuze and Guattari, the territory the refrains draw, or express, as they also put it, function as a signature, and this "signature" is significant because it enters into "shifting relations" with other refrains. Moreover, these refrains "expressed" their relations to one another and to the "exterior milieu of circumstances" (317).

24. For more on the reciprocal presupposition of the regime of bodies and the regime of signs, see Deleuze and Guattari (1987:108).

25. "The elementary unit of language—the statement"—say Deleuze and Guattari, "is the order-word." (Guattari, 1987:76), that is, that which accomplishes an action.

26. "The polyphonic modes of subjectivation actually correspond to a multiplicity of ways of "keeping time" (1995:15).

27. While there is a proliferation of functions in this thesis; the existential, the aesthetic, the performative, the pragmatic and the literary, and so on, there is a precedent to this in Deleuze and Guattari's writing, which hosts the terms "schizoanalysis, micro-politics, pragmatics, diagrammatism, rhizomatics, cartography" (Deleuze and Guattari, 1987:125). These different terms all share a proximity to one another and in respect to Deleuze and Guattari's work, which involves "the study of lines, in groups and individuals" (125). The lines to which Deleuze here refers are the lines of which we are made. They include segmentary lines: lines of detours, modification, becomings (these lines do not have "the same rhythm as our 'history'") (124). The third type of line is a line of flight. A proliferation of terms also occurs in Derrida's work as with "gramme," "writing," "trace," and "cinders" (see Patton, 1996:125). As Patton explains, the concept of "cinders" is itself used by Derrida to explain that in every concept there is the remains of others that lose their "form" (figure) in the process of the creation of a new concept. It is through the proximity of terms that the meaning of the old terms may be extended. Writes Patton, "[b]y forcible extension of ordinary concepts such as writing, trace, supplement and difference, and by grafting the newly generalised sense onto the ordinary concept, deconstruction 'discovers' what Gasché calls the quasi-transcendental 'infrastructure' of all language, experience and thought" (1996:125).

28. The earlier postmodern and cultural-critical moments mapped by this book form a genealogy that is seen to influence the approach taken toward the

literary by literary and cultural studies today. The publication *Futur*Fall*: *Excursions into Post-Modernity*, ed. E. A. Grosz, et al. (1986), echoes the idea of postmodern noncommitment spoken about by Guattari. In this publication, Baudrillard writes of the postmodern, "Events no longer have consequences because they go too quickly—they are diffused too quickly, too far, they are caught up in circuits—they can never return as testimony for themselves or their meaning (meaning is always a testimony). On the other hand, each totality of events or culture must be fragmented, disarticulated in order to enter into the circuits; each language must be resolved into the binary system, 0/1, in order to circulate no longer in our memories, but in the electronic and luminous memory of computers. No human language withstands the speed of light (Baudrillard, 1986:19)

29. "There is not much to say about the center of signifiance, or the signifier in person, because it is a pure abstraction no less than a pure principle; in other words, it is nothing." And, "the infinite set of all signs refers to a supreme signifier" (1987:114–115).

30. The following chapter deals in great length with the issue of mimesis in cultural studies and so this theme will not be further developed here.

31. Austin's contribution to communication theory nonetheless has links of extreme importance to the nature of the performative being developed here. While Austin did depend on context for meaning, Derrida points out that this also led him to "free the…performative from the authority of the truth value, from the true/false opposition, at least in its classical form, and to substitute for it at times the value of force….For [this]…reason, at least, it might seem that Austin has shattered the concept of communication as a purely semiotic, linguistic, or symbolic concept" (1988: 13).

32. Ibid.

33. In discussing Foucault's extensive work on the conditions of statements and discursive formations Deleuze notes that "he excluded…any subject of enunciation. The subject is a variable, or rather a set of variables of the statement" (1988:55).

34. Both Deleuze and Guattari draw upon the linguist Louis Hjelmslev's notion of the form of content and the form of expression. See *A Thousand Plateaus; Capitalism and Schizophrenia* (1987:108), and *Chaosmosis; an Ethico-aesthetic Paradigm* (1995:23). See also, Umberto Eco, *The Search for a Perfect Language* (1995).

35. See Derrida (1988:13).

36. As already mentioned, Austin indicates that the performative is driven by the value of force, rather than "the authority of the truth value," disrupting "the concept of communication as a purely semiotic, linguistic, or symbolic concept."

37. See also, *A Thousand Plateaus, Capitalism and Schizophrenia* (1987:86).

38. Deleuze and Guattari point out that Austin's theses on performativity and the illocutionary has made it impossible to conceive of speech as the communication of information: to order, question, promise, or affirm is not

to inform someone about a command, doubt, engagement, or assertion but to effectuate these specific, immanent, and necessarily implicit acts (1987:77).

39. This they often refer to as "schizopragmatics."

40. For further consideration of the place of the aesthetic, see also, *Revenge of the Aesthetic: The Place of Literature in Theory Today* (2000), Berkeley and Los Angeles, University of California Press.

3   The Literary Function and the Cartographic Turn: Performative Philosophy

1. See Deleuze and Guattari, "The First Positive Task of Schizoanalysis" (1996), for a thorough account of the machinic unconscious.

2. *Literary into Cultural Studies* (1991), by Anthony Easthope, is an example of this shift.

3. First published in English in 1972.

4. Bosteels notes that analysis turns toward territoriality when the question of reference is brought to the fore, as it is when a textual approach is used. Examples he gives of such territoriality are: J. Hillis Miller, *Topographies* (Stanford, CA: Stanford University Press, 1995), Nicholas Alfrey and Stephen Daniels, eds., *Mapping the Landscape: Essays in Art and Cartography* (Nottingham: University Art Gallery, Castle Museum, 1990), and Geoff King, *The Mapping of Reality: The Exploration of Cultural Cartographies* (Basingstoke, England: Macmillan, 1995).

5. The example Deleuze and Guattari give of a theory based upon structural causality is that of Louis Althusser. David Pharies in *Charles S. Peirce and the Linguistic Sign* (1985) explains that in the Peircean notion of semiosis, "The sign is considered to be addressing somebody in a real situation" (20). Writes Pharies: "[t]he immediate object, as well, as a mere representation of the dynamical object, can be neither explicit nor complete enough to meet the requirements of all interpretive tasks. These insufficiencies must be overcome by recurrence to what Peirce called 'collateral experience.' This may be thought of as an encyclopaedic store of knowledge, compiled during a lifetime of interpretation, about various aspects of reality (various dynamical objects), this store being available for use in the deciphering of signs.... Collatoral experience also includes purely contextual information.... [T]he system [then] has at its disposal premises from the interpreter's entire body of collateral knowledge, including...purely contextual information" (19–20).

6. Opposing Althusser's structural causality is Deleuze and Guattari's notion of transversality. Says Deleuze: "One must pursue the different series, travel along the different levels, and cross all thresholds; instead of simply displaying phenomena or statements in their vertical or horizontal dimensions, one must form a transversal or mobile diagonal line" (Deleuze, 1988:22, also quoted in Bosteels).

7. Take, for example, the finding by Gunter Kress that in the Mills and Boon romance, *I* am the subject of sexist discourse (1985).
8. Emphasis in original.
9. Such a methodology echoes the Empiricism of pre-modern analysis. Patrick Fuery and N. Mansfield note that, "Empiricism believes that the world can be understood and analysed by patient and systematic—usually statistical—observation and description." However, Empiricism generally does not take into account the "observer's situation and prejudices" upon what was observed (Fuery and Mansfield, 1997:108). Poststructuralism's concern that writing is not so much a transcription of "reality" but a reproduction of a set of structures and convention seems to have brought us full circle, back to a literary mode of representation.
10. Ulmer's specific topic, his research, is for the experience of justice.
11. "The issue, the challenge to artificial intelligence, and to teaching as well, is how to simulate expertise, the way experts, 'after years of experience, are able to respond intuitively to situations in a way that defies logic and surprises and awes even the experts themselves'" (Ulmer quoting H. L. Dreyfus and S. E. Dreyfus, 1994:349).
12. While Wittgenstein's "common logical pattern" may appear to be a universal matheme, of which this thesis has been critical, by this chapter's end it will be apparent that Ulmer's use of Wittgenstein's Miranda pattern does not result in a universal matheme. Ulmer's Miranda uses parts previously tangentially associated (like the duck and rabbit of Wittgenstein) but the result is not one of a reduction or conformity between parts but rather a display of their irreducibility. Ulmer's Miranda, as it will be explained, draws its own discourse outside of itself—and thus, away from its own isomorphism—when it juxtaposes hitherto nonassociated assemblages and events. To quote de Certeau from later in this chapter, the discourse "allows us to see what dislodges it from its privilege" (1988:2).
13. This aspect of "depicting," and its significance to the literary function, is explored later with respect to Foucault's concept of "the visible."
14. Deleuze and Guattari write of the concept that "there is no longer projection but connection.... This is why the concept itself abandons all reference so as to retain only the conjugations and connections that constitute its consistency.... The concept is not paradigmatic but *syntagmatic*" (1994:90–91).
15. This mode of connectionism when applied pedagogically enables writers to go beyond the organizing and reductive articulation of genre.
16. See Deleuze and Guattari on the percept, *What Is Philosophy?* (1994), and Bakhtin's notion of the dialogic imagination, in *Dialogic Imagination* (1981), for an understanding of the compositional nature of the literary.
17. One can compare Deleuze and Guattari's notions of singular and double articulation to Certeaus's notions of *Space* and *Place*, respectively; see earlier.
18. This compares to Deleuze and Guattari's notion of singular articulation: There is a "statistical order" made of these "substances" to produce a "form."

19. Mills and Boon romances are an example of the serial in prose fiction. The author's name is secondary to the publishing company, which, of course, is consistent, and the covers are also consistent in form making these works of fiction serial in type. The recurring romance plot also makes the Mills and Boon a serial form.

20. For Deleuze, Foucault's love of description puts him in the long-established tradition that "claims there is a difference in nature between statements and descriptions (for example Russell)" (Deleuze, 80). Writes Deleuze: "[o]riginating in logic, this problem has seen unexpected developments in the novel, the 'new novel' and then in cinema" (80).

21. Deleuze's describes the work of archaeology as deconstructive, it is to: "break open words, phrases or propositions and extract statements from them." Writes Deleuze, " The task…is double: it must open up words, phrases and propositions, open up qualities, things and objects. It must extract from words and language the statements corresponding to each stratum and its thresholds, but equally extract from things and sign the visibilities and 'self-evidences' unique to each stratum" (52–53).

22. De Certeau notes that "[t]he erosion and denigration of the singular or the extraordinary was announced by *The Man without Qualities*" (1988:1).

23. Roland Barthes (1996:97) also discusses the novel in respect to its conditioning of the modern subject. He notes that the modern novel is increasingly impersonal (its use of the third person Barthes describes as a "negative degree of the person"). He notes that the novel was "an act of fidelity to the essence of language, since the latter naturally tends towards its own destruction…. We therefore understand how 'he' is a victory over 'I,' inasmuch as it conjures up a state at once more *literary* and more absent" (my italics).

4   The Literary Function and Society I: Affirmation of Immanent Aesthetics

1. There is a vast array of approaches to this problematic, including those writers who theorize writing technologies, such as David Bolter, *Writing Space: The Computer in the Histroy of Literacy* (1990), and Gregory Ulmer (already mentioned), Mireille Rosello, "The Screener's Maps: Michel de Certeau's 'Wandermanner' and Paul Auster's Hypertextual Detective" (1994), among many others. There is the mapping carried out by Marxist, Feminist Postcolonial and, more recently, Queer theorists, which has many entry and exit points. There are histories of the theorization of the aesthetic, one of which is Terry Eagleton's *The Ideology of the Aesthetic* (1990). The recent philosophical writings of Jacques Derrida, Deleuze and Guattari, de Certeau, Jean-Luc Nancy, Maurice Blanchot, and others have further considered this problematic. The political importance of this problematic is evidenced by this plethora of writing and this is why the question continues in this book.

The question of ethics in relation to aesthetics is ultimately a question of the text and society.

2. This binary construction is odd considering literary studies has not been traditional since the Birmingham School—which, not incidentally, gave cultural studies its theoretical "hardware." Such a methodology when claiming an identity can only indicate a legitimacy along metaphysical lines.

3. Foucault is referring here to Roland Barthes's and Maurice Blanchot's approach to literature, which saw it as intransitive.

4. Pfeil's article "Icons for Clowns: American Writers Now," in *Another Tale to Tell: Politics and the Linguistic Sign* (1990), was originally written in 1977. It is useful here as it arrives at the beginning stages of cultural criticism and clearly points to at least one context from which cultural criticism emerges— that is, off the back of the literary fallacy. See also, Anthony Easthope, *Literary into Critical Theory* (1991), and John Docker, *Postmodernism and Popular Culture, a Cultural History* (1994) for more recent accounts of this paradigm.

5. Pfeil's writing before postmodernism was also accused of being obscure and elitist, but such criticism comes out of thinking such as Pfeil's.

6. However, while Foucault is critical of an autotelic approach to the literary text, he does not lose sight of the aesthetic in relation to ethics. That is, he maintains a pragmatic interest in the aesthetic, as this book at various times, bears witness.

7. This quote echoes the sentiments of a well-known statement by Marx, " '[t]he philosophers have only *interpreted* the world in various ways; the point is to *change* it,' " (cited in Selden and Widdowson, 1993:70).

8. See also, Lance Olsen's (1990) "Pragmatism, Politics, Postmodernism" in *Circus of the Mind in Motion*, in which Olsen compares the abstract, universal narratives of Freud's to those of history, in particular, those of a holocaust victim. Freud's narratives were condemned because they were of little use to the subject situated in the narratives of the holocaust.

9. Opposed to this self-contained history of literature, *extrinsic* literary history specifies "the forces that caused, governed, entailed, or were expressed by literary texts…and the routes by which these forces exerted their influence upon literature" (Patterson, 1990:250). In America, literary historians have turned to extrinsic literary history in response to the types of problems with postmodernism and deconstruction that Olsen alludes to (Patterson, 1990).

10. Olsen puts aesthetics into a bag with systems in general, including political, occult, and psychoanalytic systems. He likens systems to fantasies and like fantasies says they are potentially dangerous, the cause of ' "senseless tumult' " (1990:124).

11. Olsen's approach to the literary text fits Patterson's description of extrinsic literary history. See note 6, this chapter.

12. In his essay "Writing and the Novel," Roland Barthes notes the parallel evolution of the Novel and History. However, Barthes is critical of these two discourses, noting their part in reducing reality to "a point of time,"

and abstracting reality "from the depth of a multiplicity of experiences, a pure verbal act, freed from the existential roots of knowledge, and directed towards a logical link with other acts, other processes, a general movement of the world" (1996:93). I would add to this, however, that the novel functions as History only when it is read in this way.

13. For example, Guattari points out that (the machinic) production of subjectivity associated with modernity (and responsible for an antimodernity sentiment) "can work for the better or for the worse...It's impossible to judge such a machinic evolution either positively or negatively; everything depends on its articulation within collective assemblages of enunciation" (1995:5).

14. I will soon address the way in which play is indeed paramount to social change and thereby a serious or real enough activity. Olsen's notion, whereby life is opposed to linguistic gaming, is countered by Brian Massumi's challenge to structural linguistics. Massumi notes that what in fact moves the system "from one unique permutation to the next" is the continuous variation of language—there being no pure and eternal linguistic realm (*langue*) outside the *speech act* it produces. For Massumi, what needs conceptualization is "the *real conditions of production* of *particular* statements." Grammar should be indexed to "relations of power and patterns of social change." This method is opposed to the conceptualization of "the *logical conditions of possibility* of statements *in general* (what standard permutations can the system produce? What can it do without ceasing to be itself?"

15. The early work of Jean-François Lyotard (1971), *Discours, figure,* is also significant for its aesthetic concerns. Julia Kristeva's work in the area of poetic language has been crucial for thinking language outside of systematics and in regard to ethics. See *Revolution in Poetic Language* (1984) and *Desire in Language: A Semiotic Approach to Literature and Art* (1980).

16. When discussing his own empiricism, which sets out to present concepts directly, Deleuze describes himself as "the one who felt the least guilt about 'doing philosophy'" (1990:89). This is a reminder of the moral pressure upon intellectual activity in the Humanities since the move away from the direct presentation of concepts.

17. See "From Text to Diagram: Towards a Semiotics of Cultural Cartography" by Bruno Bosteels (1995), for an excellent account of the importance of Hjelmslev to Deleuze and Guattari's (particularly Guattari's) pragmatics.

18. As Guattari writes, the "old Lacanian motto according to which 'a signifier represents a subject for another signifer,' could serve as the epigraph for this new ethics of non-commitment" (1986:41).

19. Guattari's concept of machinic assemblages of enunciation is also very close to Bakhtin's notion of Dialogism; "Dialogism is the characteristic epistemological mode of a world dominated by heteroglossia. Everything means, is understood, as a part of a greater whole (i.e., formal machines)—there is a constant interaction between meanings, all of which have the potential of conditioning others. Which will affect the other, how it will do so and in what degree is what is actually settled in the moment of utterances"

(Bakhtin, 1981:426). Heteroglossia is like Guattari's abstract machine, producing utterances, which are similar to Guattari's "substance of Expression." Both are indefinite in number.

20. See Lyotard, *Discours, figure* (1971:41–82). See also note 85.
21. "Simulation is no longer that of a territory, a referential being or a substance. It is the generation by models of a real without origins or reality: a hyperreal" (Baudrillard, 1983:2).
22. See Terrence Hawkes, *Structural Semiotics* (1989:79).

5   The Literary Function and Society II: Community and Subjectification

1. Guattari demonstrates this with his own ethico-aesthetic approach to theory. Guattari states his is not a scientific discourse (1995:10). The aesthetic, in Guattari, becomes not a net cast over content (capturing content), as it is envisaged by Olsen, say, but rather, an ethics based upon the creative or "creation" (1995:7), upon the experiential and experimental. The result is the production of a singularity (which, I believe, could be responsible for why his writing has been, at times, conveyed to me as being impenetrable) and not a repetitious model.
2. In his chapter "On the Production of Subjectivity" (1995), Guattari draws upon Mikhail Bakhtin, "Content, Material, and Form in Verbal Art," in *Art and Answerability: Early Philosophical Essays by M. M. Bakhtin* (1990).
3. The term "subjectification" has been used by the translators of the writing of both Deleuze and Guattari, however, in *Chaosmosis: An Ethico-aesthetic Paradigm,* Guattari the translator has used the term "subjectivation." In this book these two terms are taken as interchangeable.
4. Guattari actually refers to the aesthetic as creative subjectivity (1995:14).
5. Guattari quoting Bakhtin notes that " 'isolation or detachment relates not to the material, not to the work as thing, but to its significance, to its content, which is freed from certain necessary connections with the unity of nature and the unity of the ethical event of being" (1995:14).
6. Bakhtin stresses that the performed act is unavailable to theoretical representation, however, a "performed act is active in the actual unique product (in an actual, real deed, in an uttered word, in a thought that has been thought...)" (1993:26–27). For example, in speaking of the relationship between the law and the once-occurrent event, Bakhtin writes that "the self-activity of a performed act is expressed in an actually effected acknowledgment, in an effective affirmation" (27).
7. This mirrors Guattari's investment in the aesthetic as inalienable.
8. See Duguld Williamson, *Authorship and Criticism* (1989).
9. The author may be a collective of people, as is often the case in the making of cinematic texts.
10. For Bakhtin, one's "own Being" is the effect of "my self-activity in a lived-experience—the experiencing of an experience as mine" (1993:36).

11. Foucault also introduces the theme of "subjectification" that involves establishing "styles of life." In *Negotiations*, Deleuze refers to this theme of subjectification as a vitalism rooted in aesthetics (1990:91). In "What Is a Dispositif?" Deleuze notes that Foucault makes allusion to "'aesthetic' criteria, which are understood as criteria for life and replace on each occasion the claims of transcendental judgment with an immanent evaluation....Could this be the intrinsic aesthetic of modes of existence as the ultimate dimension of social apparatus [*dispositifs*]?" (Deleuze, 1992:163).

12. In "What Is a Dispositif?," Deleuze discusses Foucault's "cruelly interrupted" exploration of the Self and its different natures depending on the social apparatuses that produce it, for example, Greek, Christian, Modern societies and so on. For Deleuze, "[t]he study of the variations in the process of subjectification seems to be one of the fundamental tasks which Foucault left to those who would follow him" (1992:162).

13. The word "self" indicate that subjectification is a process belonging to social production and not an "individual" subjectivity, given as in-itself.

14. In discussing the nonhuman part of subjectivity in Deleuze and Foucault, Guattari states that it's a question of being aware of the existence of machines of subjectivation which don't simply work within the "the faculties of the soul," interpersonal relations of "intra-familial complexes...but also in the large-scale social machines of language and the mass media—which cannot be described as human" (1995:9). Guattari warns against taking Deleuze and Foucault as antihumanists.

15. Deleuze makes the point that "It is not certain that all social apparatuses [*dispositifs*] comprise these (subjectifications)" (1992:161).

16. Patterson points out that this thinking within cultural criticism—and of central importance to recent literary historian—was "encouraged by the Foucauldian conception...of discursive formations, which are seen as organized according to structures of dominance and subordination that replicate the structures of society as a whole and so allow for no external purchase that might make possible a reformation or even reversal of power relations" (1990:261).

17. Guattari's poetic function (with its transformative powers) marks a shift from that of the formalists'. For Roman Jakobson, the poetic function, "by promoting the palpability of signs, deepens the fundamental dichotomy of signs and objects" (1960:356).

18. Deleuze and Guattari point out that the collective utterance is one of the primary elements of what they have termed "Minor Literature." See *Kafka, Towards a Minor Literature*.

19. This ethics, of course, brings to mind François Lyotard's notion of paganism, found in *Just Gaming* (1985), and *The Lyotard Reader* (1989).

20. As reflexive and revisionist as works like Douglas Coupland's *Generation X* may be, they do not do away with the system of their "languages." In the case of Coupland, this has taken central stage. *Generation X* forfeits plot with each of the characters many anecdotal stories making up the text. In foregoing plot (there is one story that is threaded in between the others but doesn't

involve them and thereby doesn't capture them) Coupland avoids the force by which fragments are made into a whole, within narrative.

21. If we now consider Pfeil's negative criticism of literature—such as Joyce's, for instance—which he says "approaches zero," we may see that in the light of the notion of a plane of consistency belonging to the aesthetic or literary, and its escape from "models of realization," such a criticism is indeed a direct capture of the literary function itself.

22. The problem with May '68 was that it was too reliant on linguistic representation, even in its efforts to fight being represented. This detracted from its existential body, which de Certeau felt so palpably, as he expresses in this utterance: "This experience happened. It is impregnable; it *cannot be taken away*" (1997:13). De Certeau does note that the event (which he also refers to as fact) "is more important than the claims or even the contestation that expressed it in terms prior to the event" (1997:13). He writes: "It is a fact that we can attest to for having seen and been participants: a throng became poetic" (1997:13).

23. Though Bakhtin does not claim the aesthetic for the performed act, I choose to focus on Bakhtin's notion of the act here since it most expertly explains the aesthetic as both myself and Guattari see it; that is, as the expressed of the processual, of once-occurrent being.

24. Deleuze explains that a line of flight is not an imaginary escape. Writes Deleuze: A flight is "also to put to flight—not necessary others, but to put something to flight, put a system to flight as one bursts a tube. George Jackson wrote from prison: 'It may be that I am fleeing, but throughout my flight I am searching for a weapon'" (Deleuze and Parnet, 1987:36).

25. The literary has, of course, long been considered a mode of language which "becomes the language of others and of another experience" (de Certeau, 1997:23). It is also, thereby, plural.

26. Guattari uses the expression "subjectivation," where I have used, subjectification.

27. There is a genealogy from Nietzsche, Lacenaive, Camus, de Quincey, and Foucault. See Foucault et al. (1975).

28. The Macquarie Dictionary, 2nd revision, 1981, Chatswood, NSW, Macquarie Library (1987).

29. "The artist: the first person to set out a boundary stone, or to make a mark" (1987:316).

30. Deleuze refers to the process of becoming precisely as an act of stealing, a capture by parallel forces not of one another but of that which is between them. This is not an instant act, an act of plagiarism or imitation or copy but "a long preparation" (Deleuze and Parnet, 1987:7). In *The Full Monty* we witness the "long preparation" in the building of the line of flight. The "troupe" of male strippers that the Carlyle character gets together do not merely copy existing acts but "employ" their own choreographer, think of their own specialty (going the full-monty!), design their own costume, and above all, their nontypicality as strippers (they are the husbands, fathers, etc., of the town

folk) is their ultimate line of flight. The town folk come to see them because of their unique offering. The wife of the chubby member of the troupe, Dave, wants to see her "big man" dance—thus barriers based upon certain body types are broken.

31. Deleuze and Guattari put it elegantly thus: "The refrain may assume other functions, amorous, professional or social, liturgical or cosmic: it always carries earth with it; it has a land (sometimes a spiritual land) as its concomitant; it has an essential relation to a Natal, a Native" (1987:312).

32. See Gilles Deleuze, "On the Superiority of Anglo-American Literature" (1987:36).

33. See Brian Massumi, A User's Guide to Capitalism and Schizophrenia (1992:41).

34. The collective utterance is always in a state of becoming and a process of negotiation, negotiation, not toward an end point or an outcome but toward a plane of consistency—because this founds the community. Once the community has a teleology, it ceases.

35. Deleuze and Guattari refer to he or she who speaks while in the assembly as being au milieu (of an environment). Though they might be "in the middle of the assembly" (1987:426), "the rules are different for those of the sovereign, who captures and speaks from on high."

36. I used authentic in relation to Bakhtin's notion of the performed act, where Bakhtin used the term "actual." I did so because, like Deleuze and Guattari, I need to make a distinction between real or authentic and actual, as I have done here.

6 The Reader and the Event of Fiction

1. Says Foucault, "[I]n a society like our own, games can be very numerous, and the desire to control the conduct of others is all the greater—as we see in family relations, for example, or emotional or sexual relationships. However, the freer people are with respect to each other, the more they want to control each other's conduct. The more open the game, the more appealing and fascinating it becomes" (1997:300).

2. "These conditions of context regarding the teller, the tale, and the hearer have been translated in the case of written cultures into more subtle variations of utterance and reception, variation of code and discourse, variations of ideology and fashion" (MacLean, 1988:4).

3. Says MacLean, "Since the original roots of both forms (drama and written narrative) are in the same tradition, that of oral narrative performance, the resemblance between them remains very great, and the homology which it is possible to establish between them is a very powerful tool in the investigation of the functioning of narrative in general and more particularly of written prose fiction" (1988:11). MacLean notes: "Studies of narrative structure have had a long relationship with the theatrical model, perhaps

because this enterprise is so firmly grounded in the study of oral narrative" (1988:15).

4. For MacLean, the doubling within fiction makes us aware that the fictional "belongs to the world of signs and only functions within the realm of discursive propositions" (1988:77).

5. "I shall try to explain the formal conditions under which we comprehend a film. This means that here the 'spectator' is not a particular person, not even me. Nor is the spectator an 'ideal reader,' which in recent reader-response criticism tends to be the most fully equipped perceiver the text could imagine, the one most adequate to all the aspects of meaning presented. I adopt the term 'viewer' or 'spectator' to name a hypothetical entity executing the operations relevant to constructing a story out of the film's representation. My spectator, then, acts according to the protocols of story comprehension....Insofar as an empirical viewer makes sense of the story, his or her activities coincide with the process I will be describing. For the comprehension of any one narrative film, of course, the 'hollow' forms I will be describing must be supplemented by many forms of particular knowledge. Moreover, my spectator is 'real' in at least the sense that she or he possesses certain psychological limitations that real spectators also possess. My spectator, for instance, undergoes the *phi* phenomenon...and thus necessarily perceives apparent motion in films. Finally, my spectator is active; his or her experience is cued by the text, according to intersubjective protocols that may vary" (Bordwell, 1985:2).

6. MacLean, in fact, counters only those logicians, literary critics, and speech-act theorists who insist on a demarcation between valid and invalid speech acts. For MacLean, both direct discourse and textual representation are language dependent and therefore both use "speech acts," only in differing contexts. The literary speech act is but *another* context involving its own speech acts and differing from that of "natural" direct discourse.

7. I refer to Jacques Laçan's theory of the transcendental signifier (the father) in *Écrits A Selection* (1985).

8. Says Foucault; "In a society like our own, games can be very numerous, and the desire to control the conduct of others is all the greater—as we see in family relations, for example, or emotional or sexual relationships. However, the freer people are with respect to each other, the more they want to control each other's conduct. The more open the game, the more appealing and fascinating it becomes" (1997:300).

9. In another context, Guattari dismisses scientific approaches to the subject. He notes that,

[i]t's no longer a question of determining whether the Freudian Unconscious or the Lacanian Unconscious provide scientific answers to the problems of the psyche. From now on these models, along with the others, will only be considered in terms of the production of subjectivity—inseparable as much from the technical and institutional apparatuses which promote it as from their impact on psychiatry,

university teaching or the mass media.... In a more general way, one has to admit that every individual and social group conveys its own system of modelising subjectivity; that is, a certain cartography—composed of cognitive references as well as mythical, ritual and symptomatological references—with which it positions itself in relation to its affects and anguishes, and attempts to manage its inhibitions and drives. (1995:11)

10. Foucault notes that the emphasis on the ethics and care for the Self became "somewhat suspect" following Christianity. Says Foucault: "Starting at a certain point, being concerned with oneself was readily denounced as a form of self-love, a form of selfishness or self-interest in contradiction with the interest to be shown in others or the self-sacrifice required" (1997:284).

11. See also MacLean (1988:148) for the doubleness of discourses.

12. This aspect of individuation and the part community plays in it is common to much recent drama including *Hamish McBeth* (1995), *Sea Changes,* and *Generation X* (1994).

13. In discussing capitalism, Guattari notes that the "valorization and finality" of individuals is equivalent to labor that is equivalent to capital. This, according to such thinking, is the source of alienation. Both Deleuze and Guattari note that regimes of that equivalence include signification as signification is formed by making diverse points resonate.

14. See Gilles Deleuze, *Nietzsche and Philosophy* (1983:189).

15. In discussing the distinction between fable and fiction, Foucualt is making his own adjustment to the cognate mappings of the field, as with the "Formalists' '*Fabula*' v. '*suzet*' (e.g. Tomashevsky 1965, p. 66), Todorov's '*histoire*' v. '*discours*' (1966, p. 126), Chatman's 'Story' v. 'Discourse' (1978, p. 19), Barthes's '*fonctions,*' '*actions,*' '*narration*' (1966, p. 6), and Bal's '*histoire*', '*récit*', '*texte narratif*' (1977, pp. 4–8)" (Rimmon-Kenan, 1985:133). Rimmon-Kenan uses Genette's model *histoire, récit* and *narration*. She labels these "story," "text," and "narration." Interestingly, Foucault replaces narrative with fiction.

16. Deleuze and Guattari point out that the State apparatus needs predisabled people, preexisting amputees. Perceptively, they point out that "accidents are the result of mutilations that took place long ago in the embryo of our world" (1987:426). By not agreeing to the overcoding of her "crippled state" (becoming a compensation recipient), the girl avoids this capture by the State.

Conclusion: Degrees of Freedom

1. John Marks notes that for Deleuze "[l]iterature is characterized by 'the force of the impersonal,' freeing us from the first and second person. The effect is that of an impersonal mode of enunciation, that is not a generality but a singularity: *a* man, *a* woman, *a* child (Marks quoting Deleuze, 1998:125).

2. Deleuze and Guattari point out that functions are created only because they are territorialized (1987:316). When we as writers seek our unique relationship

to the world, and a subjectification ensues, we bring into being the literary function, which does not, as though in some formula preexist the territory. This is not to say that functions do not have particular aspects, but that they only function when territories are made. For functions to result there needs to be an "emergence of proper qualities (color, odor, sound, silhouette...)" (Deleuze and Guattari, 316).

3. Notably, Linda Hutcheon's *A Theory of Parody: The Teachings of Twentieth-Century Art Forms* (1985). Fredrick Jameson, *Postmodernism or the Cultural Logic of Late Capitalism* (1992), also places a significant weight upon the issue of parody. Examples of the discussion of postmodernism and parody (literary or otherwise) are many, such as Nigel Wheal, ed. *Postmodern Arts: An Introductory Reader* (1995).

4. Roland Barthes criticizes the novel for the use of the preterite, which, he argues "reduces reality to a point of time, and...abstract[s], from the depth of a multiplicity of experiences, a pure verbal act, freed from the existential roots of knowledge." This verbal act is "directed towards a logical link with others acts, other processes, [and forms] a general movement of the world," the aim of which is to maintain "a hierarchy in the realm of facts" (Barthes, 1996:92). This account of the novel by Barthes is clearly the obverse of the account being given here of pathic knowledge and as that is being attributed to the literary function. However, this is a good opportunity to reiterate that the literary function is not defined by genre. The novels of which Barthes speaks are those of the nineteenth century and in particular, those of Balzac. This issue of the preterite, and the texts of which Barthes speaks, however, needs to be revised with consideration given to the literary function and pathic knowledge.

The postmodern text certainly stages syntagmatic discursive links that divert discourses "from their signifying, denotational and propositional incidences" (Guattari, 1995:60). Bret Easton Ellis is a fine example of such linking. In *Glamorama* (1999), for instance, Ellis links different narratives, genres, and settings.

5. In discussing writing technologies in relation to space and the subject, Mireille Rosello notes that linear texts, which are produced by the joining of points, mirror the travel map. The travel map comprises fixed and immobile roads/texts, and it is along these roots a body must circulate, between one fixed point and another (1994:130). The subject cannot create its own map or use of this official *space*. Thus, the map bears no relationship to the terrain or environment over which it is laid, and instead *space* becomes an empty vessel; it functions as a "neutral receptacle of the network" (243).

Bibliography

Agamben, G. 1995. *Homo Sacer, Sovereign Power and Bare Life*. Stanford, CA: Stanford University Press.

Agger, B. 1992. *Cultural Studies as Critical Theory*. London, Washington, DC: The Falmer Press.

Auster, Paul. 1999. *Timbuktu, a Novel*. New York: Picador USA.

Austin, J. L. 1962. *How to Do Things with Words: The William James Lectures delivered at Harvard University, 1965*. Ed. J. O. Urmson. Oxford: Clarendon Press.

Bakhtin, M. M. 1981. *The Dialogic Imagination: Four Essays*. Ed. M. Holquist. Trans. C. Emerson and M. Holquist. Austin: University of Texas Press.

——. 1990. *Art and Answerability: Early Philosophical Essays by M. M. Bakhtin*. Ed. M. Holquist and V. Liapunov. Austin: University of Texas Press.

——. 1993. *Towards a Philosophy of the Act*. Ed. V. Liamunov and M. Holquist. Trans. V. Liapunov. Austin: University of Texas Press.

Barthes, R. 1957. *Mythologies*. France: Les Lettres Nouvelles.

——. 1968. *Writing Degree Zero*. New York: Hill and Wang.

——. 1984. *Image Music Text*. London: Flamingo, Fontana Paperbacks.

——. 1996. "Writing and the Novel." In *Essentials of the Theory of Fiction*. Ed. M. J. Hoffman and P. D. Murphy. London: Leicester University Press, 92–99.

Baudrillard, J. 1983. *Simulations*. New York: Semiotext(e).

——. 1983. *In the Shadow of the Silent Majorities*. New York: Semiotext(e).

——. 1986. "The Year 2000 Will Not Take Place." In: *Futur*Fall: Excursions into Post-Modernity*. Ed. E. A. Grosz, et al. Sydney, Australia: Power Institute of Fine Arts, University of Sydney and Futur*Fall, 18–28.

Belsey, C. 1991. *Critical Practice*. London, New York: Routledge.

Bennett, T. 1979. *Formalism and Marxism*. London, New York: Methuen.

——. 1990. *Outside Literature*. London: Routledge.

Benveniste, E. 1971. *Problems in General Linguistics*. Trans. M. F. Meek. Coral Gables, FL: University of Miami Press.

Bertens, H. 1995. *The Idea of the Postmodern, a History*. London, New York: Routledge.

Blanchot, M. 1982. *The Space of Literature*. Trans. A. Smock. Lincoln, London: University of Nebraska Press.

Bogard, W. 1998. Sense and Segmentarity: Some Markers of a Deleuzian-Guattarian Sociology." *Sociological Theory*16: 52.

Bogue, R. 1989. *Deleuze and Guattari*. London, New York: Routledge.

Bogue, R. 1990. *Writing Space: The Computer in the History of Literacy*. Hillsdale, NJ: Lawrence Erlbaum.

———. 2007. *Deleuze's Way: Essays in Transverse Ethics and Aesthetics*. Aldershot, UK: Ashgate.

Bolter, J. D. 1990. *Writing Space: The Computer, in the History of Writing*. Hillsdale, NJ: Lawrence Erlbaum.

Bordwell, D. 1985. *Narration in the Fiction Film*. Madison: University of Wisconsin Press.

Bosteels, B. 1995. "From Text to Diagram: Towards a Semiotics of Cultural Cartography." In: *Semiotics 1994*. Ed. C. W. Spinks. New York: Peter Lang, 347–359.

———. 1998. "From Text to Territory: Félix Guattari's Cartographies of the Unconscious." In: *Deleuze and Guattari: New Mappings in Politics, Philosophy, and Culture*. Ed. E. Kaufman and J. K Heller. London, Minneapolis: University of Minnesota Press, 145–174.

Boundas, C. V. and D. Olkowski, eds. 1994. *Gilles Deleuze and the Theatre of Philosophy*. New York, London: Routledge.

Bourdieu, P. 1993. *The Field of Cultural Production: Essays on Art and Literature*. Ed. R. Johnson. New York: Columbia University Press.

Broadhurst, J. ed. 1992. *Deleuze and the Transcendental Unconscious*. *Warwick Journal of Philosophy*, University of Warwick, England.

Burke, S. 1992. *The Death and Return of the Author*. Edinburgh: Edinburgh University Press.

Casterton, J. 1998. *Creative Writing: A Practical Guide*. 2nd ed. London: Macmillan.

de Certeau, M. 1988. *The Practice of Everyday Life*. Trans. S. Rendall. Berkeley, Los Angeles, London: University of California Press.

———. 1997. *The Capture of Speech and Other Political Writings*. Trans. T. Conley. Minneapolis: University of Minnesota Press.

Childers, J. and Hentzi, G., eds. 1995. *Columbia Dictionary of Modern Literary and Cultural Criticism*. New York: Columbia University Press.

Clark, M. P. 2000. *Revenge of the Aesthetic: The Place of Literature in Theory Today*. Berkeley, Los Angeles, London: University of California Press.

Cook, P. 1998. "Thinking the Concept Otherwise: Deleuze and Expression." *Symposium* 2 (1): 23–35.

Coupland, D. 1994. *Generation X*. London: Abacus, a division of Little, Brown and Company.

Cull, Laura, ed. 2009. *Deleuze and Performance*. Edinburgh: Edinburgh, University Press.

Dawson, P. 2003. "Towards a New Poetics in Creative Writing Pedagogy." *Text* 7 (1): 1–10. (electronic journal, at: http://www.gu.edu.au/school/art/text/april03/lafemina.htm)

Deleuze, G. 1983. *Nietzche and Philosophy*. New York: Columbia University Press.

———. 1988. *Foucault*. Trans. S. Hand. Minneapolis: University of Minnesota Press.

———. 1990. *Negotiations*. Trans. M. Joughin. New York: Columbia University Press.

———. 1991. *Cinema 2*. Minneapolis, University of Minnesota Press.

———. 1992. "What Is a dispositif?" In: *Michel Foucault: Philosopher*. Ed. T. J. Armstrong. Hartfordshire: Harvester Wheatsheft, 159–168.

———. 1993. *The Fold: Leibniz and the Baroque*. Minneapolis and London: University of Minnesota Press.

———. 1994. *Difference and Repetition*. Trans. P. Patton. New York: Columbia University Press.

———. 1997. "Literature and Life." Trans. D. W. Smith and M. A. Greco. *Critical Inquiry* 23 (4): 225–230.

Deleuze, G. and Guattari, F. 1983. *Anti-Oedipus, Capitalism and Schizophrenia*. Minneapolis: University of Minnesota Press.

———. 1986. *Kafka, Toward a Minor Literature*. Trans. D. Polan. Minneapolis: University of Minnesota Press.

———. 1987. *A Thousand Plateaus, Capitalism and Schizophrenia*. Minneapolis: University of Minnesota Press.

———. 1994. *What Is Philosophy?* London, New York: Verso.

Deleuze, G. and Parnet, C. 1987. *Dialogues*. Trans. H. Tomlinson and B. Habberjam. New York: Columbia University Press.

Dentith, S. 1995. *Bakthinian Thought: An Introductory Reader*. London, New York: Routledge.

Derrida, J. 1976. *Of Grammatology*. Baltimore, MD: John Hopkins University Press.

———. 1988. *Limited Inc*. Evanston, IL: Northwestern University Press.

———. 1992. *Acts of Literature*. Ed. D. Attridge. New York, London: Routledge.

———. 2000. "A Self-Unsealing Poetic Text: Poetics and Politics of Witnessing." In: *Revenge of the Aesthetic: The Place of Literature in Theory Today*. Ed. M. P. Clark. Berkeley: University of California Press, 180–207.

Docker, J. 1994. *Postmodernism and Popular Culture, A Cultural History*. Melbourne, Cambridge, New York: Cambridge University Press.

Ducrot, O. Todorov, T. 1979. *Encyclopedic Dictionary of the Science of Language*. Baltimore, MD: Johns Hopkins University.

Eagleton, T. 1985. *Literary Theory, an Introduction*. Oxford: Basil Blackwell.

———. 1990. *The Ideology of the Aesthetic*. Oxford: Blackwell Publishers.

Easthope, A. 1991. *Literary into Cultural Studies*. London, New York: Routledge.

Easton, B. E. 1999. *Glamorama*. New York: Alfred A. Knopf.

Eco, U. 1995. *The Search for a Perfect Language*. Trans. J. Fentress. Oxford: Blackwell.

Flew, A. 1979. *A Dictionary of Philosophy*. London: Pan Books.

Foster, H. 1996. *Return of the Real: The Avant-Garde at the End of the Century*. Cambridge and London: MIT Press.

Foucault, M. 1963. *Raymond Roussel*. Paris: Gallimard.

———. 1973. *The Order of Things: An Archaeology of the Human Sciences*. New York: Vintage Books.

———, ed. 1975. I, *Pierre Rivière, Having Slaughtered My Mother, My Sister, and My Brother…A Case of Patricide in the 19*th *Century*. Trans. Frank Jellinek. Lincoln: University of Nebraska Press.

Foucault, M. 1977. *Language, Counter-Memory, Practice: Selected Essays and Interviews.* Trans. D. F. Bouchard. Ithaca, NY: Cornell University Press.

———. 1979. *Discipline and Punish: Birth of the Prison.* Trans. A. Sheridan. Harmondsworth: Peregrine.

———. 1988. *Michel Foucault: Politics, Philosophy, Culture: Interviews and Other Writings 1977–1984.* Ed. L. D. Kritzman. New York: Routledge.

———. 1997. *Ethics: Subjectivity and Truth. Essential Works of Foucault 1954–1984.* Vol. 1. Ed. P. Rabinow. New York: The New Press.

———. 1998. *Michel Foucault, Aesthetics, Method, and Epistemology.* Vol. 2 Ed. J. D. Faubion. New York: The New Press.

Fuery, P and Mansfield, N. 1997. *Cultural Studies and the New Humanities.* Melbourne: Oxford University Press.

Gould, T. 1995. "The Unhappy Performative." In: *Performativity and Performance.* Ed. A. Parker and E. Kosofsky Sedgwick. New York: Routledge, 19–44.

Grenville, K. and Woolfe, S. 1993. *Making Stories: How Ten Australian Novels Were Written.* North Sydney: Allen & Unwin.

Grosz, E. A., et al., eds. 1986. *Futur*Fall: Excursions into Post-Modernity.* Sydney, Australia: Power Institute of Fine Arts, University of Sydney and Futur*Fall.

Grosz, Elizabeth. 2008. *Chaos, Territory, Art: Deleuze and the Framing of the Earth.* New York: Columbia University Press.

Guattari, F. 1986. "The Post Modern Dead End." *Flash Art* 128: 40–41.

———. 1995. *Chaosmosis, an Ethico-Aesthetic Paradigm.* Trans. P. Bains and J. Pefanis. Sydney: Power Publications.

———. 1996. *The Guattari Reader.* Ed. G. Genosko. Cambridge, MA: Blackwell Publishers.

———. 1984. *Molecular Revolution: Psychiatry and Politics.* Harmondsworth, Middlesex: Penguin.

Hardt, M. 1993. *Gilles Deleuze: An Apprenticeship in Philosophy.* London: UCL Press.

Hawkes, T. 1989. *Structuralism and Semiotics.* Bungay, Suffolk: Routledge.

Hoggart, R. 1958. *The Uses of Literacy.* Harmondsworth: Penguin.

Holquist, M. 1990. *Dialogism: Bakhtin and His World.* London: Routledge.

Hoogland R. 2003. "The Matter of Culture: Aesthetic Experience and Corporeal Being." *Mosaic, a Journal for the Interdisciplinary Study of Literature* 36: 1–18.

Hutcheon, L. 1985. *A Theory of Parody: The Teachings of Twentieth-Century Art Forms.* London, New York: Methuen.

Jakobson, R. 1960. "Closing Statement: Linguistics and Poetics." In: *Style in Language.* Ed. A. Thomas, Sebeok. Cambridge: MIT Press, 350–377.

Jameson, F. 1981. *The Political Unconscious: Narrative as a Socially Symbolic Act.* Ithaca, NY: Cornell University Press.

———. 1992. *Postmodernism or the Cultural Logic of Late Capitalism.* London, New York: Verso.

Kress, G. 1985. *Linguistic Processes in Sociocultural Practice.* Melbourne: Deakin University Press.

Kristeva, J. 1980. *Desire in Language: A Semiotic Approach to Literature and Art.* New York: Columbia University Press.

——. 1984. *Revolution in Poetic Language.* New York: Columbia University.

Kuhn, T. S. 1962. *The Structure of Scientific Revolutions.* Chicago, IL: University of Chicago Press.

Lacan, J. 1985. *Écrits, a Selection.* London: Tavistock Publications.

——. 1991. *The Four Fundamental Concepts of Psycho-Analysis.* London: Penguin Books.

Landow, G. P., ed. 1994. *Hyper/Text/Theory.* Baltimore, MD, London: John Hopkins University Press.

Lodge, D. 1996. "Mimesis and Diegesis in Modern Fiction." In: *Essentials of the Theory of Fiction.* Ed. M. Hoffman and P. Murphy. London: Leicester University Press, 348–371.

Lukács, G. 1989. *The Historical Novel.* London: Merlin Press.

Lyotard, J.-F. 1971. *Discours, Figure.* Paris: Klincksieck.

——. 1984. *The Postmodern Condition, a Report of Knowledge.* Manchester: Manchester University Press.

——. 1985. *Just Gaming.* Manchester: Manchester University Press.

——. 1989. *The Lyotard Reader.* Ed. A. Benjamin. Oxford: Blackwell Publishers.

Lyotard, J.-F. and Thébaud, J.-L. 1985. *Just Gaming: Theory and History of Literature, Vol. 20. Deleuze, Vitalism and Multiplicity.* London, Sterling, VA: Pluto Press.

McEwan, I. 1998. *Amsterdam.* London: Jonathan Cape.

MacLean, M. 1988. *Narrative as Performance.* London, New York: Routledge.

Macquarie Library. 1981. *The Macquarie Dictionary.* 2nd revision. Chatswood, NSW.

de Man, P. 1981. "Pascal's Allegory of Persuasion." In: *Allegory and Represent-ation.* Ed. S. J. Greenblatt. Baltimore, MD, London: John Hopkins University Press, 1–25.

Manovich, L., 2001. *The Language of New Media.* Cambridge, MA: MIT Press.

Mansfield, Nick. 2003. *Subjectivity: Theories of the Self from Freud to Haraway.* Crows Nest: Allen and Unwin.

Marks, J. 1998. *Gilles Circus of the Mind in Motion: Postmodernism and the Comic Vision.* Detroit, MI: Wayne State University Press.

Massumi, B. 1992. *A User's Guide to Capitalism and Schizophrenia, Deviations from Deleuze and Guattari.* Cambridge, MA, London: A Swerve Edition.

Massumi, B., ed. 2002. *A Shock to Thought: Expression after Deleuze and Guattari.* London: Routledge.

Milner, A. 1996. *Literature, Culture and Society.* St. Leonards: Allen and Unwin.

Nancy, J.-L. 1996. *The Inoperative Community.* Ed. P. Connor. London, Minneapolis: University of Minnesota Press.

Olsen, L. 1990. *Circus of the Mind in Motion: Postmodernism and the Comic Vision.* Detroit, MI: Wayne State University Press.

O'Sullivan, S. 2008. *Art Encounters Deleuze and Guattari: Thought beyond Representation.* New York (State): Palgrave Macmillan.

Myers, D. G. 1993. "The Rise of Creative Writing." *Journal of the History of Ideas* 54 (2): 277–297.

Patterson, L. 1990. "Literary History." In: *Critical Terms for Literary Study*. Ed. F. Lentricchia and T. McLaughlin. Chicago, IL: University of Chicago Press, 250–262.

Patton, P. 1996. "Strange Proximity: Deleuze et Derrida dans les parages du concept." *The Oxford Literary Review* 18 (1–2): 117–134.

Patton, P., ed. 1996. *Deleuze: A Critical Reader*. Oxford, UK: Blackwell Publishers.

Pfeil, F. 1990. *Another Tale to Tell: Politics and Narrative in Postmodern Culture*. London, New York: Verso.

Pharies, D. 1985. *Charles S. Peirce and the Linguistic Sign*. Amsterdam, Philadelphia, PA: John Benjamins Publishing Company.

Recanati, F. 1987. *Meaning and Force: The Pragmatics of Performative Utterance*. Cambridge, New York, New Rochelle, Melbourne, Sydney: Cambridge University Press.

Rimmon-Kenan, S. 1985. *Narrative Fiction: Contemporary Poetics*. London, New York: Methuen.

Rorty, R. 1982. *Consequences of Pragmatism*. Minneapolis: University of Minnesota Press.

Rosello, M. 1994. "The Screener's Maps: Michel de Certeau's 'Wandermanner' and Paul Auster's Hypertextual Detective." In: *Hyper/Text/Theory*. Ed. G. Landow Baltimore: John Hopkins University Press, 121–157.

Schirato, T. and S. Yell. 2000. *Communication and Cultural Literacy, an Introduction*. 2nd ed. St. Leonards, NSW: Allen and Unwin.

Selden, R. and P. Widdowson. 1993. *Contemporary Literary Theory*. 3rd edn. New York, London: Harvester Wheatsheaf.

Seltzer, M. 1998. *Serial Killers: Death and Life in America's Wound Culture*. New York, London: Routledge.

Serres, M. 1982. *The Parasite*. Trans. L. R. Schehr. Baltimore, MD: John Hopkins University Press.

Singleton, J., ed. 1996. *The Creative Writing Handbook*. Basingstoke, England: Macmillan.

Smith, B. 1978. *On the Margins of Discourse*. Chicago, IL: University of Chicago Press.

Smith, D. W. 1998. "The Place of Ethics in Deleuze's Philosophy: Three questions of Immanence." In: *Deleuze and Guattari, New Mappings in Politics, Philosophy, and Culture*. Ed. E. Kaufman and K. J. Heller. Minneapolis, London: University of Minnesota Press, 251–269.

Thomas, D. M. 1981. *The White Hotel*. New York: Viking Press.

Ulmer, G. 1985. *Applied Grammatology*. Baltimore, MD, London: John Hopkins University Press.

———. 1994. "The Miranda Warnings: An Experiment in Hyperrhetoric." In: *Hyper/Text/Theory*. Ed. G. P. Landow. Baltimore, MD, London: John Hopkins University Press, 345–377.

Varela, F. 1980. *Autopoiesis and Cognition: The Realization of the Living.* Dordrecht, Holland; Boston, MA: D. Reidel Publishing Company.

———. 1992. *Understanding Origins: Contemporary Views on the Origins of the Mind and Society.* Dordrecht, Holland; Boston, MA: Kluwer Academic Publishers.

Wheal, N., ed. 1995. *Postmodern Arts: An Introductory Reader.* London; New York: Routledge.

Williams, R. 1958. *Culture and Society.* London: Chatto and Windus.

———. 1965. *The Long Revolution.* Harmondsworth: Penguin.

Williamson, D. 1989. *Authorship and Criticism.* Sydney: Local Consumption Publications.

Reference to video, film, and broadcast, by year

Southern Comfort, 1981. Film. Directed by W. Hill. usa: Cinema Group.

Hamish MacBeth, TV-Series, 1995. Produced by D. Keir. UK: BBC, Scotland.

The Sweet Hereafter, 1997. Film. Directed by A. Egoyan. Canada: Ego Film Arts.

The Full Monty, 1997. Film. Directed by P. Cattaneo. USA: Twentieth Century Fox Film Corporation.

Out of Sight, 1998. Film. Directed by S. Soderbergh. USA: Universal Pictures.

The Apostle, 1998. Film. Written & Directed by R. Duvall. USA: Universal October Films.

SeaChange, TV-Series, 1999–2001. ABC-TV. Executive Producers: A. Knight and A. Denholm (Artist's Services) and S. Masters (ABC). Australia: Artist's Services and ABC.

Reference to web pages/sites

UTS, 2003. *BA in Arts and Communication (Writing and Contemporary Cultures)* [online]. University of Technology, Sydney. Available from: http://www.uts.edu.au/index.html. (Accessed February 13, 2003).

Index